I0762623

Praise for
HOW TO BUILD A HAUNTED HOUSE

"As someone who lived in one of these haunted houses, I found Caitlin Blackwell Baines's book a remarkable document of the truth. All houses are haunted, but she singles out notable sites of spectral activity and writes about them with a glorious matter-of-factualness."

—Philip Hoare, author of
William Blake and the Sea Monsters of Love

"An interesting cultural exploration of some of the best-known houses where things are said to go bump in the night."

—Edward Parnell,
author of *Ghostland*

"This has that exhilarating quality that you get from the very best nonfiction. Fascinating, intriguing and thought-provoking, beautifully and intelligently written, it's as absorbing and seductive as any fictional ghost story. An absolute must-read."

—Bridget Collins, bestselling
author of *The Binding*

"Entertaining. This is just the sort of book to read over Halloween, as the shadows lengthen and the candle flickers. The author, an art historian, is less interested in whether ghosts are real than in how they and their dwellings gained such a grip on our imaginations."

—*The Daily Mail*

"With irresistible flair, *How to Build a Haunted House* is chillingly clever, richly atmospheric, and a feast of gothic curiosity. Baines gives voice to houses that whisper."

—Lucy Rose, bestselling
author of *The Lamb*

"A fascinating study of some of the world's most famously haunted houses. Caitlin Blackwell Baines give us the facts, which seldom align with the legends, while communicating the mysterious appeal of haunted places. I finished reading with a strong desire to take up ghost-hunting myself."

—Lisa Tuttle,
author of *My Death*

"From New Orleans to the silver screen, these houses are haunted by more than ghosts: Caitlin Blackwell Baines unpicks the spectral stitches of a gothic staple and reveals the political turbulence, commodification of tragedy, and commercialization of fear in this ectoplasmic exploration of the humble haunted house. Every horror fan, coffin boffin, and certified creep needs to read this book."

—Alice Slater, author of the *Sunday Times*
bestseller *Death of a Bookseller*

HOW TO BUILD A HAUNTED HOUSE

HOW TO BUILD A HAUNTED HOUSE

The History of a Cultural Obsession

CAITLIN BLACKWELL BAINES

PEGASUS BOOKS
NEW YORK LONDON

HOW TO BUILD A HAUNTED HOUSE

Pegasus Books, Ltd.
148 West 37th Street, 13th Floor
New York, NY 10018

First Pegasus Books cloth edition April 2026

Library of Congress Cataloging-in-Publication Data is available.

ISBN: 979-8-89710-078-1

10 9 8 7 6 5 4 3 2 1

Printed in the United States of America
Distributed by Simon & Schuster
www.pegasusbooks.com

To my beloved husband, Bobby, who doesn't believe in ghosts,
but has always believed in me

Contents

Author's note

When I was ten, my parents and I took a road trip from our home in south-western Ontario to the American South. Our main port of call was Charleston, South Carolina, once one of the largest and wealthiest slave-trading centres in colonial America, and now a thriving tourist mecca, known for its elegant nineteenth-century architecture and rich antebellum history. While there, we stayed in the quintessential Southern structure – a plantation house-cum-bed and breakfast. As a budding history buff I was enchanted by our accommodation: a two-and-a-half-storey glimmering white Greek revival mansion, set in a lush waterfront estate. Once an eighteenth-century orange grove that had played host to one of the bloodiest duels of the period (between Generals Christopher Gadsen and Robert Howe), today the estate hosts tourists, film crews and lavish weddings.

On our first evening, we explored the decadent antique-filled interiors in the fading Southern sunlight. The glittering chandeliers and gilt mirrors reflected the low light and cast intriguing shadows across the damask curtains and mahogany furniture. My father and I posed for photos in this atmospheric environment, which have survived as my only physical mementos of the place. While there was nothing outwardly unnerving about the house – it was opulent, yet warm and inviting, just as the original owners and modern proprietors intended – for some reason, I was overtaken by a nervous energy. Perhaps because our days had been spent touring the surrounding area, visiting historic sites steeped in violence, my hackles were up, my mind swimming with stories of bloody revolutionary skirmishes, cruel slave-owners and other sordid tales of the decadent lives of the Southern oligarchy.

As night fell, my nervous excitement morphed into genuine fear. I was shown where I would be sleeping – a small attic bedroom, no doubt once the accommodation of a scullery maid or house slave, since transformed into a chocolate-box children's room. I remember it as a shadowy garret with a brass four-poster bed, diminutive dressing table and antique rocking horse (though the extant photos prove that my memory invented many of these details). As I recall, the doily-covered lamp shed a dull, eerie glow across the tiny bedroom. In that moment, I decided that nothing could make me cross the threshold into this unsettling space, so convinced was I that it was haunted. And so I spent the night in my parents' room. Thankfully, it passed uninterrupted by spectral visitors, as did the rest of our stay at the plantation. There was nothing that ever confirmed my feeling that the place was haunted – no anecdotal evidence later recounted by the proprietors or posters on ghost-hunting internet message boards. I didn't experience a ghost that night – nor have I ever, before or since. It was just a sensation born out of the atmosphere, the architectural aesthetic, the historical context … and my own imagination.

And so began my lifelong obsession with haunted houses. This isn't to say that I'm a wholehearted believer in the supernatural; far from it. The obsession is more likely born out of my passion for social, cultural and architectural history (as well as, perhaps, a slightly macabre sensibility). More dynamic than the military monument or the national history museum, haunted houses offer a unique portal to the past: an intimate point of entry to the daily lives of those who came before us – those who just might still be communicating with us from the beyond.

What is it that makes a house look or feel haunted? And why do certain houses attract a reputation for being haunted? Setting aside the possibility of the actual existence of ghosts, is there some recipe of ingredients that makes a building take on this identity? This book is not, strictly speaking, a book about the paranormal. It is not a collection of personal and second-hand tales of things that go bump in the night. Rather, it is a book about a cultural concept, a literary trope, an iconic image, and a particular kind of place that looms large in our shared imagination.

Regardless of your beliefs about the afterlife – my own is a kind of hopeful agnosticism – you will have at some point engaged with the concept of the haunted house. It is ubiquitous in our society and culture; it serves as the subject and setting for countless short stories, novels and films; it is a long-time fixture of our urban legends; and today, it is even its own cottage industry. Countless visitor attractions and businesses thrive on the publicity of a good ghost story, while television producers capitalise on the entertainment value of watching others romp through a spooky old building.

In the English-speaking world, especially, the concept of the haunted house is so familiar that the term evokes a relatively fixed set of images and ideas which many of us accept without question. However, if we take a closer look at the historical sources that have shaped this concept, we can unlock its deeper meaning and cultural relevance.

This book explores how, and why, we have come to a collective understanding of what a haunted house is. In it, we will look to some of the most famous haunted houses in Britain and America (and further afield) for answers. Our hunt for the haunted house will take us on a journey through history from medieval Scotland to Enlightenment-era London; from Victorian rectories in rural East Anglia to plantation houses in pre-Civil War Louisiana; and finally, to the affluent suburbs of modern Tokyo. We will find them in Shakespearean theatre, Romantic novels, Edwardian short stories, late-twentieth-century Hollywood blockbusters, and contemporary reality television programmes. Over time and space, medium and genre, the haunted house adapts and morphs, but always remains intrinsically the same.

Although the haunted house of our shared imagination comes in a variety of subtly differing forms, they all have certain commonalities. Almost invariably, they are old, they are large, and were once or continue to be single-family homes. They are spaces that force us to confront the (sometimes disturbing) past; they are spaces that subvert our expectations of the house (or 'home') as a place of safety and privacy, a setting for domestic bliss; they are spaces that are simultaneously familiar, yet forebodingly strange.

What is a haunted house? Ultimately, it isn't as much a certain style of building as it is an immutable emblem – simultaneously embodying our way of life and our collective anxiety about the afterlife, the destination of our immortal souls. That a house might contain the spirit of a previous occupant is an oddly compelling notion. It offers the tantalising possibility that life continues after death, and that we might have some means of communing with the past. On the other hand, the thought that a soul might be eternally trapped in a house is profoundly unnerving. If a house is meant to be a *home*, a sanctuary from the dangers of the world, then where can we retreat in the haunted house? Perhaps there is no escaping its terrifying power, and that is why we, as a culture, can't seem to resist peering through the shadowy door.

Introduction

> All houses wherein men have lived and died are haunted houses.
>
> *Henry Wadsworth Longfellow (1807–1882)*

The concept of the ghost – that is, the disembodied spirit of a formerly living human being – is a nearly universal idea, as old as human history. Indeed, in the first century CE, the Roman author and natural philosopher Pliny the Younger recorded what is widely believed to be the first written account of a haunted house. But the idea has continued to evolve, even thrive, in our increasingly secular, technologically advanced world. To some extent, a good ghost story, whether 'true' or fictional, is simply a tale designed to amuse or playfully scare the audience. But of course, it is more than that. The concept of the ghost exists to serve as some way of explaining, easing (or possibly sometimes exacerbating) the anxiety we feel about the great unknown that is the afterlife.

Social historians, literary theorists, folklorists and parapsychologists have filled volumes devoted to the subject of ghosts – covering the what, why and how of this cultural phenomenon, as well as offering scientific or quasi-scientific inquiries into whether or not ghosts actually exist. Today, a quick search of Amazon reveals some 40,000 books on ghost-related topics, ranging from the popular regional tales of 'Haunted [insert locality here]' to more serious scholarly considerations of the subject.

Meanwhile, considerably less attention has been devoted to the study of the ghost's assumed natural habitat – that eternal home and earthly prison known as the haunted house.

The concept of a haunted house is similarly ubiquitous. There are examples of famously haunted dwellings all over the world, from Höfði House in Iceland to Château de Brissac in France to the Laperal

White House in the Philippines. But, as a cultural icon, the haunted house looms especially large in the West. In the English-speaking world in particular, the haunted house has a specific connotation and a unique cultural history, and it is with this history – the history of the haunted house of Great Britain and North America – that this book is primarily (though not exclusively) concerned.

The Anglo-American haunted house is a concept built on a foundation of folklore, narrative fiction, and social and architectural history. A construction process spanning centuries, the concept continues to evolve to this day. As the story of its evolution will demonstrate, the haunted house is more than just an arbitrary symbol; a simple signifier of something we collectively find scary. Its enduring power reveals just as much about us and our modern way of life as it does about our collective attitudes and anxieties towards death. The 'house' part of the phrase is as significant as the 'haunted', for in no other culture in the world is the supernatural so indelibly linked to the domestic dwelling.

'Haunted houses have been familiar to man ever since he has owned a roof to cover his head,' claimed Andrew Lang, a Scottish poet turned psychical researcher writing in the late 1890s, when the spiritualist craze was sweeping Britain and America, and the field of parapsychology was in its excited infancy.

It's a grand statement, but convincing enough on the surface. Ghosts were the subject *du jour* in Lang's time, and virtually everyone in Victorian Britain would have heard, read stories about or seen pictures of reputedly haunted residences. Indeed, the same could be said today. So it might be natural for us to assume that, as Lang tells us, they've simply always existed. Or, at least, they've existed for as long as the house itself. And this, he suggests, is a global phenomenon.

Quoting Lang over a century later, paranormal researcher David Taylor wrote: 'Every community in every corner of the world has a "haunted house", a building that has become a strong cultural icon both within our conscious and subconscious minds.' Again, it is a persuasive statement. Well, it is if we judge it purely on our own cultural assumptions.

But actually, the statement is only true-*ish*. Yes, there are examples of supposedly haunted structures in most parts of the world. And yes, some of those buildings are 'houses' – domestic structures in some capacity. But is the haunted house of our present, Western understanding – a multi-room, multi-storeyed domestic structure, occupied by a nuclear family and haunted by the spirits of its past occupants – truly global? Timeless?

Lang slightly undermined his own argument when, in his 1897 tome *Dreams and Ghosts*, he followed his declamatory statement on the longevity and universality of the haunted house with a number of tenuous examples. 'The Australian blacks [sic] possessed only shelters or "lean-tos", so in Australia the spirits do their rapping on the tree trunks,' Lang reported. So, more of a haunted *tree*, really…

He went on to list the 'perched-up' houses of the Dayaks – the indigenous peoples of Borneo, who traditionally lodged in communal dwellings on stilts that accommodated up to thirty families. He cited the monasteries of medieval Europe, huge ecclesiastical complexes that housed dozens of men bound by faith rather than blood. And finally, he provided 'palaces and crofters' cottages' as his only examples that realistically stand as the precursors to our present understanding of the haunted house.

When it comes down to it, our version of the haunted house is really just a reflection of the way many of us live today: a warped mirror image of the average single-family home. Yet it's only relatively recently that anyone outside the very wealthiest of European society could afford to live in any other way. In England, it wasn't until towards the end of the seventeenth century that the working poor were able to move out of their one-room wooden hovels into more durable, permanent dwellings made of stone or brick, with glass windows and chimneys – comforts that were once the sole preserve of the upper classes.

Even today, much of the world is either unable to, or unaccustomed to, living this way. To say nothing of the unfortunately vast number of people across the globe who are involuntarily homeless, transient or temporarily displaced. Many citizens of developed and developing nations are simply unfamiliar with life in a single-family house.

In modern-day China, the majority of the population live in multi-unit complexes – even those considered to be of middle- or upper-class status. Some estimates suggest that over 90 per cent of the Chinese population reside in urban apartment buildings. Space restrictions and the desire to live in cities preclude people from living in detached or semi-detached homes. In Japan, over 110 million people live in either small houses or apartments, as the majority of the country's population is concentrated in big cities such as Tokyo.

In East Asia, belief in haunted houses is less prevalent than in the Western world. Granted, there is some talk of 'tainted' homes – called *hongza* in Cantonese and *jiko bukken* in Japanese – and these properties tend to rent or sell for as much as 40 per cent below average house prices. Japan has its own equivalent of the haunted house, called *obake yashiki*, but, as we will learn, this is distinct from the Western version, and for the most part, Japanese supernatural traditions are far less focused on domestic spaces.

According to Japanese folklore expert Zack Davisson,

> *There are two kinds of ghosts [understood in Japanese culture]. The jibakurei or earthbound spirits who are bound to their location, but those are less common ... Most Japanese ghosts (yurei) are furei or free-travelling spirits. They go wherever the person they're haunting goes. It is rarer for Japanese ghosts to haunt locations. Much more common for them to haunt people.*

Similarly, in Mexico, where people have famously strong spiritual beliefs, ghosts are somewhat more apt to be free-floating entities. This is unsurprising when you consider that nearly 34 per cent of the population live in poverty, unable to afford spacious single-family accommodation. Around 34 million Mexicans live more than two people to a room in houses built from weak, impermanent materials such as cardboard and reeds in shanty towns on the outskirts of urban centres. Mexican spiritual beliefs reflect a unique hybrid of Roman Catholic and pre-Columbian Aztec and Mayan traditions, the lines of which have gradually blurred over time. For that reason, perhaps, historians are divided over the true origin of Mexico's best-known supernatural tradition, *Día de Muertos* or Day of the Dead, an annual festival usually celebrated from 30 October to 2 November, during which family members gather to pay homage to their ancestors.

Whether the celebration is a vestige of pagan belief or derived from the medieval Christian tradition of All Soul's Day is unclear. But in either case, this ritual imagines the souls of the dead returning to the earthly plane once a year to receive gifts and offerings from the living. These ghosts are deceased loved ones, rather than forbidding strangers; they are meant to be embraced and revered, rather than feared, and they are in no way tethered to their former domiciles. If their descendants move house, the ghosts simply follow, visiting them at their new address.

Similar festivals of the dead are celebrated worldwide, from the islands of the South Pacific to Nepal to Eastern Europe, suggesting that this is a far more common conception of the spirit world than the Anglo-American haunted house model.

This doesn't mean that we in the West are entirely unique in our belief that ghosts are rooted to location; across the globe there are scores of examples of haunted bridges, roads, forests, lakes and, yes, houses. But we certainly seem to be the most fixated on the notion that the ghost's natural environment is their former home.

As we will see, this widely held viewpoint emerged partially as a result of the development of our own religious traditions – an, at times, uncomfortable transition from the ritualistic ceremony and superstitious realm of Roman Catholicism to a more prosaic, predominantly Protestant belief system. Notably, however, belief – or, at least, *interest* – in the haunted house rapidly accelerated at a time when more and more Britons and Americans could afford their own homes.

The Industrial Revolution, which transformed manufacturing processes across Europe between *c.* 1760 and 1830, paved the way for a newly dominant middle class – a large segment of the population that owned and operated businesses and lived more comfortably than their working-class predecessors and present-day employees. They could afford spacious, clean and – perhaps most crucially – *private* homes in which to raise their nuclear families.

Where there was little space for privacy in the cramped conditions of a medieval peasant's cottage (or, for that matter, in the communal great hall of a castle), the average Georgian and Victorian house provided discrete, demarcated spaces for the homeowner and their kin to retreat to.

Thus, the house became the hallowed ground of personal and familial autonomy; a safe haven from the wider world. It became more than just a *house* (an impassive pile of bricks and mortar); it was now, in the fullest sense of the word, a *home* (the Anglo-Saxon meaning of the word connotes both a physical place to live and an abstract state of being: a place of belonging).

And on this site of newly important symbolic significance, bourgeois Brits and Americans projected all their most cherished values: their hopes and dreams, as well as their most profound anxieties. Deep-rooted feelings that largely persist today.

In the words of cultural geographers Alison Blunt and Robyn Dowling:

> *Home ... is a place, a site in which we live. But more than this, home is also an idea and an imaginary that is imbued with feelings. These may be feelings of belonging, desire and intimacy ... but there can also be feelings of fear, violence and alienation.*

So, if the archetypal family home was born out of the Industrial Revolution, and its terrifying inverse – the haunted house – followed relatively quickly, then it should make sense that the most familiar version of the haunted house is one that dates from precisely the same time period.

When asked to picture a haunted house, most people will come up with roughly the same image – a Gothic Victorian mansion. Indeed, if you run a Google image search on the term 'haunted house', the first hits you will get are of clip art illustrations depicting the shadowy silhouettes of dilapidated weather-boarded houses, featuring castle-like towers, oculus windows and expansive porches, flanked by decaying trees (and possibly a few bats and a tombstone or two).

According to the creator of one such image, Italian graphic artist, Daniele Montella, 'Each year at Halloween, I get [many] requests for use of the image, even from sites of paranormal research, or even by groups claiming to be ghostbusters.' As inventive as it is, the picture is not purely a product of the artist's imagination. He acknowledges it to be a creative interpretation of a real house: Carson Mansion in Eureka, California.

Built in 1884 for the eccentric lumber magnate William Carson, the eponymous Carson Mansion looks a bit like a fairy-tale castle. It is a chaotic collage of turrets, towers, cupolas and ornately carved timber pillars, brackets and bargeboards, which mimic the intricately carved masonry of earlier medieval and Renaissance structures. Carson Mansion is a prime example of what is known as Queen Anne Revival architecture – a misleading term, given that it bears no real similarity to the sober structures built under the reign of the early-eighteenth-century English queen. Instead, it is an experimental building style incorporating a variety of pseudo-historical influences including Gothic, Romanesque, Renaissance and baroque architecture.

The houses made in this style – and they were mostly domestic structures in late-nineteenth-century America – can be described as eclectic, asymmetrical and highly ornate. Carson Mansion is held up as the movement's highest (and most extravagant) achievement, and to some, it is a whimsical masterpiece. To others, it is a testament to Victorian excess and questionable taste. Whatever your opinion, it is not hard to see why it has become one of the most photographed Victorian houses in the world.

But why has it become a visual shorthand for the haunted house? Unlike many of the houses discussed in this book, it doesn't boast a particularly well-known ghost story. Yet, as we will see, that is not necessarily a compulsory component for the haunted house. Sometimes a shadowy old edifice containing just enough dark nooks and crannies is enough to set the mind racing, creating its own ghost story.

What's more, although it is American, and post-dates most of the other buildings discussed in this book, Carson Mansion is linked with the earlier English origins of Gothic Revival architecture, and indeed, with the Anglo history of the haunted house itself.

The Carson Mansion model is one of the most familiar images we have of the haunted house. Gothic Revival architecture and the many high Victorian derivations of it are unquestionably important. As we will discover, this is tied up with the prevailing values, attitudes and interests of the society that created this architectural aesthetic. The newly powerful symbolic significance of the family home, as well as a renewed interest in medieval history, antiquarianism, and the birth and rise of spiritualism, had a strong impact on the trajectory of the haunted house concept and its associated iconography.

But we may have other related, and competing, images of haunted houses in our minds. There is the medieval castle (a precursor to, and influencer of, Gothic Revival and subsequent related styles) and the later baronial castle (a nineteenth-century Scottish version of Gothic Revival), both of which conjure up images of the ghost of Banquo roaming the halls of Cawdor Castle in *Macbeth*. Or perhaps we picture a different sort of building altogether – the Tudor or Jacobean palace, or even the neoclassical country house so ubiquitous in England's rural landscape (and in the vast portfolio of the National Trust).

And so, the haunted house of our collective consciousness is at once fixed and fluid. Perhaps the best evidence of its subtly changing face can be found in, of all unlikely settings, Disneyland. 'Haunted house' fairground attractions have existed since at least the early 1900s, when they popped up in the pleasure parks of England and America, in places such as Liphook, Hampshire and Coney Island, New York. By the mid-twentieth century they were a fairground fixture and so, in 1951, when artists Harper Goff and Ken Anderson were tasked with designing the new Disneyland theme park in Anaheim, California, they naturally thought to include a ride of this type. The first design they put forward was a dilapidated version of Carson Mansion, but Walt Disney was not comfortable with the idea of including a derelict house in his park. Instead, Carson Mansion would serve as the basis for the park's train station clock tower, while the haunted house ride would be a New Orleans-style Greek Revival mansion, a neoclassical building inspired by Anderson's extensive research of Southern American architecture and his visit to the unconventional Winchester Mystery House in San Jose, California (see Chapter 8).

This original Haunted Mansion attraction, which opened in 1969, would be carried over to four other Disney theme parks around the world, though in slightly altered form. At Disney World in Orlando, Florida, the mansion built in 1971 was a red-brick Dutch Gothic building intended to evoke the high Victorian architecture of upstate New York. At Tokyo Disneyland, opened in 1983, the house was an updated version of the Florida mansion. At Disneyland Paris, the Phantom Manor opened in 1992 was a Second Empire mansard-roofed mansion based on the Fourth Ward School, a late-nineteenth-century building in Virginia City, Nevada. And finally, at Hong Kong Disneyland, the Mystic Manor opened in 2013 was a Queen Anne-style house based on Bradbury Mansion in Los Angeles, a now-demolished home built by the same architects as Carson Mansion.

All were a bit different, all were a bit scary.

Architectural style and visual iconography undoubtedly play a big role in our conception of the haunted house, but other forms of cultural production – namely novels and films – also contribute to and reinforce our shared understanding.

The ghost, of course, has been a mainstay of our oral storytelling tradition for centuries, so it should come as no surprise that they also figure in some of the oldest surviving examples of written literature in human history. They are etched into Ancient Egyptian papyruses; they crop up in classical Greek and Roman poetry and theatre; and they even play a role in the Old Testament.

Though it would be centuries before the haunted house itself became the standard setting for the ghost story, there are some notable early precedents. The first-century BCE play *Mostellaria* – sometimes referred to as 'The Haunted House play' (though the title translates from Latin as simply 'ghostly') – is widely regarded as the earliest known work to feature a haunted dwelling. Penned by Roman playwright Plautis, *Mostellaria* is believed to be based on an even older play – a lost comedy by the third-century BCE Athenian poet, Philemon.

Yes, that's right, the first haunted house in Western literary history was a setting for high jinks, not horror. But there were no ghosts in the play at all – it was an elaborate hoax pulled off by the protagonist Philolaches, the spendthrift son of an Athenian merchant, and his mischievous slave, who together invented the haunting in an effort to avoid a debt collector and Philolaches' disapproving father.

In England, the best-known early imaginings of the haunted house come from the seventeenth-century works of William Shakespeare, who was inspired by the Roman tragedian Seneca, for whom (unlike Plautis) ghosts were no laughing matter. They were vengeful wraiths and harbingers of ill-fortune with dire warnings for hubristic mortals.

But while contemporary audiences tend to assume that *Macbeth*'s Cawdor Castle and *Hamlet*'s Elsinore Castle are haunted by the ghosts of Banquo and Old Hamlet respectively, we might once again be projecting our own modern assumptions. As art historian-cum-historical ghost expert Susan Owens points out, Elizabethan audiences had a complicated understanding of the spirit world, shaped by both pre-Reformation Catholic beliefs and more modern Protestant lines of thinking. When religious reformers of the sixteenth century 'did away with the [Catholic] notion of purgatory and replaced it with the idea that after the death of the body the soul proceeded directly to heaven or hell, they struck a heavy blow at common ideas and expectations,' Owens explains. 'Gone were purgatory's permeable borders, which occasionally allowed souls to slip through and find ways of communicating with the living.'

Old habits die hard, though, and while some of the more progressive audience members at the Globe Theatre would have interpreted Old Hamlet's ghost not as the tormented soul of the deceased king but rather a supernatural entity assuming the guise of Old Hamlet, others would have fallen back on earlier understandings of the ghost as a dead human being. Even so, they probably saw these spectral visitors as just that – temporary visitants of the *Dia de Muertos* kind, as opposed to permanent ghostly residents.

Of course, it's possible that Shakespeare never intended for his ghosts to be interpreted literally. Famed Shakespearean scholar W. W. Greg was of the opinion that the Bard's ghosts were meant to represent the tormented psyches of his angst-ridden protagonists. In this interpretation, the characters are the ones who are haunted, not the castles.

For most of the early modern period (*c.* 1400–1800), literary ghosts wandered at will. They paid fleeting visits to living loved ones; they sporadically returned to the sites of their (usually violent) deaths; and, more often than not, they simply flitted about cemeteries and churchyards, bearing silent witness to their earthly remains. Walls did not seem to confine them. At least, not until the second half of the eighteenth century, when a new literary genre changed the rules. This was the birth of the Gothic novel – and it was the Gothic that pushed the ghost indoors.

Gothic fiction is characterised by themes of horror, death and love, and often harkens back to a romanticised earlier period of history. It is so named because of its association with the style of building that frequently serves as its setting: the medieval Gothic castle or neo-Gothic manor house. In fiction, as in life, these structures reflect the popularity of the medieval aesthetic in late Georgian and Victorian society, but they also provide an atmospheric backdrop against which to meditate on more universal subjects: mortality, identity, and the indelible link between the past and the present.

The emergence of this popular new genre marked the first time in the ghost story's long history that the *site* of the haunting would prove as important as the ghosts themselves.

The first Gothic novel is generally acknowledged to be Horace Walpole's *The Castle of Otranto* (1764). It tells the story of Manfred, the fictional Italian ruler of Otranto, who is determined to secure the castle and save his progeny from its mysterious curse. As we will find out in Chapter 1, Walpole's Otranto had an irrevocable impact on the literary haunted house. Despite the fact that his ghosts are largely unfamiliar to modern audiences – giant sword-wielding spooks rather than shadowy wisps gliding silently down hallways – everything else is exactly what we would expect. In short, an ancient edifice occupied by a living family who are tormented by the ghosts of previous residents.

More than a century after Walpole's pioneering work came Henry James's classic novella, *The Turn of the Screw* (1898), published at the apex of Victorian spiritualism. It tells the story of a naive young governess charged with the care of Miles and Flora, orphans who have been abandoned in their uncle's gloomy ancestral country house, alone but for the servants and the possible presence of some spectral residents.

Where Walpole's work traded on the melodrama and spectacle of the supernatural, James's eerie tale is cloaked in a quiet ambiguity, forcing us to question both the heroine's senses and our own expectations of the haunted house. Here, the ghosts are silent spectres who are only seen at a distance – high up in a tower, descending a tall staircase, peering through windows – making them simultaneously 'there', yet 'not there'; real, yet illusory. A perfect metaphor for the way the events of the past leave a pale but perceptible mark on the present.

James's work, in turn, inspired many of the most celebrated haunted house stories of modern times, including M. R. James's *Lost Hearts* (1904), Shirley Jackson's *The Haunting of Hill House* (1959), Susan Hill's *The Woman in Black* (1983), Sarah Waters' *The Little Stranger* (2009), and many more. Like Walpole's and James's seminal works, most of these books describe the experiences of unwitting visitors or new occupants of old houses that seem to be possessed by the spirits of former occupants – by now, the standard plot device of the haunted house story.

Intriguingly, in cinema, one of the most famous haunted houses appears in a film that is not based on any of these literary precedents, but on an allegedly true story. The setting for this macabre tale, 112 Ocean Avenue, Amityville, Long Island, is, on the face of it, a relatively unassuming structure. Although an attractive example of Dutch Colonial Revival architecture, characterised by its sloping 'Dutch barn' roof and quarter-moon-shaped double windows (now synonymous with demonic eyes, thanks to the memorable imagery in the film), it is not a particularly grand or exceptional building, especially when compared with its Californian counterpart, Carson Mansion. But the events of 13 November 1974 would change its reputation forever, launching it into architectural infamy.

On that night, a troubled young man named Ronald DeFeo Jr shot dead his entire family as they slept peacefully in their quaint suburban home. The following year, the ill-fated Lutz family moved in, pleased to have secured their dream house for a bargain price. They were completely unprepared for the supposedly supernatural forces that would send them packing just twenty-eight days later.

Their story, as recounted to author Jay Anson, became the basis for his book *The Amityville Horror: A True Story* (1977). This was first adapted for the screen in 1979, and over the next three decades numerous sequels and remakes followed. Though later believed by many to be a complete work of fiction – a hoax devised by cash-strapped home buyers and a duplicitous family lawyer – it is striking that it includes all the same themes and plot devices as the literary haunted house narrative, making the film a striking case of art imitating life imitating art.

Throughout this book, we will constantly be reminded of the central importance of the 'house' part of the 'haunted house'.

Granted, in Britain and America, lots of building types are deemed to be haunted – pretty much any place in which humans have existed; any place where people have loved, lost, suffered and died. In almost every city, town and village in Britain (and to a lesser extent in the younger nation of America) there are reputedly haunted hotels, pubs, restaurants, theatres and schools. Indeed, it seems that if a building has stood for at least, say, 100 years, something significant has happened there. It is therefore possible that some residual energy of the beings that once occupied the space remain. This is called the 'stone tape' theory of paranormal activity: ghostly manifestations attributed to a kind of visual or auditory recording of human energy which replays itself over and over again in perpetuity.

Yet, as we are discovering, there is a reason that the phrase most commonly used is 'haunted house', not 'haunted building'. Domestic dwellings are the intimate settings in which people not only carry out all their normal day-to-day activities, but also endure the most dramatic experiences of human existence. Historically, most people were born and died at home. They raised their children there, hosted their friends and families there, and had sex there (or maybe even conducted affairs there). Statistically, the home remains the place where most violent deaths and murders take place – no doubt the dramatic, yet all too common, result of familial dispute and dysfunction. The home is where most people spend the majority of their lives, whether they are happy there or not.

The dwellings discussed in this book are of the grandest and most spectacular sort – castles, palaces, stately homes and plantations – mostly because they are the most recognisable, historically important and architecturally significant examples. But regardless of their scale and expense, they were also homes belonging to real people: people who may – or may not – still wander the halls.

STRAWBERRY HILL HOUSE

THE BIRTH OF 'GLOOMTH'

1

...a god [or] at least a ghost was absolutely necessary
to frighten us out of too much senses...

Horace Walpole (1717–1797)

Inventing an ancestral home

Early one morning in the summer of 1764, the English author, art historian and statesman Horace Walpole awoke from a strange dream. Lying alone in a bedchamber in his home in Twickenham to the south-west of London, the lifelong bachelor blearily took in his surroundings. The pale light of dawn passed through the familiar stained-glass windows emblazoned with the coat of arms of the ill-fated queen, Anne Boleyn, casting muted colours across his collection of antique furniture, ancestral portraits, and framed prints of stately homes and castles.

Through the partially open door, he could just make out the outline of the banister at the top of the staircase, with its ornately carved newel posts adorned with antelopes – a symbol taken from the Walpole family crest.

In his drowsy haze – thanks to the previous night's dose of laudanum, taken to treat a gouty foot – Walpole felt as though he occupied a shadowy liminal space between the waking world and the world of dreams. Here, the past and the present, the living and the dead, seemed to temporarily coexist.

Ghosts are famous for frequenting such 'liminal spaces': places that exist at or on both sides of a threshold, hovering on a kind of boundary. Staircases, hallways, doors, windows: these transitional areas of the home are thought to be the ghost's favourite hangouts – no doubt because they are so used to existing on the threshold between life and death.

Some months later, Walpole recounted the experience – a vivid dream – to his friend and fellow antiquarian William Cole in a note accompanying the gift of a copy of his new book – the book inspired by that dream. Of the dream itself, he wrote: 'All I could recover was that I had thought myself in an ancient castle (a very natural dream for a head like mine, filled with Gothic story), and that on the uppermost banister of a great staircase I saw a gigantic hand in armour. In the evening, I sat down and began to write, without knowing in the least what I intended to say or relate.'

The result of Walpole's feverish writing was a 'Gothic story' – the first of its kind – a tale of a haunted castle that was not so very different from his own.

That he dreamed his dream in this house – the shadowy, neo-Gothic mansion he had built for himself in the countryside near London and filled with eclectic historical bric-a-brac – lies at the heart of what this chapter – and, indeed, this book – is all about. What is it that makes a house feel haunted? And is an actual ghost a prerequisite?

Strawberry Hill House and its aesthetic, so at odds with the neoclassical, Enlightenment-era values of his day, almost certainly inspired Walpole's dream. The dream, in turn, inspired him to write his genre-defining novel, *The Castle of Otranto*. And today, whether or not we know of his house or his novel, they nevertheless live on in our shared imagination.

Horace Walpole might be credited as the inventor of the modern haunted house. His contribution to the concept is indisputably important. Yet, as innovative and idiosyncratic a character as he was, Walpole was not working in a bubble. His architectural and literary creations were shaped by the society in which he lived. And so, with the eccentric author as our phantom guide, we will delve into Horace's world – a paradoxical place characterised by stiff rationalism and wild imagination.

'Do you know anything about Horace?' asks a friendly room guide at Strawberry Hill House, a historic visitor attraction to the south-west of London, which has been open since 2012. It's a fair question. Although Horace Walpole wielded the kind of cultural power in the eighteenth century that a social media influencer might have today, he's hardly a household name.

'I know a little bit,' I say, politely downplaying my familiarity. The truth is, as a PhD student studying Georgian art, I could hardly avoid old Horace. Not only was he a highly respected art historian – the author of *Some Anecdotes of Painting in England* (1762), one of the first published studies of British art, still regularly consulted by students and scholars today – but he was also a man about town, invited to all the most important social events in Georgian England. The well-connected Horace Walpole was the youngest son of Sir Robert Walpole, 1st Earl of Orford, Britain's first and longest-serving prime minister.

On top of this, Horace Walpole had a *lot* to say, and much of it is recorded in the thousands of enlightening (and often gossipy) letters he wrote to family, friends and colleagues over the course of his life. This treasure trove of correspondence, filling some forty-eight volumes (published by Yale University Press in the early twentieth century), makes Walpole an invaluable social commentator of his time; indispensable to anyone interested in eighteenth-century English history.

So, yes, I know a bit about Horace Walpole, though perhaps not as much as my companion this day does: Carole Tucker, Strawberry Hill's archivist and librarian.

'I do know an awful lot,' Carole tells the room guide, who didn't recognise her. 'I've been here since 2010.'

The guide bashfully absents herself.

Carole has agreed to give me a private tour of Walpole's architectural magnum opus – a glimmering white miniature castle, originally serving as both summer home and repository for Horace's vast collection of fine art and rare historical artefacts. Today it is best known for being one of the first Gothic Revival homes in Britain. Carole is prepared to cover all the usual highlights, but she's also aware that I've come with specific questions in mind. Questions about ghosts, haunted houses, and the inspiration behind history's first Gothic novel.

Strawberry Hill is where, in the summer of 1764, Horace Walpole wrote *The Castle of Otranto*. This is the building that informed the story's pivotal setting and, while the two buildings are not exactly mirror images, the fictional castle and the real one have much in common. They both hark back to a romanticised earlier period; they both trade heavily on mystery and melodrama; and they are both underpinned by their creator's apparent obsession with familial lineage. Crucially, it is from both sources that we get the precursor of the modern haunted house.

Walpole's dual creations were revolutionary in his day – dramatic reactions against the prevailing modes of building, writing, even *thinking*. He is considered to be the grandfather of the modern Gothic literary and architectural movements, and his influence in the realm of all that is spooky is still felt today.

In the words of historian and ghost expert Susan Owens: 'In binding together ancient history, old buildings, ruins and ghosts … Walpole invented a new, highly charged way of looking at the world – one that has had consequences for the way in which ghosts have been thought about ever since.'

As Carole and I stand in the main hall, at the bottom of the staircase where, 250 years ago, Horace had his ghostly dream, I cannot help but wonder at the subtle irony of my surroundings. From where I stand, I have a perfect viewpoint of where Horace's hand in armour appeared, in that space between dreaming and waking. I can feel the richness of my environment, as if I were bathing in history itself. Yet Walpole was a famous sceptic. In spite of his masterpieces – both house and story – he never came close to believing in ghosts.

The antelope newel posts are still here, as is the hand-painted wallpaper designed to mimic medieval carved stone. Almost everything in the house has been painstakingly restored or reproduced based on Walpole's meticulous notes and records, which allow modern visitors the opportunity to experience the house just as Horace and his guests would have when it was newly built. The restoration project, launched in 2010, took two years and £9 million of grants, donations and crowdfunding to achieve – five times what it cost Walpole to construct the castle in the first place (about £20,720, or £1.8 million in today's currency).

'When Horace Walpole purchased this property [initially just 5 acres of land with a small existing house], he was looking for an escape from summer in London,' explains Carole. A London summer in the eighteenth century was a sweltering cesspool to be avoided at all costs, so his desire made sense. That was exactly what most well-to-do Georgians did anyway, especially men whose professional duties were completed at the end of the parliamentary season.

Whether it was to a long-held family home in a far-flung place such as Northumberland, or a newly acquired retreat near London, escaping to the country was essential to stave off boredom and discomfort.

'[Horace] was very keen on coming to this area,' says Carole, referring to Twickenham, which, in Walpole's time was a mostly rural area south of the Thames – a bucolic spot, just two hours by horse-drawn carriage from the city. Today it is a densely populated commuter suburb.

'He was very much into history,' Carole continues, 'and in this area, within easily commutable distance, there were historically important big houses like Richmond Palace, Kew Palace, Hampton Court, Syon House.'

In other words, an ideal location for a summer getaway for a man enchanted by the grandeur of the past. That the area had a long and noble history was of particular significance to Walpole. Not only was he a history buff, he was also keenly engaged in the practice of *creating* history. Conscious of both past and future, Horace's aim was to create something unique, important and impactful.

Carole turns to a door behind us and unlocks it to reveal a small white-walled courtyard. Pointing to the archway beyond, she remarks, 'Once you had crossed through there, you would have left the modern world behind. You left all the activity of the coaches and horses, all the barges down on the river … and you stepped into this sort of quiet ecclesiastical space.'

This was Strawberry Hill's main entrance, the portal through which Walpole invited his guests into his magical little world. As we walk on, Carole explains how Horace assigned each room its own story ('In this one, you've come into the Medieval Hall…'), and I find myself suddenly aware of how incongruously small and dark the space is for the formal entrance to an aristocrat's country villa.

'Deliberately dark!' Carole exclaims as I voice my thoughts. 'He coined the word "gloomth" – a portmanteau of the words "gloom" and "warmth".' (Or possibly 'depth', according to some scholars.)

Horace certainly had a way with words. His much more famous contribution to the lexicon is 'serendipity' (a 'happy or fortuitous accident'), a word that has become so commonly understood that it has been translated into multiple languages and has even served as the title of a Hollywood film in which such 'happy accidents' drive the plot and bring the romantic leads together. The word 'gloomth', on the other hand, never really took off in the same way – though, for our purposes, it is far more significant.

The first of only a handful of times Walpole employed the term was in April 1753, in a letter to his dear friend Sir Horace Mann, then an ambassador in Italy. In the letter, Walpole writes of the 'satisfaction of imprinting the gloomth of cathedrals and abbeys' on his home. He doesn't provide a clear definition for his invented word, but we can surmise that he was referring to a certain atmosphere we might expect to encounter in a very old building, created by the effect of dim or diffuse lighting. In distinction to the existing term *gloom*, with its exclusively negative connotations, gloomth was apparently – to Walpole – a desirable quality. An exciting contradiction. A *feeling*. Simultaneously eerie and enticing, it was the very essence of the haunted house.

Evoking the shadowy cloisters of medieval monasteries and the candlelit corridors of ancient castles, Walpole's desired gloomth is felt throughout his home. One of the most obvious effects of gloomth is the result of the extensive use of stained and painted glass, found in windows in almost every room of the house. Nearly 400 pieces of sixteenth- and seventeenth-century Netherlandish glass were carted back from Flanders in the 1750s to help set the ambiance. They cast ever-changing shafts of soft colour and strange shadows across the interior of Strawberry Hill. Walpole revelled in such theatrical effects.

Another of Walpole's eccentric design choices gives another, more prosaic reason as to why Strawberry Hill's entryway seems so small and dark. The current house – now a twenty-four-room mini-mansion – was built around a rather more modest pre-existing building, a small seventeenth-century dwelling; 'little more than a cottage', as Walpole described it, on which he took out a lease in 1747. The following year, he purchased the house outright. The long-departed original owner, a coachman to the Earl of Bedford, allegedly named the house Chopped Straw Hall, in reference to the rumour that he had amassed a small fortune from selling Bedford's hay to the public while feeding his employer's horses cheaper, less nutritious straw. Walpole later changed the house's name to the far more charming Strawberry Hill.

Moving into the Great Parlour, Walpole's formal dining room, we stop in front of a grand chimney piece which, at first glance, appears to be made of solid, elaborately carved stone. In fact, it is wood, painted to look like stone, one of many such cost-saving measures in the house.

After all, Horace was 'wealthy, not *very* rich', Carole explains. He lived on a moderate, yet steady, income based on a number of government sinecures arranged by his father. These were basically lifetime appointments that required little actual work, or work that could easily be farmed out to lower-level civil servants. He also served as a Whig MP from 1741 to 1769, though this would have made no difference to his finances, as the role was unsalaried at the time.

So, Walpole had *some* money and a lot of free time on his hands. And while the illusions created by features such as the chimney piece were economical, they were also an expression of Horace's playful spirit. He delighted in the element of surprise.

All around the room, Walpole's family members gaze down at us from stately gilt-framed portraits. There are pictures of his father, Lord Orford, his beloved mother, Catherine Shorter, his brothers, sisters, nieces, nephews and, most intriguingly for our purposes, his paternal aunt, Dorothy, Viscountess Townshend, better known as the 'Brown Lady' – the ghost that allegedly haunts Raynham Hall (see Chapter 6). How serendipitous.

Though the room itself is actually lighter, brighter and altogether less gloomth-y than much of the rest of the house, there's something unnerving about being here, surrounded by pictures of Walpole's long-dead relatives. They hover above us like a circle of looming spectres. Of course, to Horace they may not have felt nearly so gloomy, and I can imagine that, in their company, he may even have felt a certain warmth. (Though, as we will see, the haunted ancestral portrait *does* play a significant role in Horace's Gothic novel.)

The importance of family in Walpole's conception of Strawberry Hill House is overwhelmingly apparent. In a 1768 letter to his old Etonian schoolmate George Montagu, Horace speaks of having been temporarily detained in London and kept from his passion project – 'the castle [I am building] of my ancestors'.

It sounds romantic, doesn't it? But what does it mean exactly?

In the eighteenth century it was standard for aristocratic families to have a 'family seat' or 'ancestral home', usually in the countryside, which provided an escape from the city in the summer months. The estates on which these houses sat were also usually lucrative agricultural income generators.

But these houses also had a symbolic purpose: to showcase their owners' illustrious lineage. The most prestigious and established noble families could trace their ancestry back many, many centuries, and most dynasties owned at least one country house dating to an earlier period. There, the modern inhabitants could not only luxuriate in the architectural splendour; they could also take heed of, and pay homage to, their ancient ancestors.

In this department, Horace was somewhat lacking. Granted, the Walpoles did have a family seat – Houghton Hall in Norfolk, an indisputably grand four-storey manor house situated on 1,000 acres of parkland – but it was decidedly modern by aristocratic standards. Built by Horace's father in 1722, it was a testament to the fact that the Walpoles were relatively new to the aristocracy, Robert having only risen from his comparably modest origins as an East Anglian country squire to the earldom in 1742.

Horace, as the youngest of three sons, was under no illusion that he would ever inherit Houghton – although in 1791, having outlived his brothers and nephews, he unexpectedly did. Regardless, he seems to have felt very little connection to the place – at least, not for a good portion of his early life, during which time he had little to do with his father or his house. He spent the bulk of his childhood with his mother at their London townhouse on Arlington Street in Mayfair.

Upon completing his formal education at Cambridge in 1739, and his cultural education on the Grand Tour in France and Italy in 1741, Horace probably returned to England with a greater appreciation for what his father had created at Houghton. Lord Orford's colossal white stone pile was a prime example of Palladianism, the architectural style favoured by the social and political elite at the time. Based on the philosophies of Venetian Renaissance architect Andreo Palladio, houses like Houghton were characterised by austerity, symmetry, and a fidelity to the architectural values of the Ancient Greeks and Romans. They expressed the 'proper' taste and ideological inspiration of their powerful owners.

Still, Houghton wasn't to be his (or so Horace thought), nor did it really *feel* like his. So, in 1748, Horace Walpole bought what he referred to as his little 'plaything house' and set about inventing an ancestral seat of his own.

This was mostly an imaginative and enjoyable exercise, but it must have been fraught with some complicated feelings; Horace was effectively building a family home for a family that didn't really exist. He was the third son of a modern nobleman, unlikely to accede to the newly created title or take possession of the house it came with, and he was also unlikely to ever have heirs of his own. At the age of thirty, Horace was unmarried. Although this was perfectly acceptable for a man of his time, he had never really shown any interest in the opposite sex – at least, no interest beyond companionship and conversation.

Whether he was a latent homosexual, asexual, or his relationships with women had been ruined by an overly doting mother, Horace likely knew he was never going to have children. He wasn't necessarily bothered about kids – he famously didn't allow them at Strawberry Hill – but it did beg the question, who was he creating a legacy for?

However conflicted Horace may have felt about the concept of family, he was certainly clear about what he wanted for his 'family seat'. On 10 January 1750, in a letter to Horace Mann, Walpole made his intentions known: 'I am going to build a little Gothic Castle at Strawberry Hill. If you can pick me up any fragments of old painted glass, arms or anything, I shall be excessively obliged to you.'

Walpole desired a 'Gothic Castle' – that is, a castle constructed in the prevailing architectural style of the high Middle Ages (*c.* 1100–1500). Though unusual for the time, this was something of a logical choice. After all, if you wanted to invent a venerable ancestral home, why not look all the way back to the Middle Ages and the pinnacle of its architectural achievements?

Emerging in France and England in the early twelfth century, the original Gothic movement developed from the simpler, more solid Romanesque style typically used for churches and castles. Where Romanesque buildings were formed of thick walls, heavy barrel-vaulted ceilings and small windows, new feats of engineering allowed for increasingly lighter, brighter and taller structures. The solid barrel vault gave way to the pointed arch and the airier rib-vaulted ceiling, and it was now structurally possible to install large expanses of stained glass, allowing a dazzling kaleidoscopic light to fill interior spaces.

Thus, rather ironically, the buildings that inspired Walpole's home were actually characterised by lightness rather than gloom. And yet, in the centuries that followed, the aesthetic became irrevocably associated with darkness, with the so-called 'Dark Ages' and with the supposedly primitive society that lived through it.

The very word 'Gothic' has long-held negative connotations. Where today the term in all its applications – to architecture, literature and aesthetics – is relatively neutral, for centuries it was a damning pejorative. The original use of the adjective was in reference to ancient Germanic peoples, the Goths, who helped topple the Roman Empire in 410 CE. Italian Renaissance authors later blamed the tribe for the demise of the classical world and all its values, which Renaissance Italy held so dear. The Goths were viewed as barbarous monsters, so anything described as 'Gothic' was too.

The derogatory term as applied to medieval art and architecture derives from a letter from Raphael to Pope Leo X in 1518, which was later popularised by the Florentine artist-cum-art historian Giorgio Vasari, who used it as early as 1530, calling medieval or 'Gothic' art a 'monstrous and barbarous disorder'. The meaning stuck. Even Horace, an ardent admirer of the style, referred to it affectionately as 'venerable barbarism'.

By the seventeenth century, Gothic architecture had fallen almost completely out of fashion in England. It had become strongly associated with a dark period of history, but it was also linked to the pre-Reformation Catholic Church and all its rituals and beliefs which, to a Protestant Englishman, seemed to be the vestiges of a strange and superstitious past.

Conscious of its negative reputation, Horace, in a later letter to Mann, attempted to justify his use of the Gothic, writing (rather condescendingly):

> *I shall speak much more gently to you, my dear child, though you don't like Gothic architecture. The Grecian [classical] is only proper for magnificent and public buildings. Columns and all their beautiful ornaments look ridiculous when crowded into a closet or a cheesecake-house. The variety is little, and admits no charming irregularities.*

Horace would be the first to propose that the Gothic was well suited to the domestic home and to *private* spaces. He would also be the first to put forward an alternative, more positive understanding of the word 'Gothic' – for him, a term used to describe a historicised and highly atmospheric environment; an adjective to go hand in hand with his invented noun gloomth.

As we pass through the door into the library, Carole pauses a moment for dramatic effect. 'Yes, so obviously this is the most Gothic room in the house,' she says, gesturing to the wall-to-wall bookcases adorned with a riot of pinnacles and crenelation. 'It was one of his very earliest builds, and you can imagine how important the library was to him.'

This is where he wrote *Otranto*. And here, prominently displayed in a spotlit glass case in the corner of the room, is an early edition of his most famous work.

Above the bookshelves – modelled after the medieval choir doors in the old St Paul's Cathedral – where traditionally there might have been paintings or busts of celebrated writers, philosophers and scientists, there are once again pictures of Walpole's family. This time the cast consists of only his *maternal* relatives.

As an author and a compulsive man of letters, this was likely the room in which he spent the most time. The most personal of spaces. And in the absence of any reference to his father, I find myself wondering if Horace had an issue with his dad. I ask Carole what she thought his feelings were towards Lord Orford.

'I think he was ambivalent,' she admits. 'I mean, he spent most of his childhood with his mother because just about the time of his birth [his parents'] marriage had broken down [and] it wasn't until after his mother had died and his father was out of power that he spent any time with him.'

There is even some debate about whether Lord Orford really was Walpole's father. Having been born eleven years after his last sibling, at a time when his parents were on poor terms, it is rumoured that Horace was actually the progeny of Lord Hervey Carr, Catherine's lover.

I tell Carole that it strikes me that Horace's little toy castle – in all its eccentricity – seems a bit like a rebellion against his father's more sober stately home.

'I think there's a strong theory about that,' she agrees. 'People always ask me why he went Gothic when the fashion was Palladian ... Horace came up with a lot of different explanations for that, but *I* think and other people think that it *was* a reaction against the Palladian house.'

In the preface to *Aedes Walpolinae or a Description of the Collection of Pictures at Houghton Hall in Norfolk* (1758), a catalogue of his late father's art collection, Horace remarks: 'Your power and wealth speak themselves in the grandeur of the whole Building' – thus acknowledging the impressiveness of both his father and his imposing abode.

And yet, in an unpublished poem penned later in the century, Walpole summed up his true feelings as follows: 'Houghton's Grandeur strikes the wand'ring sight / but Strawberry Hill is seen with pure delight.'

So, was Walpole's home a revolt against his father's? More than that, was it a rebellion against the very age in which he lived?

Strawberry Hill seems to run counter to everything the Age of Enlightenment (*c.* 1685–1810) represents. This was an era in which blind faith and superstition had supposedly been pushed aside in favour of empirical evidence and rational thought. It was a time when men like Horace's father stoically presided over their tastefully austere homes, modelled after the villas of learned Renaissance princes and classical philosophers. Here, they pored over books on modern politics and ancient philosophy, amassed collections of botanical specimens, and conducted amateur science experiments – all the while feeling smugly superior to their ignorant (not to mention tasteless) medieval predecessors.

Where Houghton typified the order and rationality of the modern age, Strawberry Hill stood for something different; it was the architectural embodiment of a mysterious and magical past. It was, in other words, out of time and place, existing in its own sort of ghostly space.

It has been said that Horace effectively reimagined the medieval era as a forgotten period of political and personal liberty prior to the constraints of the Enlightenment-era present. Here, imagination and self-expression reigned free. Some historians have even gone so far as to interpret Walpole's embrace of the anachronistic Gothic idiom as a 'high-camp defiance of normal conventions' – or more plainly, a rebellious expression of his supposed homosexuality.

On the library's timber ceiling, alongside heraldic symbols and images of crusaders, is a Latin phrase, allegedly Horace's maternal family motto. *Fari quae sentiat* loosely translates as 'Do as you want to do'. A rebel call, if ever I've heard one.

Carole and I are standing on the landing across from Horace's bedroom. From here, we have a clear view of the doorway through which Walpole glimpsed his dream phantom. This area of the house, known as the armoury, is populated by suits of armour and items of medieval weaponry – all very dramatic, and probably the prompt for Horace's vision of a 'gigantic hand in armour'.

'You'd think if there were any ghosts around, there would be some here. But to be perfectly honest, there are no ghosts.' Carole seems almost apologetic, as if she's somehow letting me down. She adds, 'I've been here plenty of times at night and it actually doesn't feel spooky to me at all.' Later, we speculate about why that is. Was it because Horace was so happy here? That there really wasn't any domestic drama within the walls of his beloved sanctuary? Even the few untimely and tragic deaths in the house seem to have left little impact. A footman who died by suicide after being caught with stolen property left Horace rattled, but, Carole tells me, 'There's no ghost story attached.'

Walpole himself died uneventfully in 1797 at the ripe old age of eighty. He was not at Strawberry Hill at the time of his passing. Some visitors report feeling uncomfortable in certain areas of the house, but Carole thinks these people are 'just being kind of imaginative'. And really, that's exactly what Walpole would have wanted.

In *Lost Treasures of Strawberry Hill*, the catalogue for an exhibition held at the house in 2018, curator Silvia Davoli writes: 'For Walpole, Strawberry Hill, with its towers and shadowy recesses, represented a theatre where the sensations of fear, surprise and suspense might be enjoyed in safety.' So, Horace's (not so) haunted house, as it turns out, was no more than an entertaining illusion.

Like the word Walpole invented to describe it, Strawberry Hill is something of a contradiction: a haunted house with no ghosts. Yet it's indisputable that Strawberry Hill was the inspiration behind the haunted house in *The Castle of Otranto*, and that its architectural legacy lives on in our modern imagining of the haunted house. And it's not an isolated example either; there are plenty of houses that are presumed to be haunted without so much as one reported supernatural experience to back this up. Some places just *feel* like they should be haunted. Perhaps this is not so much of a contradiction as it first appears, either. Perhaps, just like gloomth, Strawberry Hill embodies two realities at once: seemingly contradictory, yet somehow unified.

We ought not be surprised by this. After all, Horace himself was a contradiction through and through. An enlightened gentleman who rejected many of the core precepts of the Enlightenment. A proud owner of a 'family seat' who had no nuclear family. A healthy sceptic who wrote one of the most influential ghost stories of all time. Horace Walpole may not have even believed in ghosts, but he delighted in the *idea* of them. And he was far from the only one.

Though it was meant to be an age of logic and reason, during the Age of Enlightenment, there was no real decline in popular interest in the supernatural. As Walpole well knew, there was an insatiable demand for tales of spirits, sorcery and witches, just as there always had been. And just two years before he penned his fictional ghost story, a 'real' one was unfolding in the nation's capital, attracting the attention of a diverse public. Horace himself was among the rapt audience.

Credulity and incredulity: a 'true' Georgian ghost story

On 29 January 1762, Horace Walpole sat down to write to his old friend and distant relation Horace Mann. The friends had met more than two decades earlier in Florence, where Walpole was making a compulsory stop on his Grand Tour and Mann was serving as British Minister at the Court of Tuscany. They apparently hit it off, and though, after Walpole's departure from Italy, they would never again see each other again in person, the two like-minded intellectuals carried on a forty-year correspondence, regularly updating one another on new and notable happenings in their respective places of residence. Much of it was pure unadulterated gossip.

On this day in 1762, Horace had what he considered a deliciously frivolous piece of news to share with his absent friend: news of a haunted house. Though he was scathingly sceptical of the supernatural claims being made, the subject seems to have made Horace almost giddy. And actually, his attitude towards the ghost story was similar to the attitudes of most members of the educated middle and upper classes. Stories of the supernatural were generally greeted with a mixture of fascination, amusement and, often, disdain. With an air of amused flippancy, Walpole sets the strange scene for Mann:

> *The reigning fashion is a ghost – a ghost, that would not pass muster in the paltriest convent in the Apennine. It only knocks and scratches; does not pretend to appear or to speak. The clergy give it their benediction; and all the world, whether believers or infidels, go to hear it. I, in which number you may guess, go tomorrow, for it is much the mode to visit the ghost…*

Here, Horace speaks of the most notorious 'haunted house' in Georgian England: 25 Cock Lane, a three-storey lodging house on a narrow, winding street in the Smithfield district of London. A far cry from Walpole's Gothic castle, this unassuming little structure is perhaps an unexpected setting for a supposedly true tale of ghosts, murder, sex and intrigue.

The story began in 1759 when William Kent, a usurer from Norfolk, and his dead wife's sister, Fanny Lynes, took up lodgings at 25 Cock Lane with Richard Parsons, the lay clerk at nearby St Sepulchre's Church. Because they were unmarried (canon law forbade marriage between former in-laws), Parsons was effectively doing them a favour by allowing them to live in sin under his roof. They returned the favour by providing him with a generous loan, albeit one that came with a staggeringly high rate of interest.

When Fanny got pregnant in the summer of 1760, Parsons' eleven-year-old daughter Betty was asked by her family to stay with her while Kent was away for business. It was around this time that mysterious scratching and knocking sounds started to emanate from the walls of the small first-floor bedchamber. The noises were temporarily forgotten, however, when William and Fanny abruptly departed Parsons' lodgings following a dispute over Parsons' unpaid debt.

The following February, Fanny and her unborn child died of smallpox. But what should have been the end to Kent's tragic tale was only the beginning. Shortly after winning a legal case against the defaulting debtor Parsons, William learned that the mysterious noises had returned to Cock Lane. This time they came with an ominous message. According to Parsons and his daughter, they were the ghostly communications of the murdered Fanny, conveyed through a series of knocks and scratches. She was allegedly seeking supernatural justice for her wrongful death. She had not died of smallpox, they claimed, but arsenic poisoning at the hands of Kent.

William Kent was not the only one astounded by such sensational claims. Soon the whole city was abuzz with the story of 'Scratching Fanny', the phantom messenger of Cock Lane. By January 1762, London newspapers were flooded with accounts of the uncanny events taking place at this outwardly ordinary urban residence. Within a matter of weeks, the news spread across the nation, sparking debate about the true nature of the supposedly unearthly sounds.

For some, the affair represented an unwanted return to the dark era before the dawning of the Age of Enlightenment. An eloquent anonymous correspondent to the *London Evening Post* expressed such a view in a letter to the editor, remarking that 'the Ghost in Cock-lane has made so much Noise as to be heard at Oxford', thus inspiring him to write a lengthy verse, which concluded with a passionate call to arms to his learned compatriots to band together in order to drive the 'ghosts and sprites' out of England (by which he meant to eradicate belief in such superstitious nonsense).

So, it seems that the champions of science had just as much at stake as William Kent when it came to the prospect of debunking the Cock Lane ghost. Of course, Kent was far less interested in disproving the existence of ghosts than he was in clearing his name. And ultimately, he would be exonerated when Parsons' conspiracy to defame his creditor was at last exposed.

In early February 1762, a committee of respected gentlemen descended upon the Parsons household to conduct a series of experiments. Among them was the famed lexicographer Dr Samuel

Johnson, who relayed the events of the night to the educated (and mostly sceptical) readers of the *Gentleman's Magazine*.

He recounted that when certain controls were put into place, such as requiring Betty to place her hands on the bed in clear view of the investigators, the sounds would inevitably stop. When they requested the alleged spirit to make a noise from the site of Fanny's internment at St Sepulchre, witnesses in the church's vault again reported only silence.

Johnson and his fellow investigators therefore concluded that 'the child [had] some art of making or counterfeiting a particular noise, and that there [was] no agency of any higher cause'. In fact the Parsons' household staff confessed to having witnessed young Betty in the act of concealing a small piece of wood on her person, which they believed had been the instrument used to produce the sounds.

Prior to its debunking, however, the Cock Lane ghost managed to whip London into a frenzy. Throngs of curious spectators clogged the narrow lane, hoping to gain entrance to the infamous residence. And it was not just the 'ignorant masses' who sought a front-row seat to the supernatural spectacle, but princes, politicians and learned authors alike. These sorts were likely outwardly sceptical, but perhaps clung to a secret wish for the ghost to be real. Or maybe they were just looking for a cheap thrill, some excitement to break the monotony of their otherwise sober existence.

As we already know, Horace Walpole was among this eager crowd. On the evening of 30 January, he paid his own visit to Cock Lane, later recounting his experience as follows:

> *I went to hear it – for it is not an apparition but an audition. We set out from the opera, changed our clothes at Northumberland House, the Duke of York, Lady Northumberland, Lady Mary Coke, Lord Hertford and I, all in one hackney-coach and drove to the spot; it rained torrents; yet the lane was full of mob, and the house so full we could not get in – at last they discovered it was the Duke of York, and the company squeezed themselves into one another's pockets to make room for us.*
>
> *The house, which is borrowed, and to which the ghost has adjourned, is wretchedly small and miserable; when we opened the chamber, in which were fifty people, with no light but one tallow candle at the end, we tumbled over the bed of the child to whom the ghost comes, and whom*

they are murdering there by inches in such insufferable heat and stench.

At the top of the room are ropes to dry clothes – I asked if we were to have rope-dancing between the acts? – they told us, as they would at a puppet-show, that it would not come that night until 7 in the morning…

That Walpole should describe the experience in theatrical terms is fitting – especially since he visited the property after an evening at the opera. For the author and his aristocratic friends, the Cock Lane ghost was little more than light entertainment on an otherwise dreary winter's night. But what really jumps out here is Horace's disdain for the small and decrepit setting in which this ghost story took place. Such a grotty hovel simply would not do for his own ghostly tale.

Two years later, back at Strawberry Hill House, Horace Walpole sat down at the writing table in his library. A freshly lit candle added to the gloaming, casting long shadows across the pen and paper before him. Though they were barely visible in the twilight, Walpole knew he shared the company of his beloved (maternal) family members in the portraits above him. There was also the august presence of past English kings – portrait heads of Charles I and II in roundels in the painted glass windows, and a picture of what Horace believed depicted the marriage of Henry IV and Margaret of Anjou in an elaborate Gothic frame above the fireplace (it was actually a portrait of an unknown saint). He couldn't quite see them, but he sensed this noble coterie was gazing down on him approvingly.

Ensconced in the gloomth of his Gothic castle, his mind dancing with visions of his recent dream, Horace felt inspired. The evocative imagery of his dream added to a building obsession, for, although it had been more than two years since he had visited the famous Cock Lane 'ghost', Horace continued to be fascinated by the affair, still making references to it in his letters as late as 1790.

The whole thing, he made clear in his correspondence, was poppycock, but it did get him thinking. Clearly there was a healthy appetite for ghost stories, not just among the working classes, but also among his intelligent and erudite aristocratic friends. The Cock Lane ghost story was an 'egregious scene of folly', in Walpole's words: a foolish fraud, a work of sensational and silly fiction. Yet it had clearly got something right; it had gained the attention of the nation. But it also got something terribly wrong. Ghosts didn't belong in cramped modern lodging houses; they belonged in cavernous medieval castles. And with this improved setting in mind, Horace set to work on his own ghost story: the story of Manfred, lord of the Castle of Otranto, a medieval Italian citadel haunted by the ghost of its embittered former owner, and a sinister curse plaguing its present occupants.

The novel opens at the eponymous castle on a wedding day: Conrad, Manfred's sickly son, is marrying Princess Isabella. Manfred is eager for his son to marry in order to secure dynastic succession and forestall an ancient prophecy warning that Otranto will pass from the current family when the true owner 'should be grown too large to inhabit it'. Manfred's plans are dashed, however, when 'an enormous helmet, a hundred times larger than any casque ever made for a human being' falls from the sky, crushing the already enfeebled Conrad to death.

Suddenly finding himself without a son and heir, Manfred decides to cast aside his own wife, Hippolita, and make the fertile young princess his new bride. He corners Isabella in the castle's Long Gallery and declares his intentions: 'My fate depends on having sons, and this night I trust will give a new date to my hopes.' He lunges towards the horrified princess, but before he can carry out his dastardly plan he is distracted by the ominously swaying feathers of the giant helmet and the sudden movement of a nearby painting.

'At that instant the portrait of his grandfather, which hung over the bench where they had been sitting, uttered a deep sigh, and heaved its breast… It quit its panel and descended on the floor with a grave and melancholy air.'

As Manfred follows the beckoning ghost of his dead relative, Isabella escapes from the castle through a secret underground passageway. With the help of a local peasant, Theodore (who looks suspiciously like Alfonso, the former ruler of Otranto), the princess makes it to the nearby church of St Nicholas, where she finds sanctuary under the protection of one Father Jerome.

The rest of the story follows Manfred's obsessive pursuit of the truant princess. He is foiled by marauding knights, the girl's disapproving father, the mysterious Theodore, Father Jerome, and, of course, various paranormal forces. In the penultimate scene, set in the castle's crypt, Manfred walks in on Theodore praying with a young woman, whom he believes to be Isabella. In a jealous rage, he stabs the woman – only to discover that it is his own daughter, Matilda. This foul deed sets off the supernatural finale.

As the walls of the castle begin to crumble, the 'form of Alfonso, dilated to an immense magnitude' appears before the frightened mortals. 'Behold in Theodore the true heir of Alfonso,' says the vision and, accompanied by a clap of thunder, it ascends 'solemnly towards heaven'. Overcome with remorse, Manfred confesses that his grandfather had usurped the throne from Alfonso. It is then revealed that Theodore is really Alfonso's grandson. Order is finally restored when Manfred abdicates and Theodore and his new bride, Isabella, assume their rightful place as rulers of Otranto.

The conclusion of the story is significant. That the conflict is resolved – and the haunting effectively exorcised – by the restoration of the castle's rightful ancestral owners is not just a reflection of the preoccupations of an eighteenth-century aristocratic author with his own dynastic issues. The novel is rife with intrigue, with soap-opera-like twists and turns. It deals with questions of prophecy, chivalry, aristocracy and justice – and in doing so, it laid the groundwork for almost all modern haunted house narratives that would follow. Above all, though, *The Castle of Otranto* is a story that resolves issues of dynasty: it ends with its protagonists assuming their rightful positions in their ancestral home, thereby exorcising the hauntings. As we will see over the course of this book, the haunted house of our collective understanding invariably hinges on some sort of disruption to the ideal *family* home.

When it was released on Christmas Eve 1764, *The Castle of Otranto, A Story*, appeared under a pseudonym and was presented as the translation of an original Italian manuscript printed in Naples in 1529. That manuscript was, in turn, supposedly based on a much earlier story dating as far back as the Crusades.

It seems that this literary conceit was adopted, in part, to protect the author from bad press. Walpole recognised the 'wildness' of the story and admitted to friends he was 'diffident of its merit'. But, hidden behind the guise of the fictional translator 'William Marshal, Gent.', he could freely indulge in his outlandish medieval fantasy without fear of it damaging his reputation.

Following its surprise success, however, Horace opted to take credit for the work, and in subsequent editions it was published under his own name, with the revised title of *The Castle of Otranto, A Gothic Story*.

This was the first time that the adjective 'Gothic' was used to describe a literary work. And in effect, Walpole had invented a new – and lasting – connotation for the word. According to historian Alfred E. Longueil, 'Gothic' had three commonly understood meanings in the eighteenth century: 1) barbarous, 2) medieval, and 3) supernatural. The latter usage only passed into popular parlance following the publication of Walpole's book.

Combining an ancient curse, aristocratic love triangles, foreboding spirits and secret identities, Walpole's sensational story was a smash hit. It radically departed from the standard literary fare on offer. As Walpole well knew, the Georgian book-reading public subsisted mostly on a type of fiction now known as the 'sentimental novel'. As the name suggests, they were gushy and maudlin, featuring scenes of heightened distress, tenderness and bathos, designed to elicit a sympathetic response from the reader. They were also typically prescriptive, containing moral messages about love, marriage, family and personal conduct. The settings were usually modern and the characters often ordinary middle-class people, much like their intended audience.

The most famous of the genre was Samuel Richardson's *Pamela, or Virtue Rewarded* (1740), published some twenty years before Walpole's own novel. Similar books were continually churned out during Horace's lifetime and well into the following century. That several sentimental novel satires appeared, including Henry Fielding's *Shamela* (1741), is further testimony to their immense popularity.

Rather than penning his own satire, however, Horace wanted to offer the reader a wholly different kind of fiction. 'A god,' he wrote, '[or] at least a ghost, was absolutely necessary to frighten us out of too much senses.'

In the preface to the second edition of *Otranto*, Walpole offered an explanation of sorts for his literary experiment:

> *It was an attempt to blend the two kinds of romance, the ancient and the modern. In the former, all was imagination and improbability: in the latter, nature is always intended to be, and sometimes has been, copied with success. Invention has not been wanting; but the great resources of fancy have been dammed up, by a strict adherence to common life.*

In other words, he was trying to combine the fantasy of the medieval romance with the realism of the modern (eighteenth-century) novel – though whether or not he achieved this is debatable.

The initial response to *The Castle of Otranto* was dramatic. The first edition was an instant bestseller. Yet, as soon as it was revealed that the story was not, in fact, an old Italian legend recorded by a Cistercian monk and later discovered in 'the library of an ancient Catholic family in the north of England' (as the original preface maintained), interest began to wane. Ironically, critics damned Horace's book for some of the same reasons they bashed the sentimental novels he reportedly abhorred, describing it as superficial, sensationalist and maudlin.

But Walpole recognised that his work was ahead of its time. Like his architectural innovations, his literary experiment was an act of defiance against the straight-laced society in which he lived. He remarked: 'I have not written for this century, which only wants cold reason.'

It turns out he was right. It would take some time for the Gothic novel to gain full traction, and though a few works emerged in relatively quick succession to capitalise on the success of Walpole's book, it would not be until the start of the nineteenth century that the Gothic novel truly came into its own.

Today, Horace's literary magnum opus, though recognised as the first Gothic novel, is by no means held up as its best example. Outside of university lecture halls, the book is rarely discussed. Instead, works such as Mary Shelley's *Frankenstein* (1818) and Bram Stoker's *Dracula* (1897) are more often cited as prime examples of Gothic fiction.

Many modern readers, like his contemporaries, find that Walpole's work lacks fully realised characters, and relies too much on histrionics and melodrama. What's more, the gargantuan ghost that dominates Horace's pages bears little resemblance to the shadowy spectres that would haunt the houses of Gothic fiction a century later. Yet, Horace's work was undeniably influential.

A decade later, the novelist Clara Reeve declared that her own tale, *The Old English Baron* (1777), was 'the literary offspring of the *Castle of Otranto* written upon the same plan, with a design to unite the most attractive and interesting circumstances of the ancient Romance and modern Novel'. She was the first of countless authors to borrow heavily from Walpole.

In succeeding years, *Otranto*'s themes and plot devices were recycled again and again. The 'transcribed manuscript' framing device, for example, was reused in Reeve's *The Old English Baron* and in William Beckford's *Vethek* (1782). The themes of aristocratic decay and dynastic crisis appear in works such as Ann Radcliffe's *The Castles of Athlin and Dunbayne* (1789) and Charles Maturin's *The Fatal Revenge; or the Family of Montorio* (1807). And even its inventive imagery of a picture coming to life was revived in Shelley's *Frankenstein*, Oscar Wilde's *The Picture of Dorian Gray* (1890) and M. R. James's *The Mezzotint* (1904).

But more than anything it was the archetypal setting of the Gothic novel that *Otranto* helped cement: the dark castle, abbey, monastery or manor house – any gloomy old building that seemed to harbour shadowy secrets. And in the very early days, it literally was *any* old pile – ecclesiastical, public or private – though over time, the domestic home became the standard setting for the Gothic novel.

Those seeking to identify the real-life location of Walpole's fictional castle seem to have little to go on, yet the author has left us some tantalising clues. In the preface to the first edition, Horace, as the fictional translator, hinted: 'The scene is undoubtedly laid in some real castle. The author seems frequently, without design, to describe particular parts.'

Later, in the note he sent to his friend William Cole with a copy of the book, Walpole wrote:

> *Your partiality to me and Strawberry [Hill] have I hope inclined you to excuse the wildness of this story [Otranto]. You will even have found some traits to put you in mind of that place. When you read of the picture quitting its panel, did you not recollect the portrait of Lord Falkland all in white in my gallery?*

With this in mind, it is easy to imagine Horace absent-mindedly strolling down Strawberry Hill's Long Gallery. Under its glittering fan-vaulted ceiling, he pauses to glance out of the windows to the elegantly landscaped grounds below, only to be distracted by a sudden movement he sees out of the corner of his eye. Eying the nearby portrait of the Jacobean statesman, Henry Cary, 1st Viscount Falkland, Walpole's fertile imagination awakens. He conjures up an image of the dour gentleman descending from his canvas and gliding across the gallery floor with the same 'grave and melancholy air' he would later ascribe to the ghost of Manfred's grandfather. The author is thus transported from his own home to the mystical environs of the Castle of Otranto.

The neo-Gothic legacy

Like his literary legacy, Horace's contribution to architecture took a little time to gain momentum. For the most part, Georgian attitudes towards the Gothic style were still largely coloured by popular opinion about the period in history from which it originated.

Anti-Catholic and anti-foreign sentiment – particularly in the aftermath of the Glorious Revolution (1688) and the Jacobite Rebellion (1708–46) – led Britons to be naturally suspicious of an architectural style that symbolised the Catholic past.

Walpole and his fellow champions of the Gothic held stridently anti-Catholic views. Indeed, in the preface to the first edition of *The Castle of Otranto*, Horace wrote that 'the principal incidents [of the novel] are such as were believed in the darkest ages of Christianity' – referring, of course, to the era before the Protestant Reformation.

It was not until the start of the nineteenth century that the British public expressed a more widespread interest in and appreciation of the medieval past. They also grew more sympathetic towards Catholicism (manifest in the series of 'Catholic Relief Bills' passed by the government in the late eighteenth and early nineteenth centuries).

A reawakening of high church and Anglo-Catholic beliefs paved the way for the later Gothic Revival movement which dominated religious and civic architecture in the Victorian period. The most iconic exemplar of British neo-Gothic is the parliamentary complex at the

Palace of Westminster, built after the original medieval structure burned down in 1834. Its towers – a defining feature of the London skyline – soar over the Thames like the spires of a magnificent Gothic cathedral. Its powerful evocation of the ecclesiastical is unsurprising given that one of the lead designers, Augustus Pugin, had recently converted to Catholicism.

Meanwhile, Horace's 'Strawberry Hill Gothic' (or 'Georgian Gothic') has come to be seen as a distinct, yet more limited, movement of its own. Only a handful of buildings can be said to copy the appearance of Strawberry Hill, with its distinctive pristine white castellated walls. The Priory Hospital in Roehampton, Surrey, constructed in 1811, probably comes closest to it.

In 1923 the great Edwardian master of ghost stories, M. R. James, chose to describe the mysterious doll's house in his Gothic short story 'The Haunted Doll's House' as being 'Strawberry Hill Gothic', thus underscoring the longevity and conceptual importance of Walpole's creation in supernatural fiction.

So why has Gothic architecture become so strongly associated with the supernatural? Walpole can't have arbitrarily picked the Gothic castle as the setting for his ghost story, and it surely can't have been a coincidence that his ghostly dream came to him at Strawberry Hill, and not at, say, Houghton Hall or his neoclassical townhouse in London. The religious connotations of the Gothic might offer one explanation for why it is often linked with the idea of ghosts. A lot of early Gothic fiction incorporates ecclesiastical buildings – abbeys, monasteries and the like – and even the later stories, which typically take place in domestic settings, feature buildings that borrow heavily from an architectural style that was once mainly reserved for religious structures.

These buildings are all inherently old, dark and mysterious. But more than that, the Gothic aesthetic, with all its Catholic associations, is linked to a particular form of the afterlife.

The Catholic concept of purgatory (long since expunged from Protestant dogma) is the belief that impure souls linger in a liminal phase, awaiting their passage to paradise. These souls are not deemed fundamentally bad; rather, they are lacking in the requisites to gain entry to heaven. They include people who died in a state of sin, those who were not given a proper burial and, until fairly recently, those who died without first being baptised.

Though there is debate within the Catholic Church about what exactly purgatory is, the popular conception of it was largely shaped by medieval writers, most notably Dante Aligheri. In Dante's *The Divine Comedy* (1321), he describes purgatory as a physical location – a third place between heaven and hell; a mountainous island in an otherwise empty sea. Officially, however, Catholic doctrine does not teach purgatory as a place, but rather a state of being, a stage in the process of life, death and eternal salvation.

So, out of the raw material of ancient religious dogma, writers of Gothic fiction (and the general public) came to conceive of ghosts as trapped souls with unfinished business. Where once those souls with unfinished business might have been thought to be tied to an abstract metaphysical space, they were now firmly connected to a literal one. A specific one: the domestic home.

The haunted house thus became a kind of purgatorial 'waiting room' from which unhappy souls could hope to escape heavenward once they had somehow set things right in the world of the living. 'Scratching Fanny', Alfonso, and the scores of Gothic ghosts to come were all cut from this same purgatorial cloth.

It is clear that the neo-Gothic in art, literature and architecture has lived on long after Horace set the ball in motion. More than a century after Walpole realised his medieval fantasy in Twickenham, another eccentric medievalist created his own on the Isle of Bute, a small island off the western coast of Scotland. It was at this extravagantly eccentric monument that I – having recently completed my doctoral studies – found myself in the autumn of 2015. I took up the role of curatorial researcher there, to study the home's unique social, architectural and art historical heritage.

The millionaire polymath John Patrick Crichton Stuart, 3rd Marquess of Bute, was the richest man in Victorian Britain. His annual income – based on mining and shipping concerns – was about

£15 million in today's currency, giving him more than enough resources to create the world's grandest neo-Gothic home.

His first attempt came in the remodelling of his Welsh estate, Cardiff Castle (which was a real medieval castle dating back to the twelfth century). Not satisfied with the genuine article, in 1868 Bute enlisted the services of the eminent Gothic Revival architect William Burgess to expand and redecorate the castle in an eclectic, pseudo-historical mode, incorporating Gothic, Byzantine and even Arabic motifs.

But it was his more ambitious architectural project at his ancestral home in Scotland that truly allowed Bute to run wild. This was Mount Stuart, a colossal red-brick palace built atop the fire-damaged ruins of the family's Georgian seat on the Isle of Bute. Between 1878 and 1900, Mount Stuart was rebuilt from the ground up using an army of architects and designers, including Burgess, Robert Rowand Anderson and Richard Weir Schultz. The new Mount Stuart boasted a colonnaded marble hall, a small jewel-like Byzantine chapel, a Gothic crypt and an indoor swimming pool with a Turkish bathhouse theme.

Like Strawberry Hill, it is an encyclopaedia of references to the former owner's favourite Gothic (and Romanesque and Byzantine) buildings, as well as being a lavish homage to Bute's adopted Catholic faith. Lord Bute's conversion at the age of twenty-one shocked Victorian society, and inspired the eponymous character in Benjamin Disraeli's *Lothair* (1870).

Fittingly, in addition to his interests in architecture, medieval history and religion, Bute was also an amateur paranormal investigator, a member of the Society for Psychical Research, and the author of *The Alleged Haunting of B—— House* (1899), which documented scientific investigations into the haunting of Ballechin House in Perthshire.

One of my first questions when I arrived at Mount Stuart was, 'Is it haunted?' A natural assumption for any visitor. After all, it seems to have all the necessary ingredients – a long history, a Gothic aesthetic, a strong whiff of Catholicism. Yet the family and staff who had lived and worked there for years were only able to offer me a few hazy encounters: the aroma of cigar smoke in the study, the sense of a benign maternal presence in the nursery, and a general feeling of disquiet in the attic.

At first, I opted to work in the nursery, as it offered a quiet retreat from the bustling activity of the archives and library a few floors below. But I also hoped to have my own encounter with the friendly ghost of a former nanny. For hours each day, I sat alone in silence at the makeshift desk I had set up, hoping to feel her loving ghostly embrace, as a Bute family member had vaguely recalled from her childhood. But I experienced nothing.

In truth, the great Gothic pile is fairly quiet in supernatural terms. It is actually the the neoclassical Dumfries House, the Bute family's secondary Scottish residence, that, the same family member told me, has a much stronger reputation for being haunted. Yet Mount Stuart *looks* haunted. And so, most years around Halloween, it hosts 'haunted house' tours, and the few flimsy anecdotes of ghostly experiences are recounted to guests by staff dressed in cheesy historical costumes.

Today, this kind of event is standard practice at historic sites with even the vaguest of ghostly associations. As archivist Carole Tucker tells me, the same kind of event is held at Strawberry Hill, even though the home has no real association with the supernatural.

I believe Carole when she says that Strawberry Hill is, quite simply, *not* haunted. But given its connection to one of the most important fictional ghost stories in British history, this seems almost inconceivable. Sure, there is a story that Horace practised necromancy, and that the perfectly circular 'Round Tower' was used to summon demons. And it is said that one nineteenth-century resident, Countess Frances Waldegrave, allegedly murdered three of her four husbands, and later returned to haunt Strawberry Hill. There is also the series of twentieth-century employees who died under mysterious circumstances, supposedly following encounters with the ghost of the murderous Lady Waldegrave. But in the end, it seems the most famous ghost to come out of Strawberry Hill was Horace Walpole himself – not a literal ghost, of course, but a symbolic spectre whose powerful presence continues to loom large over the cultural history of the haunted house.

CHILLINGHAM CASTLE

BESIEGED FROM WITHIN

2

The feudal castle and phantom forms have so long been associated that one almost suggests another…

Leonora Bennet, Countess Tankerville (1872–1949)

Once upon a time at a haunted castle...

In the autumn of 1896, under a leaden Northumberland sky, Leonora Bennet approached the gates to her new home, Chillingham Castle. A somewhat unnerving scene greeted the American expat, who had only recently married her aristocratic paramour, George Bennet (the future 7th Earl of Tankerville) in her native Washington state, after which they had moved to the north of England. While the landscape she viewed from her carriage window on the way to the castle had been barren, desolate moorland, the immediate environs of Chillingham were softer and greener. A long avenue of oak trees might have been a reassuringly familiar reminder of the leafy Pacific Northwest – though, as Leonora would later learn, these were 'hanging trees', the primitive gallows once used to torture, execute and display the kingdom's enemies and traitors.

Chillingham Castle, located in the far north of England, a stone's throw from the Scottish border, has a long and violent history. The medieval stronghold turned stately home had a reputation for being haunted, and Leonora would experience paranormal activity there almost immediately.

In fact, her first supernatural encounter with Chillingham had occurred several years before she even took up residence. In a dream, Leonora's deceased brother-in-law (whom she had never met, but later recognised in photographs) greeted her at the gates of her soon-to-be marital home. When she finally visited the place on that autumn day, Leonora mused: 'This is the second time I find myself approaching the gates of Chillingham Castle, but strangely, it's the first time I have actually been here.'

In her first days at Chillingham, Leonora felt a mixture of excitement and apprehension in assuming her role as the mistress of a *bona fide* medieval castle. As a relatively ordinary upper-middle-class American, a music teacher and daughter of a dentist, this would have been a highly unusual environment, like no home she had ever lived in before.

'I was raised in Spokane in Washington state, and we do not have castles there,' Leonora wrote in her journal. 'I have seen them in my travels, of course, and I have imagined them from the time I was a little girl dreaming of princesses and handsome knights, but now that I am living in one, nothing seems to be quite as it should.'

Indeed this was no fairy-tale castle. It was a decidedly darker sort.

Over 100 years after Lady Leonora's arrival, and 800 more after its original construction, Chillingham Castle is now a popular visitor attraction. Despite its remote location, the castle still pulls in a steady stream of tourists keen to explore its battlements and ramparts. While neither the biggest nor best-known castle in the region, it has a unique charm. And it probably doesn't hurt that it is situated near the more popular site of Alnwick Castle, the seat of the Duke of Northumberland – or, as it is more popularly known, the stand-in for Hogwarts School of Witchcraft and Wizardry in the Harry Potter films.

Chillingham's present owner, Sir Humphry Wakefield, 2nd Baronet, purchased the ancient edifice in 1982 for his wife, Katherine, a direct descendant of the noble family who had once owned it. Given that the castle had been abandoned for nearly five decades, she may not have fully appreciated the romantic gesture at the time. A cramped, crumbling citadel comprising four corner towers, connected by crenelated walls surrounding a small central courtyard, Chillingham seemed to have changed little since its early days as a fortified defence against Scottish invaders. But Sir Humphry quickly recognised its unusual potential.

He soon set to work renovating the old pile, a process that took several years just to make it habitable. Wary of whitewashing hundreds of years of history, Wakefield used a gentle touch, carefully preserving the castle's authentic character, embracing the old and the odd. Using his resources as a London antiques dealer, the baronet filled his home from floor to rafter with a vast assortment of oddities (medieval torture equipment, suits of armour, taxidermised animal heads, and the like), creating an aesthetic that one commentator went so far as to compare to the campy 1970s children's classic, *The Ghosts of Motley Hall*.

Capitalising on the recent rise in popularity of ghost-themed tourism and television programming, Chillingham is currently marketed as the 'Most Haunted Castle in Britain', hosting some 20,000 visitors a year for candlelit ghost tours, spooky overnight stays and Gothic-themed weddings.

Although visitors to Chillingham Castle range from serious history buffs to curious holidaymakers, most who come to the castle have at least a passing interest in ghost stories. Many hope they will see or experience something spooky. And as it happens, quite a few of them do, indicating that either Chillingham really *is* haunted, or its unsettling ambiance has the power to persuade even those who profess not to believe.

One such unwitting convert was Tracy Barlow, a qualified nurse from Hull specialising in wound care, who visited Chillingham in October 2018. Given her line of work, she's clearly not squeamish or easily frightened. She's also fiercely practical. 'I have never believed in the paranormal,' Tracy tells me. Though she admits that, as a child, she had an interest in ghost stories and horror films, even then she was never quite convinced of the existence of ghosts. Over time, her scepticism grew, and by the time she was an adult, she found herself almost annoyed by the credulity of others. 'I got so sick of it, I actually went out of my way to prove that ghosts were not real. I was the opposite of a ghost hunter.'

With this goal in mind, Tracy and her equally sceptical husband, Lee, planned a three-night stay at Britain's most haunted castle. The first two nights they spent in the Grey Apartment – one of seven self-catering guest suites at Chillingham – passed completely uneventfully, as they expected. On the third night, however, after a day of sightseeing and a pleasant meal at a local pub, Tracy and Lee returned to their accommodation to find that the atmosphere had changed. Where it had previously been warm and welcoming, it now felt somehow ominous.

'I can't explain it, but it was unsettling, and I felt like we were being watched,' she recalls. 'We were sat watching TV and both of us kept looking behind us, as it felt like someone was there...' To ease her mounting anxiety, Tracy got up from the sofa and went to look out of the window. As she watched a family of tourists playing on a cannon, something inside the room caught her eye. It was one of the many antiques in the apartment. 'Suddenly, the mandolin that was on the window ledge turned to face me by itself,' she maintains. 'It didn't spin or slip; it literally turned slowly to face me.'

Ever the pragmatist, Tracy felt that there must be some natural explanation. So she tried to push it to the back of her mind and settle back down to the nightly news. But as soon as she took her seat, she felt something brush against the back of her hair. Then they heard an 'almighty bang' from the bedroom. It sounded as though someone had thrown a table against the wall. Yet when they checked the room, the couple found it completely undisturbed.

Neither of them were particularly looking forward to going to sleep that night, but when the time came, they calmly carried out their regular night-time rituals before climbing into bed. Needless to say, they did not have a peaceful night's rest. Moments after they switched off the light, a nearby wardrobe began rattling and banging as if someone was trying to open it. Then came the 'unmistakable sound of fabric dragging along the carpet, backwards and forwards across the room'. The banging wardrobe got louder. Lee rolled over to Tracy and suggested that perhaps they had better head home early in order to 'beat the traffic'. It was 3 a.m.

However, despite the unearthly noises in their bedchamber – and the sound of bagpipes and horses' hooves from the courtyard outside their window – the couple stayed the night, managing to get a few broken hours of sleep. At 6 a.m. they got up and promptly checked out.

So, after her unforgettable stay at Chillingham Castle, had Tracy changed her beliefs about the supernatural? 'Well ... there is something off about that place,' she admits. Though she won't go so far as to say she believes in ghosts, she can't explain away all that she experienced in the Grey Apartment. That night got Tracy wondering 'whether dark histories can leave a residue. Not ghosts as such,' she muses. 'But maybe a residue from the past that present-day people can pick up on.'

This is a popular hypothesis for the occurrence of supernatural phenomena, expounded by believers and sceptics alike. It's known as the 'stone tape' theory, and it posits that so-called hauntings are really just 'tape recordings': mental impressions of emotional or traumatic events recorded in the stone (or bricks and mortar) of a house, castle or other building, which are replayed under certain conditions. So, if a particularly violent or harrowing incident took place in a building, its walls could soak up the bad energy. In Chillingham, there was quite a lot of bad energy to soak up.

In a 2008 episode of *Ghost Hunters International*, one of the hosts, Donna Lacroix, describes Chillingham's dark past in horrifyingly grisly detail:

> *In history, it was a strategically placed line of defence against the Scots. Thousands of prisoners were tortured and slaughtered here in the most horrific ways. We're talking everything from men having their arms and legs ripped off, thrown down a 20-foot hole and left to die. Prisoners resorting to cannibalism, forced to eat their own flesh to survive. Some were even put into barrels with spikes and rolled around until the flesh was ripped right off their bodies.*

This, Donna maintains, is why Chillingham is so haunted.

But there's a problem with this theory. The ghosts that reputedly haunt Chillingham Castle are not hideously disfigured prisoners. They're not Scottish, not soldiers, not even men. They are, by and large, women and children. A forlorn countess; a little boy dressed in blue; a pallid woman desperate for a drink of water. These are Chillingham's most famous ghostly residents. And they seem to have very little to do with the castle's history as a military stronghold and everything to do with its past as a family home.

So, what *does* make Chillingham so haunted? Like scores of other castles of a similar age and pedigree, it has had this reputation for years. Several of the ghostly legends associated with it seem to coincide with Lady Leonora Bennet's tenure at the castle at the start of the nineteenth century, making her a key player in Chillingham's story. And this makes sense: as a spiritualist with an avid interest in the supernatural, Leonora may have helped to shape the castle's reputation. That she was a wife and mother – an American expat struggling with her domestic duties in a strange new environment – might explain why the ghosts who are reported to manifest are women and children.

And yet, three years before Leonora took up residence in 1896, the *Globe* newspaper ran a story on Chillingham's 'Radiant Boy', the mysterious child in blue who is still said to manifest in a certain bedroom over a century later. It is one of the most enduring legends connected to the castle, which evidently preceded the time of the ghost-enamoured American countess.

So, the exact origins of Chillingham's haunted reputation remain unknown. Regardless, we can still identify a few of the main factors at play. There's its violent history, of course; but there's also its architectural aesthetic, its atmospheric setting, and a folkloric and literary tradition that places the medieval castle at the heart of so many scary stories. For although it was in the eighteenth century that Horace Walpole popularised castles as the standard setting for Gothic fiction, such structures had already long been associated with the ghostly.

Why is this? How and why did we inherit this assumption that all medieval castles must be haunted? Perhaps the very essence of the castle as a structure lends itself to the scary, its dissonance making us feel instinctively ill at ease. At once fortress and family home, theatre of war and backdrop for domestic drama, the castle can be a confusing and chaotic space.

And as Lady Leonora would discover, a forbidding fortress like Chillingham was far from the ideal place to raise a family.

It must be said that Chillingham isn't a haunted *house*, per se. It's a haunted *castle*. And while the word 'castle' is often used interchangeably with words like 'palace' or 'mansion' to refer to a grand and important residence, the term is strictly defined as 'a large structure, typically of the medieval period, fortified against attack with thick walls, battlements, towers, and in some cases, a moat'.

Chillingham was constructed in this manner in the early thirteenth century, when it was one of almost 100 fortifications that dotted the bleak borderlands of England and Scotland, a turbulent territory suffering from repeated raids from both sides of the border for centuries until the Act of Union of 1707 brought the kingdoms together.

It was here at Chillingham in 1298 that Edward I launched his attack on William Wallace during the First War of Scottish Independence. A century later, Edward III granted the original owners, the Grey family, a Licence to Crenelate, allowing the construction of battlements that transformed the formerly small stronghold into a fully fortified castle. These battlements were marked out by regularly spaced 'crenels' (rectangular gaps designed for shooting arrows or firing cannons at an enemy below), giving Chillingham the jagged toothlike walls most of us associate with medieval castles.

But even in this tumultuous age, when such defensive structures were essential for the survival of kings and communities, the castle almost always also served a domestic function alongside its military one, as the home of the lord and his family. Chillingham was the residence of the powerful Grey family (later the Earls of Tankerville), descendants of the kinsmen of William the Conqueror. Within this working castle, tucked away from guardrooms, weapons stores, kitchens and the communal Great Hall, were the small private quarters of the lord and lady, where they conducted their regular everyday lives.

As time wore on and the kingdoms of Europe experienced more prolonged periods of peace or decided to conduct their battles further afield, the need for a fortified dwelling decreased, so many former fortresses were gradually converted into more comfortable family homes (though, as Lady Leonora would learn, there was only so much that could be done to suitably domesticate a crumbling fortress like Chillingham). At any rate, the case can be made that castles have always been *homes*, at least, if not houses.

Today, the term 'castle' may conjure up two fairly distinct images in our minds. The first is the fairy-tale castle – or Disney princess castle, if you will. This was probably the sort that Leonora envisioned as a little girl growing up in America. It is the kind comprising soaring circular towers, steep spires and white crenelated walls – motifs deriving from the Flamboyant Gothic style, a late Gothic derivation used in many French and German castles built in the sixteenth and seventeenth centuries.

These buildings might properly be called palaces rather than castles, given that they were not actually fortified and served almost exclusively as dwellings. But they nevertheless referred back to their medieval precursors, retaining the battlements and towers that were once used for military purposes, but that were now mostly ornamental.

Because of their whimsical quality, these castles have long been associated with fairy tales and epic legends. And rightly so, considering that most of our canonical fairy tales are set in a utopian version of medieval Europe, making the stylised variant of the castle the perfect backdrop. Since at least the nineteenth century, these fantastical structures have inspired numerous book illustrations. Cinderella's iconic castle – seen both at Disney's Magic Kingdom and in the logo that appears at the beginning of every Disney film – was likewise modelled after castles of this type; specifically, Château d'Ussé, a seventeenth-century chateau in the Loire Valley in France, and Neuschwanstein Castle, a nineteenth-century Flamboyant Gothic Revival palace perched atop a hill in southern Bavaria.

Somewhat ironically, the castle aesthetic now widely associated with sweet children's stories about princesses and fairy godmothers was almost certainly also an influence on Walpole's Strawberry Hill House. The fictional castle in his novel, on the other hand, seems to take more of its aesthetic cues from our second type of castle.

The second sort is the more rustic, rough-hewn castle with solid grey stone walls, long battlements, arrow slits, trapdoors, secret passageways and dungeons. This is the kind we picture looming over a stark northern landscape, on the watch for marauding attackers – an ancient, fortified castle, like Chillingham. And it is this type of castle that is most commonly associated with ghosts.

When Leonora Bennet came to her castle home for the first time at the end of the nineteenth century, the concept of the haunted castle was already firmly entrenched in the popular imagination. Though she may have been hoping for the fairy-tale version, she would certainly have been familiar with its more ominous counterpart. The appearance of the castle prompted her to ask her new in-laws, 'Have you any ghosts?' The stoic response Leonora received from Countess Olivia Tankerville, her stony-faced mother-in-law, was: 'We do not allow them.' The reaction of the aged Charles, 6th Earl of Tankerville, on the other hand, suggested that Leonora's instincts may have been right after all. 'My father-in-law's eyes twinkled and sparkled despite his age,' Leonora remarked, 'and his wry smile hinted of hidden mysteries that had been swept under the carpet a generation past.'

The origin of the haunted castle myth is impossible to pinpoint. It has been part of the British folkloric tradition for aeons. And along the borderlands, in northern England and southern Scotland, where so many decaying old fortresses litter the landscape, it is fully embedded in the vernacular culture. Take, for example, a legend first documented in the early twelfth century describing supernatural activities at Alnwick Castle, Chillingham's neighbour 10 miles to the south. The story goes that the lord of Alnwick (or in some versions, a gentleman friend of the lord) was a jealous, paranoid man who feared his wife was unfaithful to him. One night he silently slipped out of his bedroom window and crept along the castle's parapet towards his wife's chamber, hoping to catch her in the act. Before he could peer in, however, he slipped and fell to his death in the courtyard below. Though he was given a proper burial, the lord soon rose from his crypt beneath the castle to wreak havoc on the mortal inhabitants of the estate, spreading plague as he went. When the frightened locals decided to exhume the lord's body, they were astonished to discover the corpse bloated with blood.

In his account of the story, recorded in *Historia rerum Anglicarum* (1196–8), the medieval chronicler William of Newburgh identified this as one of a flurry of contemporary reports of revenants. A 'revenant' – from the French word *revenir*, meaning to return – wasn't a ghost exactly, but an animated corpse who returned from the dead to torment the living. While popular belief in such creatures waned towards the end of the Middle Ages, legends like 'the vampire of Alnwick Castle' would be reborn centuries later in Gothic fiction. Their ancient settings would be revived, too.

The haunted castle was finally catapulted to the forefront of popular culture at the end of the eighteenth century, thanks to Walpole and his Romantic-era literary successors. By the nineteenth century, the spooky setting was cropping up everywhere, from cheap chapbook publications (the 'pulp fiction' of the day) to more sophisticated short stories, poetry and novels devised for more educated readers. At one end of this spectrum were products such as *The Haunted Castle; or the Child of Misfortune: A Gothic Tale* (1801), an obscure 54-page anonymously published novella that sold for sixpence (about £1.10 in today's currency). At the other end was Bram Stoker's *Dracula* (1897), perhaps the most famous horror novel of all time.

In its first American edition, published in 1899, *Dracula* featured a frontispiece illustration depicting a black crenelated tower perched atop a hill, shrouded in mist and a cloud of bats – a simple, yet enduring embodiment of the haunted castle (notably having much in common with the later iconography of the haunted house). This frontispiece was based on Stoker's descriptions of the fictional Transylvanian residence of the titular Count Dracula: 'A vast ruined castle, from whose tall black windows came no ray of light, and whose broken battlements showed a jagged line against the sky…'

Castle Dracula quickly upstaged its Gothic forerunner Otranto as the ultimate haunted castle (admittedly, one that was home to a vampire, rather than a ghost). The book was an immediate critical success, praised for its masterful storytelling and evocative settings, including Dracula's sinister seat, which would later be immortalised in more than fifty film adaptations (as well as a popular video game franchise called *Castlevania*). It even helped put Transylvania, a formerly obscure region of Romania, on the cultural map, drawing tourists to the castles that had apparently inspired the book – despite the fact that the author had never actually visited them.

Instead, the Dublin-born Stoker spent much of his time prior to writing *Dracula* in northern England and Scotland – in Whitby in North Yorkshire and Cruden Bay in Aberdeenshire. In fact, it was New Slains Castle, a sixteenth-century manor teetering on a cliff above the North Sea, a mile north of Cruden Bay, that is believed to have informed the layout of Stoker's fictional castle. Thus, it was actually the dramatic, windswept landscape of northern Britain, with its crumbling castle ruins, cold sea and calamitous history, that was the true Gothic backdrop for Stoker's story. And at precisely the same time he was composing his classic tale of terror, Lady Leonora Bennet was embarking on her own at Chillingham Castle.

Spirit lady: Leonora Bennet, 7th Countess Tankerville

The legend of Chillingham Castle has an unexpected central protagonist – not the ghost of a marauding Scotsman or a medieval princess, but a comparatively modern (living) person – the turn-of-the-century mistress of the manor, Leonora Bennet, wife of the 7th Earl of Tankerville, who lived there from 1896 to 1931. Leonora was, at once, a conventional upper-class woman of her day and a fish out of water. In this respect, she makes an ideal historical tour guide.

When she arrived at Chillingham in the autumn of 1896, the worldly, well-educated expat brought with her just enough knowledge and prior experience to intellectually understand the environment she would soon call home. However, while Leonora had learned all about castles as a young girl and had even visited a few while on holiday in Europe in her youth, no amount of armchair tourism or childhood sightseeing could have prepared her for the harsh reality of living in a 700-year-old fortress. She would have to find coping mechanisms – some of which, as we will learn, involved invoking the supernatural.

Leonora Bennet (née van Marter) was born in Zurich, Switzerland, on 19 November 1872. Her American parents were James Gilbert van Marter of New York and Sophia Albers of Missouri. While it was reported in the British press that Leonora was an heiress, and that her father was a magnate of some description, James was actually a dental surgeon who, rather unusually, specialised in the study of ancient dental artefacts. At some point he moved to Europe, spending time in Switzerland as well as Rome, where he studied ancient Etruscan dentistry. It is not clear whether the family was, as the *Manchester Courier* stated, 'fabulously wealthy', but they were certainly cultured.

The details of Leonora's early life are hazy, though thanks to her copious diary-keeping as an adult we know that she spent an impressionable part of her youth in Spokane, Washington. She seems to have flitted between the two American coasts, and made regular excursions to Europe. According to some reports, she was educated in Germany and France. By the mid-1890s, she was living in New York, where she received a certificate in teaching the piano-forte. It was also around this time that, at a dinner party in the city, she met her future husband, George Montagu Bennet. Rumour had it that the eccentric future earl had somersaulted over a sofa and into the lap of his would-be bride.

Remembered by his nickname, the 'Singing Earl', Lord Bennet was a legendary figure who began his varied career as a naval officer before entering the army and serving as the Lord Lieutenant of Ireland's aide-de-camp. Upon retiring from the military, he travelled to America in the 1890s and fell in with some Christian revivalists – evangelicals with a strong belief in their personal connection to God, often expressed through impassioned hymnal music. While in New York, Lord Bennet studied under the Italian opera singer, Giovanni Sbriglia, perfecting the rich baritone voice for which he would become renowned. At other times during his lengthy sojourn in America, Lord Bennet was reputed to have worked as a cowpuncher on a south-western ranch and as a clown in a travelling circus. He also had an artistic side, expressed through intricate woodcarvings and painted miniatures which he occasionally exhibited at the Royal Academy.

George Bennet was clearly a bohemian at heart, though blue blood coursed through his veins. His seventeenth-century ancestor, John Bennet, 1st Baron Ossulston, married into the eminent Grey family of Chillingham, who, during the Hundred Years' War, earned the earldom of Tankerville for helping to defeat the French at Tancarville in Normandy. Through his paternal grandmother, the legendary beauty Corisande de Gramant, Lord Bennet was also a descendant of the French King Henry IV, from whom he was said to have inherited his brooding good looks. His charming eccentricities were likewise attributed to his noble French ancestry.

By the end of the nineteenth century, the Tankervilles' fortunes and prestige may have been on a downward ebb, like so many aristocratic families of the time. And they surely benefited from the influx of American funds to help maintain their ancient northern pile. Yet the assumption that Lord Bennet followed in the footsteps of his cash-strapped peers by deliberately seeking out an American heiress seems unfounded. For one thing, it was reported in *Hearth and Home* magazine in October 1895 that the Tankerville estates were still intact, ranking 'second only to those of the Duke of Northumberland in that county...'

Moreover, George's adopted faith placed little emphasis on material wealth. Reportedly, he preached to villagers in Chillingham and to sailors aboard ships docked in Tacoma harbour, near his wife's family home, indicating that he was committed to a missionary life rather than a life of luxury. But crucially, it seems, in Leonora van Marter, George Bennet found a kindred spirit: a fellow music-loving eccentric to join him on his unconventional life journey. Quite simply, it was a love match. They married in Tacoma, Washington, on 23 October 1895.

Leonora's arrival at Chillingham would not occur for another year; ever the eccentrics, she and her new husband spent the first year of their marriage on the American continent, on honeymoon in Canada and then back in the States, where they participated in missionary activities at the Tacoma docks.

The earliest evidence of their presence in England comes in a news report of 17 September 1896, which describes a homecoming celebration held at Chillingham, during which the Earl and Countess Tankerville presented their son with a silver bowl commemorating his recent marriage. Lady Leonora, however, was not in attendance. She remained in London due to 'indisposition' – probably a Victorian euphemism for pregnancy or miscarriage (a daughter she conceived earlier that year had died in childbirth).

They likely decided at the time that Leonora was in no state to make the long and arduous journey up north, where she could take the train only as far as Wooler, a small Northumbrian town at the foot of the Cheviot Hills, then would have to endure a rocky carriage ride for the remaining 7 miles to Chillingham. When she did finally make the trip, she travelled in a dilapidated coach pulled by an old shire horse called Bobby.

Leonora arrived childless, and apprehensive about the prospect of starting a family at Chillingham. But however uneasy she felt, she could never have anticipated the trouble that awaited inside her new marital home – a place that was meant to bring her happiness, comfort and security, but in the end only brought hardship and heartache.

Chillingham Castle would be Leonora's place of residence for the next thirty years, but it could hardly be described as her 'home' in the conventionally positive sense of the word.

*

At some point early in her residency at Chillingham, Lady Leonora sat down at a writing desk in the library in the old south tower and carefully drafted a page of notes, outlining a proposed health and housekeeping regime for life at the castle. These jottings seem to form a kind of personal pep talk: a strategy for survival in her strange new environment. She begins on a positive note: 'Chillingham can be recommended because of its bracing air, the country life and the mental effect of being in the long-looked-for home.' But, Leonora caveats, 'Some precautions must be taken.'

Truth be told, Chillingham Castle was in a somewhat shabby condition. Granted, there was ample evidence of the extravagant sums that had previously been spent on the castle in anticipation of royal visits, namely the construction of the Great Hall in honour of James VI in 1603 and its lavish redecoration two centuries later for the future Edward VII. But after more than 150 years of peace with Scotland, Chillingham was no longer strategically significant. It was now little more than a remote and impractical family home. A home with dungeons in place of water closets and arrow slits instead of bow windows.

Leonora was clearly conflicted about her new surroundings. On the one hand, she marvelled at the sheer age of the decrepit old pile and the many visible reminders of the countless souls who had passed through its corridors over the centuries.

'We still see on the dungeon walls ancient initials and lines scratched in by [the prisoners] to count the number of weary days of their imprisonment,' she remarked in wonderment. But with these intriguing novelties came considerable drawbacks. There was no electricity, no heating system, and far too many stairs (access to much of the castle required scaling steep spiral staircases). Life at Chillingham Castle, it seems, was not so different in 1896 to life there in 1296.

In her memorandum, Lady Leonora lists some of the inconveniences of living in a draughty 700-year-old stronghold, along with possible remedies. 'I must avoid repeated chills and congestions, both by arranging for ventilation without draughts and a means of heating the most used rooms (bedroom, bathroom and sitting room) to keep them temperate and dry... Baths and hot water form an important part of the regime.'

As well as alleviating these physical discomforts, Leonora was keen to circumvent the potentially negative psychological effects of her situation. This would require 'times of rest and quiet, alone, supplemented by periods of relief from the responsibilities, and rest in London, at recognised intervals and *before* any signs of breakdown'.

One of the major causes of stress at Chillingham was domestic unrest. Though her marriage seemed to be solid, Leonora's relationship with her aged in-laws was fraught. The incumbent Earl and Countess Tankerville were still the castle's official owners, and they were reluctant to cede control to the next generation. Countess Tankerville, in particular, was deeply resentful about the prospect of handing over her home to her son and his American wife. It seems that she had never been that fond of George, who was actually her second-born son; her first, Charles, had died of cholera while in military service in India in 1876 (this was the deceased brother who had appeared in Leonora's portentous dream).

Leonora's feelings of discomfort at the castle were only exacerbated by this sense of not belonging. In journal entries, she bitterly recalls her mother-in-law's hostile treatment towards her, recounting that in her first years at Chillingham she could scarcely 'walk through the drawing rooms without hearing the words "This shall never be your home".'

In her book *Co-habiting with Ghosts: Knowledge, Experience, Belief and the Domestic Uncanny* (2014), cultural geographer Caron Lipman cites a lack of ownership as a major contributing factor in purported haunted house cases, with people living in borrowed or rented houses tending not to properly 'bond' with their place of residence, causing them to feel perpetually ill at ease. So even if there were no actual ghosts to speak of, it might be possible for Leonora to imagine that the castle was haunted, possessed of a negative energy that prevented her from feeling at home there.

But, of course, at Chillingham there *were* ghosts. Or at least, Leonora and others believed there to be… Again, her feelings on the matter were mixed. At times, she took the view that at least some of the spirits at Chillingham were malevolent – and that one in particular threatened real harm. After the death of Countess Tankerville in 1922, Leonora became increasingly convinced that a dark force had gained control of the castle, causing general calamity and misfortune to befall the Tankerville family. This was directly attributed to the spiteful spectre of her dead mother-in-law.

The late Countess Tankerville notwithstanding, most of Chillingham's resident spectres were regarded as relatively harmless. In much of Lady Leonora's extant writings, she treats the topic of ghosts remarkably casually. Rather than malevolent forces, they are simply a source of curiosity to her. Indeed, right from the start, ghost stories proved a welcome distraction from an otherwise dreary existence. Leonora's diary entries documenting her first days at Chillingham capture a mixture of boredom, discomfort and anxiety, brightened only by her daily discoveries of hidden secrets and supernatural wonders.

'Despite the rain, the men have gone to look at wild cattle,' Leonora writes on her second day, referring to the castle's renowned herd of Chillingham wild cattle, a rare breed that had lived on the estate since the Middle Ages. 'These things do not interest me much because we do have a few beasts of our own in my home country,' she explains. Though the beasts were evidently interesting enough to attract the attention of the famed animal artist Edwin Landseer, who painted the cows in 1867, Leonora felt she had better things to occupy her time:

> *What news of Ghosts? I managed to speak to the old housekeeper whose age is unknown and whose years of service can only be guessed at ... But what a fountain of knowledge! There is not an object in the castle she has not cleaned at least one hundred times over and there is not a story or secret she hasn't heard. There are many black family scandals from years gone by of which she would tell me nothing, but when asked about ghosts she was extremely forthcoming. Bless her.*

With the aged housekeeper as her guide, Leonora embarked on her first ghost hunt that afternoon. Later that evening, while in the relative warmth of the library, she updated her diary. 'All afternoon I have been visiting the locations of ghost sightings according to the old housekeeper,' she writes breathlessly. 'I had no idea there could be so many apparitions living under one roof.'

There was the ghost of an old woman, believed to be a victim of poisoning or plague, who frequently appeared begging for water; an apparition of a small child, who wailed in sadness every night; and the aroma of rosewater, believed to be the calling card of the 'Grey Lady', Mary Berkeley, wife of the 1st Earl of Tankerville. All of this would provide excellent fodder for Lady Leonora's diaries and notebooks for years to come, and fuel a growing obsession that would soon lead her to attempt to make contact with the ghostly residents with whom she shared a home.

Séances, spiritualism and spirituality

That a worldly woman like Leonora Bennet should be so fixated on the supernatural might seem strange. In her day, however, it wasn't just quirky New Age types who obsessed over the spirit world. In Victorian Britain and America, spirits were widely believed to be everywhere – in the dimmed parlours of London's modern town-houses, in the walls and rafters of quaint New England farmsteads, and even in the presidential apartments at the White House. This, after all, was the golden age of spiritualism.

To understand the peculiar cultural environment that Lady Leonora was steeped in, we must first travel back across the Atlantic to her native land. Here, the story of spiritualism begins, rather precisely, on the evening of 31 March 1847 at an unassuming cedar-clad farmhouse in the tiny hamlet of Hydesville in upstate New York – a world away from Chillingham Castle.

It was the night before April Fool's Day and farmer John Fox, his wife Margaret and their two youngest daughters were preparing for sleep in their shared family bedroom. Kate, aged eleven, and Maggie, aged fourteen, were mischievous little sprites who delighted in playing pranks on their parents and older sister, Leah, aged thirty-one. On this night, however, the younger girls were apparently worn out from play and were resting peacefully when a chorus of thumps and knockings erupted throughout the house. The strange sounds seemed to emanate from the floor and walls all around them, with no clearly identifiable source.

Rather than cowering beneath their bedsheets, the girls sprang into action. The youngest, Kate, began to challenge the mysterious noise-maker, demanding that it follow her instructions. 'Mr Splitfoot,' she declaimed, using an old-timey nickname for the devil, 'do as I do.'

She clapped. It rapped back in response. She then decided to test the sentience of the being, asking a series of simple questions. Once it had succeeded in such challenges as rapping out the girls' ages, the questions became more probing.

'Is this a human being that answers my questions so correctly?' Silence.

'Is it a spirit? If it is, make two raps.' Two raps.

'Is it an injured spirit?' Two raps.

'Were you injured in this house?' Two raps.

'Is the person living that injured you?' Two raps.

'Will you continue to rap if I call my neighbours, so they may hear you too?' Two enthusiastic raps.

The obliging poltergeist was true to its word, and soon after performed on command for an enraptured audience of neighbours. Using the same method of call and response, the villagers of Hydesville were able to ascertain that the noisy spirit was a thirty-one-year-old pedlar called Charles Rosna, who had been murdered for money five years earlier in the east bedroom. His throat had been slit and his body had been hastily interred in the cellar below. Although an impromptu excavation of the supposed burial site uncovered only a scattering of animal bones and a pool of well water, many members of the community remained steadfast in their belief in the pedlar-spirit. They also believed in the special powers of the Fox sisters, who seemed to possess an uncanny ability to communicate with the dead.

This was how the Fox farmhouse became the birthplace of the modern seance – a key component of the subsequent spiritualist movement, and a fashionable activity that would soon be practised in the darkened drawing rooms of homes all over the Western world, including at Chillingham Castle.

Today, we often think of seances as a kind of innocent parlour game, the sort you might play as a pre-teen at a sleepover with friends, crowded around a Ouija board in a candlelit living room. And this was pretty much what early nineteenth-century seances were like. Before they became a heavily commercialised form of public spectacle, seances started out as an amateur activity, typically performed with friends and family in the privacy of the home. Seances required no special equipment; they didn't require leaving the house; and everyone theoretically had the capacity to call forth the souls of the dead if they wanted to (though some were obviously better at it than others).

Young Kate and Maggie Fox became instant celebrities for their mediumistic abilities. Initially, the girls were removed from the family home to keep them safe from supernatural forces and undue media scrutiny. But as soon as they had they fled the farm, they were being trotted out like a circus sideshow. It seems that the murdered pedlar wasn't the only spirit willing to talk to the Fox sisters, and nor were the knocks and raps confined to their Hydesville home. Under the management of their elder sister Leah, Kate and Maggie embarked on a lengthy tour of the north-eastern states, providing paying punters with the opportunity to communicate with the dead. They were the first of countless professional mediums to offer this unusual service.

The enterprising Fox sisters were largely responsible for kickstarting the nineteenth-century mania for seances. But they were hardly the first little girls to play at mediumship; after all, nearly a century earlier in London an artful eleven-year-old called Betty Parsons had used the very same means to communicate with the ghost of Cock Lane. And just like their Georgian forerunner, the Fox sisters would eventually be exposed for fraud – or rather, Maggie Fox would expose herself. In 1888, after more than forty years as a celebrity of the spiritualist world, she confessed that it had all been a hoax. 'When we went to bed at night, we used to tie an apple to a string and move the string up and down, causing the apple to bump on the floor,' Maggie recalled. 'Mother listened to this for a time. She would not understand it and did not suspect us of being capable of a trick because we were so young.'

This stunning admission might have been a death blow for mediumship, had it not been for the fact that the seance was by now a firmly established practice for followers of a rapidly growing religious movement. With their April Fool's Day prank of 1847, Maggie and Kate had unwittingly set the course for the establishment of a new religion based on the simple premise that the living were capable of conversing with the dead. What started as a small group of loosely organised non-conformists with an interest in the mediumistic abilities of the Fox sisters and others grew to an international legion of devotees. By the end of the nineteenth century, the spiritualist movement had an estimated 8 million adherents in America and Europe, most of whom were from the middle and upper classes.

So how did a pair of pre-teen pranksters, the daughters of a modest New York farmer, manage to launch a global religion? Though they may not have known it, the Fox girls lived in the midst of a hotbed of religious reform. Their Hydesville farm was located in the middle of a region of New York that is now known as the 'Burnt Over District', in reference to the spiritual fire that swept the area in the first half of the nineteenth century. This was the birthplace of Mormonism, Millerism and the Seventh Day Adventist Church, and was also a haven for radical Quakers and Shakers. It was the setting for the 'Second Great Awakening', the early-nineteenth-century revival that shaped the form of evangelical faith practised by Leonora and her husband.

While none of these other denominations showed much interest in talking to the dead, what they did have in common was a desire for a more personal connection with the spiritual world. Free from the trappings of traditional organised religion, with no formal deity, place of worship or strict code of conduct, spiritualism offered perhaps the most direct connection of all. For this reason, some of its earliest adherents were converts from these other like-minded faiths.

Though it managed to attract participants of both sexes, spiritualism quickly became the special domain of women. This was partly to do with the widespread belief that the so-called 'softer sex' was somehow more sensitive and receptive to the spirit world. It was probably also related to the notion of the female body as a vessel, a conduit for life, and maybe also for the spirits of the dead. So, while both men and women went to mediums for spiritual guidance, it was typically women who performed the service. That Lady Leonora herself claimed to possess the ability to see 'beyond the veil' was probably not that unusual for a woman of her day.

Ultimately, the appeal of this new movement was simple. It presented the tantalising opportunity to reconnect with lost loved ones – a desire that transcended religion, sex, nationality, age and social station. A desire that took on an increased sense of urgency in a world that seemed increasingly shrouded in death. The Crimean War (1853–6) saw the loss of some 16,000 Britons; in the American Civil War (1861–5) 600,000 Confederate and Union men died, while outbreaks of cholera, tuberculosis and yellow fever on both sides of the Atlantic caused the death toll to soar higher still. No one was left unaffected. And so the men and women of Britain and America flocked to the salons of famous mediums, attended 'trance lectures' by renowned spiritualist speakers, or simply held private seances in the comfort of their own homes – all in a desperate bid to speak to the uncountable dead.

In June 1912, Lady Leonora Bennet (now Countess Tankerville) had as good a reason as any to contact a spiritualist medium. She had had more than her fair share of encounters with death. There was the stillbirth of her daughter in 1896, the passing of her father-in-law in 1899, the sudden loss of another infant daughter in 1900 and the death of her own father in 1902. And, of course, there were the many nameless dead who shared her castle home. But her motivation for wanting to make contact with the other side that summer may have been more pointed. From the moment she set foot in the castle, there were murmurings of a dark family secret. For years, no one would break their silence, not even the dutiful old housekeeper, who would happily regale her new mistress with ghost stories but refused to air the Tankervilles' dirty laundry.

With the death of her father-in-law more than ten years earlier, the incumbent Countess Tankerville must have felt she had gained a little more control of the castle (even with the crusty old dowager still holding court). Yet, she had a niggling feeling that someone or something was working against her. Jewellery and family heirlooms kept disappearing; money seemed to be seeping from the estate at an alarming rate, and shady individuals employed by the dowager always seemed to be skulking in the background. The greatest blow came in the summer of 1910 when the Tankervilles discovered they had been cheated out of nearly £20,000 (approximately £1.5 million today) in a fraudulent mining investment scheme. All of this spelled bad news for the new earl and countess. According to the late Lord Tankerville's will, if they failed to maintain the castle to a satisfactory standard, they would be forced to forfeit the estate to a distant cousin. Lady Leonora needed help, and she hoped it might come from the spirit world.

That the souls of the deceased could reveal hidden knowledge was a common belief among spiritualists. Based on the earlier writings of Emanuel Swedenberg (an eighteenth-century proto-spiritualist), many adherents to spiritualism maintained that the dead acted as intermediaries between the living and God. Through this connection, the spirits could share an omniscient perspective of the world with their earthbound communicants. And so, if you sought answers to the mysteries of life, or even if you just wanted to find your missing house keys, all you had to do was talk to a dead person.

Lady Leonora's pious husband was somewhat nervous about dabbling in the 'dark arts', having previously warned his wife of the dangers of mysticism and the occult. He pointed to the nefarious influence of his mother's strange companion, Miss Henrietta Elout, a Dutch-born missionary who had allegedly come to Chillingham to convert the dowager to evangelism, but instead seemed to be teaching her some form of witchcraft. Suspiciously, the same Miss Elout had also allegedly invested in the scam that lost so much of the Tankerville fortune. Nevertheless, the earl evidently allowed his wife to go forward with her plan, perhaps recognising that spiritualism had something in common with his own religious persuasion.

In advance of her seance, Leonora had already learned a bit about the skeletons in the Tankerville family closet. This was revealed not by a spirit source, but a living relative. On his deathbed, Lord Robert Montagu (or Uncle Bob, as he was affectionately known), the dowager's brother, finally confessed to his beloved nephew George the reason for his mother's mistreatment of him. According to Uncle Bob, his sister had been keeping a terrible secret. George was really his father's first-born son and had been the rightful heir all along. Meanwhile his elder brother, Charles Bennett, Lord Ossulston, had been the product of the countess's extramarital affair. And in her grief over the sudden passing of her favourite (albeit illegitimate) child, Countess Olivia confessed his parentage to the conniving Miss Elout, who used it as a powerful source of blackmail.

What other secrets did Chillingham hide? And how could its dark spell be broken? It was Leonora's belief that only the spirits could say.

There is no record of the identity of the medium Leonora called upon that summer, but a 12-page transcript preserved in the Northumberland Archives gives us some idea of how their seance was conducted. He or she (but almost certainly she) was tasked with both contacting the spirits and cleansing the castle of its negative energy. Where seances were more typically conducted in a room in which participants gathered around a table, this one was mobile, progressing through the castle room by room, providing us with a kind of virtual ghost tour.

The record, however, is light on contextual detail. We don't know the exact date, the people present, or their reactions to the experience. We don't even know the time of day the seance took place, but it's probably safe to say it was after dark. The summer of 1912 was one of the wettest on record, so it is very possible that it was an appropriately dark and stormy night at the castle. If so, the sound of the driving rain and howling wind would have only heightened the already unsettling atmosphere. We can imagine the seance party, guided by candlelight, slowly moving through the ancient building, with cracks of thunder occasionally punctuating their solemn vigil. Shadowy corners and frightened faces would momentarily be awash in the eery bluish-white glow of lightning.

According to the transcript, the seance began in what was called the Audit Room, the castle's administrative office, where estate tenants went to pay their rent. Here, the medium hit upon something supernatural almost immediately, both seeing and sensing the pain of a tortured soul. She said:

> *After a moment of prayers revealed a lady in white – with pale face – so pale that from the pallor and psychometrical conditions I take it she was very slowly poisoned... The craving I have is now of thirst, that thirst which one feels would come if one's inside was inflamed. I cannot get her name – she throws herself down to show me she died here, in this very spot.*

The medium apparently possessed 'extrasensory perception' or a 'sixth sense', meaning that she could perceive images and information not through purely physical means, but through the power of the mind. While the darkened office may have appeared empty and unremarkable to the average person, the medium claimed it was teeming with energy: the residual energy of a woman whose sickly pallor hinted at her untimely end. A figure who largely lined up with an established legend attached to the castle: a pale woman, desperate for water, who had famously accosted a footman guarding the family's silver in the pantry. At first believing that the woman was a guest of the family, the footman went to fetch her drink. When he returned, she was gone. And he was suddenly acutely aware that the pantry was locked from the inside, preventing any intruders from gaining access to the precious heirlooms within.

As skilled in her craft as she may have been, the medium was unable to make out the whole picture. The spirit world is shadowy and mysterious, and like most of its phantom inhabitants, the pale lady was coy and unwilling to reveal too much of herself. She withheld her name, the exact manner of her death and the identity of her assailant, admitting only that her 'distress has been great'. The ghost was, however, willing to share some of her special spirit wisdom: 'Tell her Ladyship that if she remarried here when *enceinte* she would not only have never brought forth a son, but she surely would have come over herself.'

This vaguely cryptic message seems to suggest that there had been plans to hold a second wedding ceremony for Leonora and her husband at Chillingham when she was pregnant and that, had she attended, she surely would have perished.

Before departing the Audit Room, the medium was accosted by another spirit – the ghost of 'dear Lord T's father', the 6th Earl of Tankerville, who was clearly agitated. Again, the spirit spoke in enigmatic riddles: 'My God, what a life I had – but it passed. Thank God – so tell my dear son my soul is heavy and yet glad – He shall see justice.' With that, the room was cleansed and the seance party pressed on with their tour of the castle, passing through sitting rooms, dressing rooms, boudoirs, dungeons and more.

For much of their progress, they were stalked by the sorrowful spirit of the 6th Earl. Like the grim spectre of Jacob Marley in Charles Dickens' classic ghost story *A Christmas Carol*, the late Lord Tankerville seemed to be tethered to the earthly realm, doomed to spend eternity roaming the halls of his former home, desperate to impart a message to his surviving loved ones. What exactly that message was remains unclear.

In a drawing room in the east tower, the Earl was joined by a 'stormy presence' – this time not a ghost, but the energy of a living woman whose 'hypnotic influence' over the dowager was still active. 'I get a name like (tho not clear) Ellen,' wrote the medium. She was corrected by Lady Leonora in an annotation that reads 'Elout'. The earl warned that this woman had 'four crates full of things which should be here', but that once she died, the 'packages of silver ... the crest ... the jewellery' would be restored to their rightful owners.

The medium's tour culminated in the bowels of the castle. Strangely, she detected no 'earthbound spirits' in the dungeon. But she did sense a hidden 'subterranean passage' beneath her feet, where she claimed a cylinder containing ancient papers and plans was concealed. Her final contact was with a ghostly white figure in a lower corridor, whom she identified as the same pale lady she had first encountered in the Audit Room. With the session concluded, the medium and her 'spirit guide' proclaimed the castle cleared of its negative energy.

We don't know whether Lady Leonora was satisfied with the services of her medium, or whether the seance succeeded in quietening the spirits – at least for a little while. The countess must have felt vindicated that the ghosts had confirmed her suspicions about the dowager and her nefarious friend Miss Elout. But in the long run, it really didn't help.

Ten years after the 1912 seance, Lady Leonora and her husband were still plagued by misfortune. The death of the dowager in February 1922 had failed to put an end to their long streak of bad luck – if anything, it was getting worse. In the summer of that year, a devastating fire broke out at Gwyds Castle, the Tankervilles' recently acquired second home in north Wales. Everything was consumed by flames, leaving not a scrap of furniture or artwork unscorched, obliterating Lady Leonora's painstaking efforts to restore the old pile to its former glory. The Chillingham scourge seemed to have followed her to what she must have considered a safe retreat from her haunted home. In a last-ditch effort to rid the castle of dark forces, Leonora ignored her husband's earlier advice and contacted an occultist for help.

On 26 June 1926, she penned an imploring letter to a Mrs Besant. This was probably Anne Besant, a leading proponent of theosophy, an occult movement loosely related to spiritualism, which incorporated belief in reincarnation, spirits and secret knowledge. Leonora's lengthy missive recounted the Tankervilles' woeful tale and sought answers to a number of pressing questions, including:

> *Is there now in the Castle some centre or concealed object from which the forces of black magic are able to exercise an influence? ... Could my [husband's mother] be set free from attraction to this place? If the family curse is an old one, can we do anything specific to bring it to an end so as to save the coming generation from those things which we have had to suffer?*

A cursed castle, an embittered ex-owner and a terrified new inhabitant – it could all have been lifted right out of a Gothic novel. Except it was real. At least, it was real enough to Lady Leonora.

Alas, she received no guidance from the occultist expert. According to the countess, her letter to Mrs Besant was 'never answered or even acknowledged'. When she later agreed to share its contents with a family friend, one Captain Pape, he declared that Leonora was 'not straight' (implying she was either not telling the truth or she was mad – or both). And it's hard to blame him. For not only was the countess's story fantastical, it also had a suspiciously familiar ring to it, combining elements from traditional folklore, popular fiction and fashionable fads. This doesn't mean she made it up, exactly. But in the wake of so many misfortunes, holed up in an odd and atmospheric environment, and immersed in a culture obsessed with the spirit world, perhaps it was inevitable that Leonora would let her imagination get the better of her.

Though she lived in a castle – a structure designed to protect – Leonora and her family were constantly under threat. Bad mother-in-law, bad financial investments, bad luck in general... None of this hardship was alleviated by the sanctuary of home – in fact, it all seemed to have occurred within its walls, which would surely be enough to drive anyone around the bend. Maybe Captain Pape was right. Perhaps the countess was not altogether 'straight'. And yet, even if her supposedly supernatural experiences were the product of an unstable mind, the fact remains, she *was* haunted, tormented by an increasingly hostile home life – which is, after all, a standard symptom in most haunted house cases.

Grey Ladies and Blue Boys: classic castle legends

By the 1920s, Countess Leonora Tankerville was increasingly eager to share her ghostly experiences with others. Not just with mediums and occultists who might be able to help her with her paranormal problems, but with an audience of like-minded people who shared her interest. She was clearly not alone.

Some seventy years after the advent of spiritualism, just a few short years after the devastation of the Great War, ghosts were the talk of the day, a subject discussed and debated everywhere from mainstream newspapers to fringe science journals, from middle-class dinner parties to the salons of the London intelligentsia. Her obsession with the afterlife put Leonora in the illustrious company of fellow noblewomen such as Anne Grenville, 4th Countess of Warwick, and Gwladys Townshend, 6th Marchioness Townshend; with great thinkers like Thomas Edison and Pierre Curie; and literary giants like Sir Arthur Conan Doyle and Charles Dickens (the former wrote to Lady Leonora to discuss their mutual obsession, while the latter was actually an avowed sceptic, despite his literary interest in the subject and his membership of the Ghost Club, a London-based paranormal research society). It was probably because of its mainstream acceptance that Countess Tankerville felt comfortable discussing the topic in mixed company.

In July 1925, the earl and countess hosted a grand fete for the Conservative Association at their castle home which attracted some 2,000 partygoers. The *Berwick Advertiser* reported that the event was a great success and that Leonora charmed her guests with 'interesting anecdotes of historical lore', which naturally included a few ghost stories. Mirroring the mood of the occasion, the tales she told were of the more romantic sort – the forlorn spectre of the long-dead Grey Lady and the mysterious Radiant Boy – rather than stories about her wrathful recently deceased mother-in-law.

Later that year, on the evening of 3 December, the countess gave a lengthy talk about her haunted home on a radio programme broadcast on the Newcastle 5NO station. The transcript of the countess's radio talk was subsequently released as an eight-page booklet entitled *The Ghosts of Chillingham Castle* (1925), published by a small Waller-based printer called J. W. Brand. In the introduction, Lady Leonora borrows from a well-known poem by the American poet Henry Wadsworth Longfellow:

All houses in which men have lived and died
Are haunted houses: through open doors
The harmless phantoms on their errands glide
With feet that make no sound upon the floors.

It is a fitting quote, not only in the literal sense but also in its underlying meaning. The poet is effectively reassuring his readers that ghosts are not the stuff of Gothic nightmares, but rather 'harmless phantoms'; mere shadows of the past that leave a faint human imprint on otherwise inanimate structures. Less about death and more about memory, the poem must have been of some comfort to the countess – an incantation to keep her darker fears about Chillingham at bay.

Leonora continues on from Longfellow in a voice that is plain yet elegant, devoid of hyperbole and sometimes surprisingly insightful – a far cry from the rantings of a hallucinating madwoman. She begins with a salient fact: 'The feudal castle and phantom forms have so long been associated that one almost suggests another.' The castle's setting, she points out, is rife with Gothic possibility: 'a district full of romance ... so close to the Borderland [that] in old times [it was] the scene of many a raid from its Scottish neighbours'. The castle's dungeons, she speculates, 'were probably seldom without some unfortunate inmate immured therein ... If there is any truth in Longfellow's contention, Chillingham should certainly afford shelter to many wraiths of its departed owners and former dwellers.'

And so, indeed, it did. This castle apparently lived up to expectations.

The remaining seven pages of the booklet are a jumble of anecdotes and observations pertaining to Chillingham's macabre past, its haunted reputation and the nature of ghosts more generally. Part ghost story, part social history, part personal essay, the countess's booklet makes for compelling – if slightly disjointed – reading. But while some of the particulars of her tales are unique to Chillingham, much of the content is familiar to the point of cliché.

Consider the tale of the Grey Lady. This was believed to be the ghost of Lady Mary Berkeley, wife of the notorious Ford Grey, 1st

Earl of Tankerville (third creation), who caused a great scandal in 1683 when he was charged with adultery for his affair with Lady Mary's younger sister, Henrietta. The story goes that the scorned wife was left abandoned in her 'dark and lonely Castle with only a fatherless baby girl as her companion'. The earl never returned, and Lady Mary, who purportedly died of a broken heart, never left. 'To this day,' Leonora reports, 'the rustle of her dress is sometimes heard along the corridors and stairs and as the disappointed and anxious wraith passes by, a chill, as of cold air, seems to sweep through one's very marrow.'

A dejected woman, an untimely death, a sorrowful spectre doomed to spend eternity wandering the halls of her former home – it's a classic castle legend, common to historic properties across Britain and beyond. There's the 'White Lady' of Samlesbury Hall, Lancashire (Lady Dorothy Southworth); the 'Green Lady' of Longleat, Wiltshire (Lady Louisa Carteret); and the Brown Lady of Raynham Hall, Norfolk (Lady Dorothy Townshend) – all colourful ladies in life, reduced to a muted palette in the hereafter.

Typically, these White/Grey/Green Ladies are mourning a loss. The death of a loved one, the demise of a marriage, or some other sort of domestic downfall. Sometimes their appearance is said to portend a tragic event: the White Lady of Berry Pomeroy Castle in Devon, who allegedly starved to death in the dungeon, now brings ill tidings to all who see her. But more often than not, they are simply harmless projections, replaying their painful past in perpetuity.

The Grey Lady isn't the only familiar ghostly trope either. There is also the Blue or Radiant Boy, a schoolboy spectre, who is said to habitually haunt the Pink Bedroom at Chillingham. There, each night at the stroke of twelve comes the sound of a sobbing child. 'Anyone sleeping there sees gently approaching them the figure of a young boy dressed in blue and surrounded by light,' claimed the countess. Though the identity of the boy was never uncovered, builders working in the Pink Bedroom one day stumbled upon a grim discovery. Behind the wall was a small skeleton, together with some scraps of blue silk, believed to be the remnants of a Jacobean-era costume. Once they had been properly interred, the boy's nightly visits ceased (that is, until Sir Humphry arrived later that century).

Like the forlorn lady, the ghost child is a mainstay of the haunted castle myth, and a stock character of horror literature and film more generally. From the hideously emaciated ghost urchins in Dickens' *A Christmas Carol* to the demonic twin girls in Stephen King's *The Shining*, dead children have been scaring us for over a century – probably more. Whether it's the loss of innocence, the disquieting thought of harm befalling such young children, or the stark realisation that death could come to us at any time, there is something fundamentally frightening about the ghost child. For parents, the fear takes on an entirely different dimension, as it must have done for Lady Leonora. It isn't clear whether she was familiar with the Radiant Boy trope, which had been popular well before her tenure at Chillingham, but she had lost two children of her own.

The roots of the Radiant Boy myth are unknown, but they seem to be of Anglo-Irish origin, with strong ties to the north of Britain. According to Richard Harris Barham in *The Ingoldsby Legends* (1840), such stories are typically associated with wealthy families in which a child heir has been murdered in order to prevent the rightful course of succession. The child returns as a harbinger of bad luck or as a warning to future generations.

John Henry Ingram states in *Haunted Homes and Family Traditions of Great Britain* (1886) that Radiant Boys are children murdered by their mothers – akin to the *kindermorderinn* of German mythology. This might explain why, as folklorist William Henderson identified in the 1870s, the legend has a hold in the borderlands, an area largely settled by Germanic and Scandinavian tribes in the ninth and tenth centuries. But the myth migrated south too, and ended up as far south as Hertfordshire, where a Radiant Boy is said to haunt Knebworth House.

Of the dozens of documented Radiant Boy myths from around the country, one stands out. It appears in Catherine Crowe's *The Night Side of Nature* (1847), where it is recounted using the common Victorian convention of censoring people and place names in order to protect the reputations of real individuals. It is the first-hand account of a Rev Henry A—— of Redburgh, who, in the winter of 1824, spent an unforgettable night at C—— Castle. This was a friend's ancestral home described as a 'border tower', implying its close proximity to Scotland. If it were not for the inclusion of a singular geographic detail in the reverend's account, we might have assumed the mystery location was Chillingham. But this castle's west-facing windows looked out on the River Eden, indicating that it was actually Corby Castle, the Cumbrian seat of the Howard family.

Situated on the bank of the river that forms the boundary between Cumbria and North Yorkshire, some 70 miles south-west of Chillingham, Corby also started life as a thirteenth-century fortress. It too could boast of hundreds of years of violent history, generations of unbroken occupancy, and its very own ghost child. Corby's Radiant Boy is described by the reverend as 'a beautiful boy, clothed in white, with bright locks, resembling gold, standing by my bedside, in which position he remained some minutes, fixing his eyes upon me with a mild and benevolent expression'.

So, here we have two castles – Corby and Chillingham – separated by less than 100 miles, with similar histories and the same type of resident spirits, differing only in the colour of their clothing. There is no historical record of a child having been murdered at either property, but then again, both castles would have witnessed scores of untimely and undocumented deaths over the centuries, as would any other building of a similar age and function.

But why is it that such buildings more often play host to the ghosts of women and children, not men? Given their historical purpose, would it not make more sense for the castle to harbour the souls of fallen military commanders or soldiers rather than lost little boys and heartbroken women? When Lady Leonora's medium scoured the halls of Chillingham in search of spectres, it was mostly female energies she encountered in the domestic quarters of the castle. She detected nothing in the dungeon, where presumably dozens of captive soldiers died before their time. Are the spirits of women and children simply more persistent at haunting? Do they cling longer to the earthly realm? Or do we, the living, keep them tethered here?

The key to explaining this phenomenon might come back to the fact that the castle has always represented two contrasting spheres – the domestic and the defensive. Where ordinarily we can separate the atrocities of war from domestic life, in the castle we cannot. Those who reside in such buildings carry out their daily activities against a backdrop of death, living with the constant reminder that the walls around them were constructed to keep the enemy at bay, but were not always successful.

Perhaps even more disturbing is the notion that the enemy can also come from within. Adultery, infanticide and other forms of familial crisis can be just as alarming as a military conflict – or perhaps even more so; the destruction of domestic stability is rather harder to parse than that of war. And so, if the forlorn lady and the Radiant Boy represent the ultimate perversions of familial life, than where better for them to roam than the castle, itself an aberration of the home?

That Lady Leonora latched onto the stories of the Grey Lady and the Radiant Boy is hardly surprising. As a wife and mother confined to a gloomy castle for decades, such narratives surely would have resonated with her. While her husband was, by all accounts, a faithful partner, the countess nevertheless endured plenty of hardship in her home. Family conflict, financial woes, death and loneliness seemed to stalk Leonora down Chillingham's dark corridors. At the times she felt especially homesick for America or uncertain of her ability to survive as the mistress of a medieval castle, we can imagine her turning to Lady Mary for solace. Perhaps the belief that her female forerunner was still present made life in the castle a little less lonely for Leonora.

But solidarity with her ghostly brethren could provide little comfort for the countess after the death of her beloved 'Singing Earl'. Following her husband's death in July 1931, Leonora promptly departed Chillingham for Edinburgh, leaving the castle empty for the next fifty years, save for its brief stint as an army barracks during the Second World War. One wonders if the officers stationed there ever awoke to see the Radiant Boy standing by their beds.

Happily ever after?

On a mild, late-spring day in 2021, I embark on my own tour of the 'most haunted castle' in Britain. Right off the bat, it's an uncanny experience. Most of the Covid-era restrictions have recently been lifted and the weather in north Northumberland is shockingly pleasant for this time of year. I have also been lucky enough to secure my own private tour with Mark Trotter, one of the castle's veteran ghost guides. A retired police detective from Durham, Trotter came to Chillingham in 2014 with a keen interest in local history but none whatsoever in the supernatural. If I had asked him a decade ago if he believed in ghosts, the no-nonsense former investigator would have replied in his thick brogue, 'Ack, no, that's twaddle.' But today he feels differently. 'I completely believe now,' he declares. You could hardly ask for a more reliable witness and guide than a man who spent thirty years of his life exposing fraud and sniffing out criminals.

My tour of the castle will be a bit different to the ones Mark usually conducts. Rather than being guided by the light of torches and candles, we will be winding our way through narrow corridors and steep spiral staircases in the noonday sun (or at least, what little of it can penetrate the thick, centuries-old stone walls). While it's not exactly scary, I can still get some sense of how it must feel for the night-time ghost hunters. Even in broad daylight, it's tricky to navigate around the mountains of artefacts and oddities crammed into the tight spaces of the castle's tower rooms. I can perfectly understand how, in low flickering candlelight, stags' heads and suits of armour might momentarily be mistaken for monsters and malevolent spirits.

As Mark shepherds me around the castle, stoically recounting its gruesome history and introducing the phantom figures associated with each room, he tells me about some of his own experiences.

In the dungeon or *oubliette* – which, as he explains, comes from the French verb 'to forget' – Mark points out a trapdoor to the bottom chamber where Scottish prisoners were once tortured or simply left to die. He recalls a time he was presenting the hatch to a small party, when suddenly his audience gasped in unison, later claiming to have seen the shadow of a dog darting between his legs. 'Now that ties in with the history, because they used to send the dogs in to clear up the mess,' he says, presumably referring to the prisoners' decaying remains.

In the undercroft, where Sir Humphry displays his prodigious collection of torture equipment (much of it replica and none of it ever used in the castle), Mark tells me about the 'scold's bridle', an iron muzzle suspended from a chain in the ceiling, which was traditionally used to silence impudent women. One night, Mark was hosting a rowdy group of ladies on a hen do. Just as he had finished explaining the purpose of the ghastly device, it began to swing violently above his head, much to the delight of his inebriated guests. 'If you try to move it yourself,' Mark claims, 'it just bobs up and down, but on the night in question it was spinning in a circular motion.'

In a room that is now set up as a chapel, but was once Lady Leonora's library, Mark tells me the sad tale of Eleanor, a young girl who is said to have been kept prisoner at the castle in the late Middle Ages (side note: there is no concrete evidence that this poor lass ever actually existed). After being abused by the soldiers who confined her, Eleanor supposedly staggered into this library-cum-chapel and died. Her presence has reportedly been felt there ever since.

On one particularly eventful evening, Mark told this story to a group of guests who were seated on the pews in front of him. He was then astonished to see a woman's hair rise into the air, as if being pulled by a playful child. The woman, to his even greater surprise, failed to react to the hair-tugging.

'You do realise that someone is pulling your hair?' he said to her.

'Oh, don't worry, it's just my friends playing a prank on me,' she replied.

'Well, you might want to turn around,' he retorted. There was no one sitting in the pew behind her.

If I'm honest, this all sounds like a bit of a lark. As much as I trust Mark Trotter, and sincerely believe that he did witness these events, the whole thing seems pretty light-hearted: an entertaining approximation of the medieval castle experience, complete with ghostly happenings, but none of it feels genuinely frightening or has anything to do with the recorded history of the castle.

So, I ask him, what of Lady Leonora? Is there any evidence that the real-life historical figure with whom I have become best acquainted has stuck around at the castle?

Well, as it happens, Mark has news from the other side. Conducting his own seances using 'divining rods' (metal rods which allegedly cross over one another when a spirit is communicating), Mark made contact with Leonora's husband, George. When Mark asked if his wife was still at the castle with him, the earl responded in the affirmative. 'I asked if she wished to communicate with me; however, she declined,' Mark explains. Several subsequent efforts to reach the countess failed too. Then one day Mark inquired whether Leonora, a paranormal enthusiast in life, could see things differently now in the hereafter. She must have liked this line of questioning, for she suddenly became a lot more loquacious.

'I communicated with her about five or six times after that,' Mark says. 'She is friendly with Eleanor, the girl in the chapel, as well as the spirit of the Blue Boy, which also remains at the castle.' Leonora is, Mark reports, 'happy here with George'.

So, in the end, maybe the countess did get her fairy-tale ending after all.

BORLEY RECTORY

NEW HAUNTS FOR OLD GHOSTS

3

Poltergeists are domestically inclined, and their chief haunts are private houses, comfortable homes, family circles... They prefer the country and quiet places to the town and noise. They are fond of farms, and can hardly keep away from rectories!

Harry Price (1881–1948)

The most haunted house in England

The Bull sisters were typical turn-of-the-century Essex girls. Though they were the daughters of a country rector residing in Borley, a sleepy parish on the Essex–Suffolk border, the Bull ladies were vivacious and sociable. They enjoyed long invigorating walks through the East Anglian countryside, shopping excursions to the nearby market towns of Long Melford and Sudbury, and attending local parties. It was on the evening of 28 July 1900 that two of the seven sisters, Freda and Mabel, were returning home from one such social engagement when they experienced something that would startle them right out of their carefree frivolity.

As they approached the back gate to their garden, they were greeted by their younger sister, Ethel, who was eager to hear news of the party. They stood at the gate for a moment, chatting about the evening's events, when suddenly all three ladies witnessed a mysterious figure in black gliding across their lawn. The sun had not yet fully set, and in the dusky midsummer light they could clearly make out the form of a young woman. Her head was bowed, as though in prayer, and she wore what appeared to be a nun's habit. Had it not been for the fact that she was effectively floating along the garden path, the Bull ladies could have sworn the figure was flesh and blood – just as alive as they were.

One of the sisters ran indoors to raise the alarm. Another sister, Elsie, who had also stayed in that evening, was having none of this superstitious nonsense. Clearly, the woman was a benevolent Sister of Mercy who had somehow lost her way while out on a charitable mission. Elsie flew out of the back door of the family's manse, planning to set the errant young woman on the right path. But before she could accost the trespasser, the figure vanished before her eyes.

Of all the unusual incidents to occur over the years at their family home, this event would stand out as the most memorable for the Bull sisters. Years later, surviving sisters, Ethel, Freda and Constance would recount their astonishing tale to the renowned paranormal investigator Harry Price. He would go on to declare their childhood home the most haunted house in England.

Borley Rectory was built in 1862 for the Reverend Henry Dawson Ellis Bull, to replace a much smaller, nineteenth-century manse. It was a solid red-brick structure, two storeys high, with steeply sloping gables, massive chimney stacks and bay windows overlooking the expansive back lawn.

While large and imposing, the Reverend Bull's home was plain and almost entirely unremarkable in architectural terms. In years to come, it would often be referred to as Gothic, but this was something of a misnomer. The rectory lacked nearly all the typical ornamental flourishes of the popular style – there were no pointed arches, tracery windows, oriels or castellated walls. Apart from the pitched roof, which might be said to recall the pointed spires of a cathedral, and a porch entrance that took the form of a small tower, there was very little about it that was conventionally Gothic. But it *was* built at the height of the Victorian Gothic Revival movement, and it was certainly 'Gothic' in the literary sense. Indeed, it served as the setting for one of the most famous ghost stories in British history. And as we know, ghosts and the Gothic go hand in hand.

Borley Rectory is now long gone, the house itself a ghost – invisible, intangible, immaterial. Despite the fact that it was demolished in 1944, it continues to attract legions of ghost hunters hoping to catch a glimpse of the spirits that once allegedly haunted the old rectory, though those who actually live in Borley have nothing spooky to report. Local historian Andrew Clarke tells me that 'no resident has ever seen anything remotely odd' – apart, of course, from the ghost hunters. 'We could only tell you about the irritation of the Halloween eccentrics,' he laments.

My pilgrimage to Borley is not your typical ghost hunt. It's a bright afternoon in the middle of May and I'm with my four-year-old son, boisterous pre-teen stepchildren and cheerfully sceptical husband. The birds are chirping, the sheep are bleating and the warm late-spring sun beams down on us, making even the graveyard we are walking through seem a cheery sort of place. As I search for the graves of the Bull family, my children play an impromptu game of hide-and-seek, excitedly ducking and darting behind the ancient headstones and monuments that scatter the grounds.

Posted on the door to the 1,000-year-old parish church to which the graveyard belongs is a laminated sign that reads:

> *In this churchyard all are at rest. The Church Building continues to be a centre for Christian Worship for the inhabitants of the small village community and their friends... There are no ghosts here. The shriven souls were laid to rest within the blessing of the Holy Mother the Church. They rest in peace.*
>
> *It is our prayer that your soul may find salvation and that you too may rest in peace when your time comes. All we ask in return is your respect for this place and what it stands for. GO IN PEACE.*

We take our cue to leave, and continue our tour of the tiny village.

Today, there is not much to see in the village at all, aside from the small Norman church, its adjoining graveyard, and a spattering of quaint cottages and farmhouses. Blink and you'd miss it. Yet, like most curious visitors, we can clearly picture what once stood on a modest rise across the road from the church. Almost everyone who visits is familiar with the iconic images of the fire-damaged rectory used to illustrate Harry Price's bestselling book *The Most Haunted House in England* (1940). The grainy black-and-white photographs capture a classic haunted house: an abandoned, derelict Victorian mansion with shattered windows, gaping holes and a missing roof.

When, in June 1929, the eccentric paper-salesman turned paranormal researcher Price visited Borley for the first time, the rectory was just sixty-seven years old. Though relatively modern for a haunted house, Borley was far from being new and sparkly. Price recounted his impression of the property that day, describing the exterior of the house as 'sombre' and 'gloomy', and the interior a 'rabbit warren' of poorly laid-out rooms. Even before its eventual decline into age and decrepitude, Borley Rectory was decidedly dark and dreary. What's more, legend had it that the modern rectory had been built on top of the ruins of a medieval monastery, leading some to speculate that the dark history of its ancient foundation had bled through to the otherwise ordinary house above.

The impetus for Price's first visit to Borley was a letter written by its inhabitant, Reverend Guy Smith, to the editor of the *Daily Mirror*. He asked for an introduction to the Society for Psychical Research (SPR), which he hoped could help with some paranormal problems he and his wife had been experiencing.

Still in operation today, the SPR is a non-profit research organisation devoted to the scientific study of phenomena commonly described as psychic or paranormal. Founded in London in February 1882 by a ragtag band of physicists, psychics, spiritualists and clerics, the society claims to be the first organised group to apply scholarly methods to the research of 'human experiences that challenge contemporary scientific models'.

From the beginning, there was no clear consensus on the group's collective goals, beliefs or overall remit. Some were die-hard believers; some were hardened sceptics; some wished to establish concrete evidence of the afterlife; others sought to disprove the dubious claims of mediums and clairvoyants; still others believed they could reveal new and natural explanations for supposedly supernatural events. Some were men (and they were mostly men) of science, some were men of faith, and some were somewhere in the middle. What they all shared, however, was an interest in ghosts – and by extension, haunted houses. Regardless of their individual beliefs, they were all keen to investigate such matters.

Today, the study of paranormal phenomena – or parapsychology – is generally perceived as fringe or pseudo-science; indeed, from its inception in the mid-nineteenth century, 'psychical research', as it was then known, regularly incurred the wrath of mainstream scientists and academic researchers. Yet, in those early days, the general public would probably have viewed parapsychology no differently than many other new and mysterious fields of scientific inquiry, including psychiatry, thermodynamics and evolutionary biology.

That the Reverend Smith and his wife hoped to secure the services of the Society for Psychical Research does not necessarily demonstrate their eccentricity or superstitiousness – in fact, it probably indicates the opposite: that they were relatively reasonable people who sought scientific answers to their mysterious problem.

The *Daily Mirror* editor's first priority was, of course, sniffing out a good story, and so, before promising the Smiths to send the help they requested, he dispatched a staff reporter, one Vernon C. Wall, to investigate the strange situation unfolding at the rectory.

The first in a series of reports on Borley was published on 10 June under the headline *Ghost Visits to a Rectory. Tales of Headless Coachmen and a Lonely Nun. The Elopers. Mysterious Happenings on the Site of Old Monastery. From our Special Correspondent, Long Melford.* In typical tabloid fashion, the headline (as well as the article itself) was clunky, sensationalist and factually dubious. Yet it was evidently enough to pique the interest of the paper's wide readership. The article began:

> *Ghostly figures of headless coachmen and a nun, an old-time coach, drawn by two bay horses which appears and vanishes mysteriously, and dragging footsteps in empty rooms. All these ingredients of a first-class ghost story are awaiting investigation by psychic experts near Long Melford, Suffolk.*

Enter Harry Price. Though he was not an official member of the Society for Psychical Research, as the Smiths had requested, he held the honorary title of Foreign Resident for the American branch of the SPR and had a loose affiliation with the University of London, to which he would bequeath his extensive library and archive (whimsically known as 'the Harry Price Library of Magical Literature'). Price had also established his own National Laboratory of Psychical Research, a rival society to the SPR, with whom he had fallen out several years earlier. His state-of-the-art research facility included a lecture theatre, a darkroom, and a seance room equipped with cameras, recording devices and all manner of new-fangled gadgets designed for testing paranormal activity.

Price's reputation then was as a staunch sceptic, famed for exposing fraudulent mediums, supposed spirit photographers, fake hauntings and the like. Though considered one of the best in the field, his fiercely critical eye and arrogant airs didn't win him many friends. He made enemies of both fellow researchers and professional psychics, whose livelihoods were put in peril by Price's tireless work. He was also considered an enemy to spiritualism, which he once witheringly described as a movement that was 'at its best a religion; at its worst a racket'.

But, while he may have come to Borley a sceptic, after more than a decade of investigation, he left a true believer... Or possibly a show-boating conman, depending on who you believe.

The afternoon that Wall's first article appeared in print, Price received an urgent phone call from the editor, who had managed to track Price down at the London home of a friend with whom he had been enjoying a leisurely lunch and a friendly debate about the nature of poltergeists. The editor brought Price up to speed on the events developing at Borley, and asked him if he wished to join the *Mirror*'s reporter at the rectory. He agreed and made plans to depart for Borley immediately.

That a seasoned veteran of the paranormal world was so quick to accept such an invitation is curious. As one of the nation's pre-eminent psychical researchers, Price must have received requests like this on a near daily basis. And, in truth, there was nothing exceptional about Borley that made it stand out from the scores of other reputedly haunted properties across the country. Disembodied footsteps, shadowy figures and dark legends were all titillating, of course, but far from unique.

Borley's principal legend, too, is one that is repeated up and down the country. The tale, as recounted by Wall, is of a young nun who fell in love with a groom (or, in some versions, a monk) at the monastery that allegedly once stood on the rectory's grounds. One day, the couple arranged to elope with the assistance of another groom, who had a coach waiting for them in the road. 'From this point, the legend varies,' claims Wall. 'Some say that the nun and her lover quarrelled, and that he strangled her in the woods, and was caught and beheaded.' In the other version, 'All three were caught in the act by the monks, and the two grooms were beheaded, and the nun buried alive in the walls of the monastery.'

As with most such stories, the origins of the Borley nun are hazy and the details unfixed. And as it turns out, the nun story is a remarkably popular trope for ghost stories. Hinchingbrooke House in Cambridgeshire, originally an eleventh-century convent and now a stately home some 50 miles due west of Borley, boasts a remarkably similar legend of a love affair between a nun and a monk, resulting in their execution (or, alternatively, the nun's suicide after she becomes pregnant). A bridge over the nearby Alconbury Brook, fittingly known as Nun's Bridge, is reputed to be where she jumped to her death, and where she continues to revisit, scaring the daylights out of oncoming motorists.

There is also the ghost nun of Chicksands Priory, a religious house in Bedfordshire, founded in the twelfth century for a community of Gilbertine nuns and canons. This nun has a name, Rosata, which is chiselled into a memorial plaque in a surviving cloister. Rosata's tragic tale is essentially the same as the others: an illicit love affair, an unwanted pregnancy, and an execution. Just like at Borley, the nun's paramour was said to have been beheaded, but in a gruesome twist, Rosata was walled up to her neck and forced to watch her lover die. The wall was then sealed up and she was left to perish. Naturally, her spirit is said to remain at the site of her grisly demise.

Still morc phantom nuns crop up in British legend and literature across time and place, and suffice to say, the order of ghostly nuns is full of spirit sisters just like the one at Borley. And that's to say nothing of her male counterpart, the headless coachman, who likewise has a rich and ubiquitous presence in European folklore – but more on him later.

As Wall hinted in his article, Borley possessed all the staple ingredients of a classic ghost story, together with the quintessential protagonists. And this must have made the sceptic Price all the more suspicious of its authenticity. The only potential peculiarity here was that, instead of being an ancient castle, convent or old country house, Borley was a relatively modern middle-class home.

Perhaps Price was eager to escape the city to an easy-to-reach, yet bucolic little corner of the country. Or maybe he looked forward to the publicity the *Daily Mirror* would throw on his work. Whatever the case, he packed hastily and made his way to the Essex–Suffolk border with his trusty Girl Friday, Lucie Kaye. Years later he would remark, 'I little dreamed that there was ten years' work ahead of me probing what was to become the best-authenticated case of haunting in the annals of psychical research.'

So, what made Borley Rectory so special? Was it really that haunted? The consensus after Price's death in 1948 was that it almost certainly wasn't. Rather than being the 'best-authenticated' haunted house ever investigated, it was widely considered to be the location of one of the most elaborate and long-lasting hoaxes of modern times. Nevertheless, the fact remains: there is something about Borley. Something that continues to draw those pesky ghost hunters nearly 100 years later. Something that makes Borley add up to more than the sum of its fairly ordinary parts.

Here, I do not seek to prove or disprove the Borley haunting (though the reader will inevitably draw their own conclusions). Nor do I attempt to offer a definitive or even fully comprehensive account of the Borley Rectory saga. There are plenty of books out there that do that. Rather, this is an attempt to tell the tale of how a house – ostensibly a fairly unextraordinary house – came to be one of the most famous 'haunted houses' in British history.

With the benefit of hindsight, it's probably not that difficult to pinpoint the set of circumstances that made Borley Rectory a landmark paranormal case. The story emerged at a time when the public were tussling with two strong and diverging impulses: the desire to move forward, and the desire to cling to what once had been.

This was an age characterised by rapid advancements in technology and scientific discovery which revolutionised the world and made modern life vastly easier and more comfortable. It was the era in which penicillin was discovered; vaccines for smallpox, polio, influenza and measles were developed; when the radio, the incandescent lightbulb, the vacuum cleaner and the aeroplane were invented, and so much more.

But it was also an age in which people lived in fear. In an increasingly secularised world, untethered from the strictures (and arguable safety) of organised religion, the interwar period of 1918 to 1939 saw one of the biggest spikes in spiritualist belief of all time. Grieving survivors were not only trying to come to terms with the loss of their loved ones during the First World War, but they also sensed the ominous clouds of political discontent forming over Europe in advance of the Second World War.

Where science represented the future, folklore and traditional religion represented a romanticised and potentially more comforting past. With Borley Rectory, the public could have both. A great gloomy pile that simultaneously embodied antiquity and modernity; supernaturalism and science; faith and fact.

Science vs the supernatural

At the heart of this story lies the tension between belief and disbelief. Borley Rectory has come to embody the ongoing debate among the British public (and global society at large) of whether or not ghosts really exist, and whether or not they can be scientifically proven. Some eighty years after the destruction of the house and the death of its most dogged investigator, the debate rages on.

Today, according to Sean O'Connor, author of *The Haunting of Borley Rectory: The Story of a Ghost Story* (2022), 33 per cent of Britons admit to believing in ghosts, with 14 per cent claiming to have actually seen, felt or heard one. O'Connor puts this forward as a considerable number, but from my experience, it seems a conservative estimate.

Whenever I'm asked what I write about, I always hold my breath, fearing I'll be viewed as a madwoman. But almost invariably, people are curious about the subject, and quite often they will have a ghost story of their own, first-hand or otherwise, which they will usually share with me with the caveat of confidentiality.

The personal paranormal anecdotes I've accumulated over the years have not just come from New Age types. They have come from successful business owners, aristocratic landowners, medical professionals, engineers and, in the most memorable instance, an academic who once moved in the same circles as Stephen Hawking. A respected professor at the University of York, the academic told me a story she had heard from a local publican who had observed on CCTV the bar stools in his ancient inn rearranging themselves of their own accord, long after the pub had closed for the night and the bar was empty. The scholar sheepishly admitted to me that she now felt slightly uneasy every time she visited this pub for a tipple.

Most of us – especially those who come from educated middle-class backgrounds – are conditioned to think that intelligent individuals do not believe in ghosts. It's been this way since at least the days of Horace Walpole and the infamous Cock Lane debacle, and it carried on through much of the following century, right up to the days of Harry Price and beyond. This may have been why the Reverend Smith and his wife, though troubled by the seemingly inexplicable torment in their house, still maintained they did not believe in ghosts.

On his hit BBC Radio 4 podcast *Uncanny*, presenter Danny Robins interviews scores of individuals who claim to have had ghostly encounters. Following the recounting of their remarkable and often unnerving experiences, Robins always asks his guests the same question: 'So, do you believe in ghosts?' And wouldn't you know it, more often than not, they say 'no' or 'I don't know'. These are the same people who have just described in detail how they've personally experienced a ghost, yet they still can't quite admit to believing in them.

It's notable too that so many fictional ghost stories feature protagonists who start out sceptical or indifferent to ghosts, but who gradually begin to question their beliefs (or sanity) as the paranormal plot unfolds.

Perhaps the most celebrated ghost story writer of the twentieth century, English author and antiquarian M. R. James, frequently employed scholarly, serious-minded central characters. Antiquarians, archaeologists, art historians, theologians and scientists all served as a foil to the supernatural. In essence, James's typical protagonist was a reflection of himself: a distinguished provost and later vice-chancellor of Cambridge University; the son of a clergyman, raised in a strict religious environment, who somehow found himself caught up in ghost stories. The works published in his earliest anthology, *Ghost Stories of an Antiquary* (1904), were based on the tales with which he regaled his students as they huddled around the roaring fire at Christmastime – a welcome diversion from the rigours of scholarly study.

James was an indisputable master of the genre, yet he claimed to have no knowledge or interest in 'true' tales of the supernatural. 'The avowedly fictitious ghost story is my subject,' he maintained, despite the fact that he may have had a supernatural experience of his own at his boyhood home, the Old Rectory at Great Livermere in West Suffolk, a seventeenth-century manse located just 20 miles north of Borley. This experience is recounted in his last published ghost story,

'A Vignette' (1935), indicating that the event had a lifelong impact on the author.

However, whenever he was asked if he believed in ghosts, James always avoided giving a straight answer, replying only: 'I'm prepared to consider evidence and accept it if it satisfies me.'

Suffice to say, while it's long been deemed acceptable to have an ironic interest in the subject, we don't often readily admit to believing in ghosts in mixed company. And we certainly don't attempt to use science in an effort to prove their existence. Or at least not without opening ourselves up to the withering criticism of sceptics.

This was also the case in the early days of psychical research in the mid- to late nineteenth century. Some of the pioneering practitioners were once respected scientists and intellects, such as naturalist Alfred Russel Wallace, a leading proponent of natural selection alongside Charles Darwin, and Sir Arthur Conan Doyle, a physician and creator of literature's most famous detective – who quickly lost the respect of their former colleagues when they began wading into the weird world of paranormal study.

Harry Price was born on 17 January 1881 at 37 Red Lion Square in the central London district of Holborn. Though the eighteenth-century square had once been home to the city's fashionable elite, by Price's time, it was not an especially desirable address. It was probably for this reason that, in his 1942 autobiography *Search for Truth: My Life for Psychical Research*, Price intimates that instead of growing up in this working-class urban enclave, he was raised in a well-to-do family home in rural Shropshire.

Much has been made of this claim; his many detractors employ it as evidence of Price's deceitful nature. However, this was probably less of a full-blown lie than an artful stretching of the truth. Price's father, Edward Ditcher Price, a former butcher turned commercial traveller, was originally from Shropshire and it's entirely possible that some of Harry's childhood was spent there.

Many of the dubious details of Price's early life have been used to paint the picture of a lifelong con artist, a self-aggrandising fraudster perfectly capable of single-handedly orchestrating the Borley Rectory 'haunting', and there's no denying that he was a bit of a grifter. But rather than listing the myriad charges against him (which can easily be found online and in the scores of other books written about Borley), let's instead focus on what led to his pursuit of paranormal research and, more importantly, what made him succeed where Alfred Russel Wallace and others had failed.

As a boy, Price attended Waller Road Infants School in New Cross, followed by Haberdashers' Hatcham Boys School. He did not attend university, leaving school at the age of fifteen, though he did, for a time, attend evening classes in photography, chemistry and engineering at Goldsmiths College.

Even though he left school young, Harry was clearly intelligent, with unusually erudite interests for someone of his background. Like his Victorian polymath predecessor, Wallace, Price didn't let his lack of formal education stop him from pursuing a variety of academic subjects. From a young age, he was an astronomy enthusiast, an avid coin collector and an amateur archaeologist. In early adulthood, however, Harry would discover that without a degree in these fields, it would be difficult to pursue a career in them. This wasn't for a lack of trying; at twenty-three, he successfully convinced the Ripon Museum in North Yorkshire of his expertise in ancient coins, leading to his appointment as honorary Curator of Numismatics.

Though he would later be exposed as a fraud, the qualities he used to pull it off – his confidence, articulacy and ambition – would serve him well in future endeavours.

It would take a little while for Harry to find his true calling. In the meantime, during his twenties and thirties, he plied the family trade, travelling up and down the country hawking everything from paper bags and adhesives to veterinary medicine. He was a natural salesman and probably could have eked out a fairly comfortable existence for himself and his wife, Constance – more than enough to fund life at their quaint village home in Pulburough, West Sussex. But where was the glory in paper sales?

At last, in his early forties, Price finally hit on it – the special skill he possessed that would earn him the fame and respect he craved. Not an academic expertise, but a childhood hobby he likely never imagined would amount to much more than an amusing diversion.

In *Search for Truth*, Price describes the pivotal moment in his early life that would pave the way for his future career. At the age of eight, suffering from toothache, Harry was taken by his mother to a medicine show – a travelling act performed by a quack doctor peddling 'miracle' cures. This one was staged by the notorious Yorkshire-born mountebank, William Henry Hartley, who performed under his Indian shaman alias, the Great Sequah. The show incorporated elaborate Native American-inspired costumes, exotic music and, most importantly, magic tricks. The greatest feat was the conjuring of a pair of 'snow-white doves' from a previously empty bowler hat.

'Though I was transfixed with wonder at the clever Sequah show, looking at the incident in retrospect, I feel that on that eventful morning I did not believe a word I heard or a thing I saw. It was the novelty of it all, rather than genuine amazement, that made such an impression on me,' Price reflects. 'The fact that I at once demanded "how it was done" is proof, I think, of [my] inherent scepticism…'

On returning home that day, young Harry asked his parents to buy him books on magic so he too could learn the proverbial tricks of the trade. Decades later, Price maintained his interest in magic, becoming an expert conjurer himself. In 1922, he was even admitted to the Magic Circle, an exclusive society of master magicians. It was with this secret knowledge that Price was able to forge a new career – that of a ghostbuster: a ruthless debunker of mediums, conjurers, clairvoyants and all manner of charlatans who had interwar Britain completely enthralled with their uncanny abilities. Ironically, the former fraudster was to make his name by exposing the fraudulence of others.

Price's first major success was in 1922, with the exposure of famed 'spirit photographer' William Hope, whom he had discovered would procure existing photographs of deceased family members and expose the 'apparitions' onto photographic plates prior to sittings with his clients.

This was followed by the debunking of French medium Eva Carrier in the same year; the Polish medium Jan Guzyk in 1923; the Austrian medium Maria Silbert in 1925; the American medium George Valentine in 1931, and so on.

By the time Price was called upon to investigate Borley Rectory, he was the nation's go-to ghostbuster, a titan in his field. He travelled Europe delivering lectures on the paranormal; he hobnobbed with the likes of Harry Houdini and Sir Arthur Conan Doyle; and he even managed to form an alliance with a respected academic institution, the University of London, which accepted his offer to equip and endow its Department of Psychical Research in 1926.

In spite of his chequered past, his lack of formal scientific training and his famously abrasive personality, Harry Price had finally made it. And the key to his success was simple: scepticism. It was what made him credible. As a result, on those occasions when he *did* claim to have witnessed authentic supernatural phenomena, he had enough respectability in the bank to be believed – for a while, at least.

The spectre of history

All haunted houses have a history. Generally speaking, they are old and atmospheric, though this is not compulsory. So long as a house has a past – preferably a violent or troubled one – there might be just enough salacious material to scrape together a haunting. As we've established, when Borley Rectory first developed a reputation for being haunted, it was barely half a century old. It was neither ancient nor particularly architecturally interesting, and its recent history was relatively uneventful. But it could – and would – lay claim to a past that long predated its Victorian-era foundations.

To some extent, in the case of Borley Rectory, it is not the actual building itself that is as significant as its location. The outwardly unassuming little community of Borley, nestled in the heart of the East Anglia region of south-eastern England, is so much more than it initially seems. Not really a village at all, but rather a very small hamlet, Borley consists of a church and a few houses. Beyond that, countryside. A soft, gentle terrain with arable fields, sheep grazing pastures and narrow, winding lanes that follow the rolling contours of the land. These tight rural alleys are lined with thick hedgerows and ancient oak trees. Skylarks sing overhead; pheasants rustle through the undergrowth below; silent swarms of gnats cloud the air. On warm summer days, when the golden sunlight dapples the dense foliage, it's almost magical.

Meanwhile, just 18 miles away, in the bustling city of Colchester, droves of tourists amble around the ruins of Colchester castle;

punters pour in and out of chain restaurants and high-street shops; and commuters board trains that get them to London in just under an hour.

And yet, nearby Borley and the surrounding countryside feel remote, almost untouched since the days when the artist John Constable could be found on the bank of the River Stour (the natural boundary between the two counties), sketching bucolic scenes for his Romantic masterpieces. In fact, this picturesque little pocket of England, nestled in the Stour Valley, is known as 'Constable country'.

But this dreamy pastoral imagery belies the region's turbulent past. While it may seem like a sleepy backwater today, this neck of the woods was once one of the busiest and wealthiest parts of the country. And where there's wealth, there's power. And where there's power, there's usually a struggle. As it turns out, the real history of this location is far bloodier than the isolated deaths of a rogue nun and her illicit lover.

Travelling back some 2,000 years to its earliest period of recorded history, we find the Stour Valley at the heart of a powerful Celtic kingdom, the territory of the Trinovante, whose land stretched from north of the River Thames into modern-day Hertfordshire, Essex and southern Suffolk. Emperor Julius Caesar himself declared it the 'strongest state in those parts', and so, in 55 BCE, the invading Romans forged an alliance with the tribe in order to squash the rest of the native population.

The Trinovantian tribal capital, Camulodunum (modern-day Colchester), later became the first permanent Roman outpost in the British isles, while Long Melford, Borley's neighbour 2 miles to the north, became the second largest settlement in the region.

Thanks to its fertile ground and easy access to the English Channel, the Trinovante's traditional lands were hotly contested, and it was here that the Romans faced the biggest and bloodiest rebellion of the Romano-British era. In 60 CE, under the fearsome command of Queen Boudica, Camulodunum was stormed and burned to the ground by a coalition of angry Celtic tribes, including the Trinovante, who resented the fact that their kingdom had been annexed by their former Roman allies.

All told, 60,000 men died in the Boudican revolt, a staggering death toll similar to that of the Battle of the Somme 2,000 years later.

Fast forward 1,000 years and we find the Stour Valley (and indeed most of the rest of Britain) under the firm control of the Normans, who had wrested power from the incumbent Anglo-Saxon rulers. Famed for their military prowess and Catholic piety, the Normans were also meticulous record-keepers, and it is thanks to their diligence that we have the earliest recorded description of Borley, a small settlement then known as Barlea, an Anglo-Saxon word meaning 'pasture' or 'field of bore'.

According to the Domesday Book (essentially an eleventh-century tax survey), Borley was then in the possession of Adelaide, Countess of Aumale and half-sister to William the Conqueror, who had forced its former owner, an Anglo-Saxon called Wihtgar Ælfricsson, to hand the property over. With it, Adelaide got a manor house, a meadow, a wood and some farmland. Her residents included 10 villagers, 5 farmers, 7 cattle, 28 pigs, 25 sheep, 24 goats and 2 beehives. Not much, really, but it was a nice little estate in a nice little corner of the country.

The next mention of Borley in the annals of history is in a land survey of 1308. By this time the land was in the possession of Edward I. It had now more than quadrupled in size, with 44 listed families in 41 households – about 230 residents. Remarkably, this is roughly the same figure recorded in a census of 1830, indicating that Borley's brief period of expansion was followed by centuries of stasis. But while it failed to develop along the lines of its closest neighbour, Long Melford – by then a prosperous market town of about 600 people – Borley was nevertheless stable and profitable.

For centuries, as Borley stood quietly unaltered, the region around it experienced extraordinary change. The surrounding area saw the rise of major religious communities at Clare, Sudbury, Ipswich and Bury St Edmunds, and around these religious communities grew thriving commercial centres built off the back of the verdant land. To be sure, the outbreak of the Black Death in 1348, followed by the Peasants' Revolt of 1381, wreaked havoc, but the village of Borley continued its slow, steady march along the path of progress.

By the fifteenth century, northern Essex and southern Suffolk were leading centres for cloth production, the kingdom's main export, making the Stour Valley one of the richest parts of England. The rows of large, brightly painted, timber-framed townhouses that can still be seen in places like Lavenham, Coggeshall and Long Melford are a testament to the success of the region's medieval merchants. Had it not been for the collapse of the woollen industry in the mid-sixteenth century, Long Melford may have continued its expansion south, blurring its rural boundary with Borley in a parade of handsome Tudor homes and shopfronts.

Still more change came with King Henry VIII's decision to sever ties with the Catholic Church. The dissolution of the monasteries between 1536 and 1541 had a huge impact on the region surrounding Borley. Almost overnight, the religious communities that had shaped the area's spiritual, social and cultural life for centuries were gone. Some were destroyed, as in the case of Bury St Edmunds Priory, once the richest monastic community in the country, while others were converted into private residences, such as Clare Priory, which became the family home of Sir Thomas Barnardiston.

This was also the fate of Borley Manor, which for some time had been in the possession of the Priory of Christchurch, Canterbury. In 1546, it was purchased by Sir Edward Waldegrave, a courtier to the future Queen Mary. It would remain in the Waldegrave family for the next 300 years.

Generation after generation, Borley stood largely untouched, always on the fringes, never quite at the centre of the political and religious tumult and violence that rocked the region. The Civil War raged, witch hunters tore through the countryside, fortunes were won and lost, and through it all, the village bore silent watch to the spectacle of history.

And so, while the rectory itself may have been a relatively recent construction, the earth on which it stood was steeped in a long, rich history. A history that, at the time of Borley's construction, was plainly visible all around – just as it is today. There were Roman ruins, medieval churches, Tudor manor houses, seventeenth-century thatched cottages, and eighteenth-century inns and public houses as far as the eye could see. It was a virtual mosaic of all the epochs to which the region had borne witness.

*

In the summer of 1862, Reverend Henry Dawson Ellis Bull, rector of Borley from 1862–92, made the decision to knock down the old rectory. A worldly and educated man with a degree from Oxford, he was also the scion of a long-established East Anglian family who could trace their lineage almost as far back as the earliest history of Borley itself. The Bulls had been hereditary rectors in the region's country parishes for many generations, and Henry was born in 1832 in Pentlow, Essex, 5 miles west of Borley, where his father and grandfather before him held a lucrative living. As such, his ambitions were lofty, with grand designs to build a house that could compete with the local gentry. Moreover, Reverend Henry had a notoriously high libido: he would soon need a large home for a large family.

If you enter the phrase 'architect of Borley Rectory' into Google, the top result will appear in a banner at the head of the page: Augustus Pugin (1812–52). That would have been a supernatural feat given that Pugin, the great neo-Gothic designer, partly responsible for the Houses of Parliament, died a decade before Borley was constructed. And even if he wasn't tied up being dead, Pugin would hardly have had the time to design a relatively minor provincial rectory when he was busy designing the most important buildings in the nation. Needless to say, Pugin had nothing to do with Borley Rectory.

The mistake appears to have originated from a Wikipedia entry in which historian Andrew Clarke put forward the idea that the rectory was built to a design 'inspired by Pugin'. Even this might be a bit of a stretch, but it does at least account for the confusion.

Strangely, few researchers have seemed remotely interested in identifying the actual architect behind the nation's most famous haunted house. Even Clarke says only, 'The architect, a Bury man, went on to design Pentlow Rectory.'

The Bury man in question was John Johnson. Pugin he was not, but he was a prominent regional architect who had some national success in the form of Alexandra Palace, a public entertainment venue built in 1873, conceived as north London's answer to the Crystal Palace. Johnson was inspired by the Gothic Revival movement and was involved in many ecclesiastical structures in Suffolk and Essex. As such, he was a natural choice for the new Borley Rectory.

The building work commenced in the summer of 1862. Merely weeks later, a report on a death inquest appeared in the *Norwich Post* involving a seventeen-year-old labourer, John Whyard, 'a carpenter working at Borley Rectory [who] with the other lads had gone to bathe ... in a river adjacent to the rectory where he was at work.' The river was deep and Whyard was cautioned not to swim out of his depth. He persisted nonetheless, then complained of a cramp, and was suddenly dragged under. His colleagues attempted to save him but were unsuccessful, and his death was deemed an accident.

It was an ominous start for the new Borley Rectory. And yet, none of the subsequent strange happenings have ever been attributed to the unfortunate Master Whyard. A drowned builder's apprentice, it seems, doesn't make for a good ghost story. Nothing compared to a beheaded monk and walled-up nun, at any rate.

In any case, the rest of the building work went off without a hitch, which was no small feat, given that, in addition to room for their eventual family of fifteen, they also needed accommodation for a large staff, a substantial kitchen, offices, and reception rooms for their many social engagements. Though the Reverend Henry was, on the face of it, a simple country vicar, he was also a member of a well-to-do family with enough social status to mingle with the local gentry. As such, he would need to have an appropriately grand setting to host the upper echelons of local society.

According to Price in *The Most Haunted House in England*, the rectory completed in 1862 was roughly L-shaped. It comprised a scullery, kitchen, pantry, dining room, library and drawing room on the ground floor, and eight bedrooms and a private chapel on the first floor. The stable block of the earlier rectory was retained and converted into staff accommodation and offices.

As the Bull family grew, the need for still more space resulted in a new wing, constructed in 1876, turning the earlier L-shaped floor plan into a large rectangle surrounding an open courtyard. The extension provided further storage space on the ground floor and three additional chambers on the first, making a grand total of eleven bedrooms.

The Reverend Henry was probably as pleased as punch with his stonking new state-of-the-art home. Though later inhabitants would complain of its dreariness and inconvenience, in Bull's day it was the height of fashion – or, at least, the height of fashion for the area.

That Bull lived out the rest of his days at Borley without making any substantial changes to his home suggests he was satisfied with what he had created. It was big, it was modern, and it was befitting of a gentleman-cleric. There was just one thing missing: a history.

Cock and bull stories: the creation of England's 'most haunted house'

It's not clear when the ghosts of Borley first came on the scene, but one of the more popular theories is that they originated with the Bull children; after all, several of the girls would attest to the sighting of the ghostly nun.

The thirteen offspring of Henry and Caroline Bull – six boys and seven girls – lived a charmed, if somewhat sheltered, existence. The bulk of their childhood was spent in and around Borley, with its centuries-old parish church, pretty little cottages and farmhouses. Though they were privileged to be brought up in such a bucolic environment, at times the Bull children must have been a bit bored.

Though Borley Rectory was not entirely without character, it certainly lacked the mystery and romance of some of the more venerable buildings in the area, like the Old Rectory at Great Yeldham, a parish just 8 miles west of Borley, where Reverend Henry occasionally preached with his children in attendance.

Four hundred years old, with thick lath and plaster walls, exposed timber beamed ceilings and a jettied upper storey, the Old Rectory had the whimsically teetering appearance we so often associate with medieval buildings. There were ancient scribblings on the exposed beams ('Cast me not away from thy presence'); a built-in window seat under which a set of human bones was supposedly uncovered; and a centuries-old cellar rumoured to have once formed part of a subterranean passage to the adjacent church.

And there were ghosts. Servants complained of lights turning on and off of their own accord; the rector's dog refused to enter a certain room; and the doorbell rang without anyone being there. All the same classic poltergeist-type activity that would later be reported at Borley. What's more, Great Yeldham had its own 'Nun's Walk' – the same moniker given to the ghostly garden path at Borley.

Given all these ingredients, one wonders why Borley and not

Great Yeldham became the better known of the haunted rectories.

So, were the bored Bull children inspired by such stories to infuse their mundane modern home with some ghostly glamour? Did they invent the legends in order to fit in? After all, almost every big house in the area had a ghost: Clare Priory (demonic monk); Melford Hall (Countess Rivers); Kentwell Hall, Long Melford (ghost child). The list goes on.

Of course, it's entirely possible that the Bull sisters' compelling account of the nun floating down their garden path was based on an actual experience. But the backstory used to explain her presence is far-fetched, to say the least. For one thing, there's no documentary or archaeological evidence to support the idea that there was ever a religious house on the grounds of Borley Rectory. Moreover, underground passageways allegedly connecting the mythical monastery to a nearby convent at Clare – thus enabling secret rendezvous between the nun and her lover – have since been proven to be flood drains.

As for the purported punishment for the nun's wrongdoings – eternal imprisonment in a bricked-up chamber – even the converted believer Price acknowledged that the idea was cribbed from a fictional source, Sir Walter Scott's epic poem *Marmion, Canto Second,* 'The Convent'. Such punishment seems to have been reserved for fiction. There is almost no evidence that the practice of immurement – that is, the act of imprisonment in a confined space until death – occurred in England in recent history, or maybe even at all. Most historians consider the numerous reported cases of walled-up nuns to be pure fantasy; titillating tales cooked up by anti-Catholic storytellers in a post-Reformation society.

And then there's the matter of the *other* Borley ghosts: the phantom coach and headless coachmen. The legend features heavily in Wall's June 1929 article in the *Daily Mirror*, in which he reports that an old-fashioned coach had been seen at least twice on the lawn by one of the Smith family servants, Mary, who claimed that it 'remained in sight long enough for [her] to distinguish the brown colour of the horses'. Wall was also told that the late Reverend Harry Bull had seen the coach one night when walking down the country lane outside the rectory. Startled by the thunderous clatter of horses' hooves bearing down on him, the cleric turned and 'to his horror [saw] an old-fashioned coach lumbering along the road, driven by two headless men'.

It isn't known who was the first to make the connection between the phantom coach and the tale of the ill-fated nun, whether it was the Bull family or the later tenants, the Smiths and their staff, but in any case, it was subsequently carried forward by Harry Price in his own writings on Borley. However, again, while intrigued by the story, Price acknowledged the potential problems with it. The general public had already picked up on the historical discrepancies; as one Freda Noble of Bridge House in Long Melford pointed out in a letter to the editor of the *Suffolk and Essex Free Press* in the spring of 1929, it was between '1529 and 1547 that Henry VIII suppressed all the smaller monasteries and nunneries in the land', meaning that even if there had been a religious house on the site of Borley Rectory, all the nuns and monks would have been evicted by the mid-sixteenth century.

Meanwhile, the first coach to be seen in England was made by Walter Rippon for the Earl of Rutland in 1555 during the reign of Mary I. Later a more elaborate one was made by the same man for Queen Elizabeth I. However, these were very primitive early prototypes of a mode of transportation then solely reserved for the kingdom's elite. So, it would seem, as Ms Noble writes, that 'the nun of Borley and the coachmen could never have met during life on earth, their only acquaintance being a ghostly one'.

And even if we were to separate the ghosts – the nun and the coachmen – we would still be left with a pair of suspiciously familiar characters.

As we already know, the lovelorn nun is omnipresent across the British folkloric landscape, with nearly every county in the country boasting at least one spectral sister skulking around a site of supposed historical significance. This can probably be chalked up to that inextricable link that has been forged between the pre-Reformation past and the supernatural. While today nuns conjure up the cheerfully benign characters of pop culture classics like *The Sound of Music* (1965) and *The Flying Nun* (1967–70), in the nineteenth century the nun was a powerful and shadowy synecdoche for the Catholic Church. She existed as a kind of ghostly vestige of a mysterious and commonly misunderstood bygone era: a mythical figure that probably seemed all the more romantic to a family of middle-class Protestants living in a decidedly ordinary modern home.

Similarly, the headless coachman and phantom coach pop up all over Britain and beyond, though their precise cultural origins are unclear. Some contend that the phantom coach (or *cóiste bodhar*) is a folk tale native to Ireland. Much like its better-known Irish supernatural cousin the banshee, the *cóiste bodhar* and its headless driver the *dullahan* were believed to be harbingers of death. According to legend, if you saw or heard the coach, it foretold your imminent demise – or that of a family member.

The *cóiste bodhar* was, in fact, a new twist on an even earlier myth. The coach part, of course, was new, reflecting a then-modern mode of transport, but the *dullahan* – which can refer to either a headless coach driver or a headless horseman – was practically timeless. Indeed, there were literary precedents for the headless horseman all over the place – in medieval Arthurian legend, in eighteenth- and nineteenth-century German fairy tales, and perhaps most famously in the classic Gothic short story, 'The Legend of Sleepy Hollow' (1820), by American author Washington Irving.

By the late nineteenth century, the headless horseman and its later derivate the headless coachman were known to all in both literary and legendary form. And for the Bull family, the spectral figure rode especially close to home, with the local legend of the headless coachmen of Acton circulating just 5 miles east of Borley Rectory.

So, even if we are to give the Bulls the benefit of the doubt and believe that they really did experience something supernatural, based on the historical inaccuracies and strong similarities to existing legends, it seems clear that, at the very least, they were inventing an acceptable framework in which to parse their encounters with the unknown. Fairy tales, folklore and a feeling of 'keeping up with the Joneses' may have made such experiences not only easier to accept, but also somewhat enjoyable.

On 9 June 1927 the Reverend Harry Bull died in his home in a first-floor bedroom known as the Blue Room. Rather predictably, he was soon after inducted into the ghostly cast of characters haunting Borley, said to be responsible for the sounds of footsteps regularly heard throughout the house.

Following Harry's death, Borley Rectory sat empty for twelve months. Bishop Guy Warman, the man in charge of filling the living, evidently found it difficult to attract viable candidates, apparently having offered the position to twelve men before finally handing it over to the Reverend Guy Eric Smith. It has been suggested that this was because of the rectory's reputation for being haunted, but there was probably a far more prosaic reason for the lack of interest: the parish was remote; the house was exceptionally large and difficult to run; it had no piped water, no gas or electricity; and it was extremely outdated.

Alas, the Reverend Smith and his wife Mabel had few options. Newly ordained and recently immigrated from his native Calcutta, the Reverend Smith was of mixed race, with a dark complexion that would have made it very difficult for him to fit in and find acceptance anywhere in England. Notably, Smith's heritage is something that Price never mentions in *The Most Haunted House in England*, describing the couple as 'very intelligent, delightful, and much travelled people, who were, like myself, utterly sceptical as regards [to] "spirits".' However, this omission was not necessarily a sign of his 'colour-blindness'. Price wished to put forward Reverend Smith as a respectable and trustworthy witness, and would have been aware of the prejudiced views of a good portion of his readership. This was a time when people of colour were disbarred from many professions and establishments and race riots had recently rocked several British cities, where unemployment was running high. A sadly large segment of the British population would have viewed an Indian immigrant as unintelligent, unsophisticated and unwanted.

In this harsh cultural climate it would have been very difficult for Smith to find employment, and he probably couldn't afford to turn his nose up at Borley. The Smiths had only left India in 1926, due to Mabel's poor health. After suffering a miscarriage, she found that she would be unable to conceive again, and purportedly fell into a deep depression. So she and her husband decided to pursue a fresh start in England, where the former civil servant Smith would immediately enrol in Chichester Theological College to retrain as a clergyman. They accepted the Borley living in October 1928.

For the couple from Calcutta, the cold, cavernous manse in rural northern Essex must have been a culture shock on a grand and powerful scale. Arriving just as winter was on its way, nothing could have prepared the Smiths for the bitter cold or the inky black nights which descended rapidly upon them as the sun dipped below the horizon as early as 4 p.m.

Historical weather reports show that November 1928 was a particularly stormy period for the whole of the British Isles, with gales ripping across the south-east of England in the second half of the month. The howling winds and groaning of the house shifting on its foundations must have added immeasurably to the foreboding atmosphere.

To make things worse, by the time the Smiths took possession, Borley Rectory was a shambles, having been stripped of its furniture and locked up empty for a year. Cupboards and walls were overrun with rats, while the cellar was riddled with lizards and toads; water damage from a leaking roof filled the air with the sour stench of damp and made several of the bedrooms entirely uninhabitable. Not that the Smiths were short on space. With just the two of them and their pet cats, much of the decrepit thirty-two-room mansion went entirely unused. It must have been a grim reminder to the Smiths that they were childless and alone in a home designed to accommodate a boisterous family of fifteen. If not haunted by ghosts, the Smiths were certainly haunted by loneliness and unease.

The first reported paranormal events experienced by the Smiths occurred shortly after they moved in. It started with disembodied whispers on the first-floor landing. Soon it escalated to the sound of moaning, then a woman's voice shrieking, 'Don't, Carlos, don't!'

The Smiths also allegedly experienced other phenomena typically associated with haunted houses: the sound of footsteps, mysterious bell-ringing, and strange lights seen illuminating upper-floor rooms that were not in use. Two of the Smiths' servants described seeing full-bodied apparitions: the phantom coach and a figure in black leaning over the back gate, respectively. One maid was so frightened that she left her employment after only two days working at Borley.

Though the Smiths themselves were sceptical, they found it increasingly difficult to wholly dismiss the rumours about their house. The gruesome discovery of a human skull hidden in a cupboard did nothing to calm Mrs Smith's already jangled nerves.

Where the Bulls' encounters with the paranormal had occurred in the rectory grounds – ethereal forms appearing to them at a hazy distance outside their home – the ghosts seem to have moved in with the Smiths. The 'traditional ghosts' – spectral figures with romantic backstories that were the stuff of legend and folklore – were no more. The unthreateningly remote spirits were replaced by a haunting that was present, personal and invasive. This haunted house was evolving, and its new inhabitants took the form of the insidiously modern poltergeist.

Though cases of such entities have been described for centuries, the word 'poltergeist' itself – deriving from the German *polten* (noisy) and *geist* (ghost or spirit) – only passed into common English usage in the early nineteenth century. Widespread interest in, and study of, these unseen forces responsible for physical disturbances and unexplained noises coincided with the advent of psychical research in the second half of the nineteenth century. But it wasn't until the twentieth century that cases of poltergeists really ramped up. They often seemed to be attached to dysfunctional, disenfranchised or otherwise unhappy families, especially those with a young, emotionally volatile female family member. Ghost expert Roger Clarke refers to them as 'council house' ghosts, in reference to a number of high-profile cases in which poltergeists were reported by working-class families living on council estates.

While far from being working class, the Smiths *were* living in a borrowed house in which they did not feel at home or wanted. Certainly, their overall attitude towards both the house and the haunting was decidedly less positive than that of the Bulls. They claimed not to be afraid of what was happening to them (in fact, they claimed not to believe in ghosts), but they definitely weren't happy about it.

On 15 July 1929, after less than a year in residence, the Smiths moved out of the rectory. The Reverend Smith continued to perform his duties at Borley Church for the next nine months, commuting from nearby Long Melford, but when a living became available in Kent, he pounced on it. Here, according to Price, the Smiths at last lived 'in peace, both mentally and physically.'

The next family to take up residence at the rectory were the Foysters – the Reverend Lionel, his wife Marianne and their adopted daughter, two-year-old Adelaide. Like the Smiths, the Foysters had recently arrived in England after living overseas (Nova Scotia) and they too would find it difficult to blend in. While Lionel was a fairly typical English country parson – grey-haired, tweed-clad, in his fifties – Marianne was no ordinary preacher's wife. She was nearly half her husband's age, striking and vivacious, with fiery red hair and full crimson lips.

Mrs Foyster cared little for village life, despised the gossipy parishioners, and took every opportunity to escape to London, where for a short time she ran a flower shop with one Frank Peerless (alias Francois D'Arles), a fairly shady former Borley lodger with whom it would later be revealed she was having an affair.

For the most part, however, Marianne was stuck in the village with few friends and a much older husband who suffered from a variety of debilitating health problems. Though improvements had been made to the house, it was still too big, too cold and too dreary.

So the unhappy wife attempted to fill the void by fostering children (evidently she and Lionel were unable to have their own) and engaging in an ill-advised tryst with a man who, as it turns out, was a pathological liar with a violent temper. Once again, the house would reflect its residents' mental and emotional turmoil.

Under the Foysters' tenure, paranormal activity at Borley rapidly and dramatically intensified. As with the Smiths, it began with strange sounds (footsteps and disembodied voices) but quite quickly escalated to full-bodied apparitions now manifesting *within* the house (Harry Bull). Soon there were objects disappearing and reappearing (jewellery, silverware, crockery), mysterious smells (lavender, fire) and cryptic messages appearing on the walls ('Marianne Please Help').

Like the Smiths before them, the Foysters decided they needed help. And so, in October 1931, on the invitation of Lionel Foyster, Harry Price and a group of colleagues paid a visit to Borley, where they witnessed a number of uncanny events. Pebbles whizzed through the air; a claret bottle was hurled down the staircase; Marianne was inexplicably locked in her bedroom; and most remarkably, a fine bottle of Burgundy was transmuted from a 'beautiful ruby *Chambertin*' to 'jet-black ink' in the glass.

Price was perplexed, but he observed that most of these events occurred either in Marianne's company or when she was conspicuously out of sight. The investigator and his associates were growing suspicious. When he told the reverend and his wife of his misgivings, Marianne was livid. Lionel was sheepish, and desperate for the opportunity to exonerate his wife. So, Price and his colleagues agreed to stay one further night to investigate, on the condition that there would be further controls put in place. All the external and internal doors and windows would be locked and sealed, the children would be confined to their rooms, and the maidservant would be sent home for the evening.

'By the time we had finished sealing the rectory, it was nearly half past nine. So I assembled the incarnate occupants of the house in the kitchen,' recalls Price. 'Everything seemed very quiet after the excitement of the previous night, [so] we thought that our control arrangements had exorcised the [poltergeist] for good and all.'

But then, at last, after nearly an hour of waiting, the sound of a service bell pealed through the still night air.

'The ringing of the bell was the sum total of phenomena we heard, saw, or felt that evening,' Price reports. 'A little later some visitors arrived, which made further investigation impossible.' One of those visitors was Frank Peerless. His whereabouts earlier that evening are unknown.

Naturally, it is the opinion of many sceptics that Marianne Foyster (possibly with the assistance of her lover, Peerless) was responsible for the 'haunting' of Borley Rectory. But of course, Marianne was not the first to claim it was haunted. She was merely one in a succession of occupants who felt, for various reasons, that there was something not quite right about the rectory. For the Bull family, it lacked history. For the Smiths, it was a symbol of what they personally lacked – children. And for the Foysters, it was the physical manifestation of their dysfunctional marriage. A large age gap, adultery, the absence of natural heirs – all these things were the inverse of domestic bliss. And Borley Rectory became a monstrous mirror reflecting back the Foysters' flaws.

Like the Smiths, the Foysters claimed not to be frightened by the things they experienced, but several witnesses described having seen Marianne in a state of distress. Price himself described her as 'hysterical', and in October 1935, the Foysters left Borley for good. Allegedly, not because of the ghosts but because of Lionel's deteriorating health. He moved into a long-term care facility. The local diocese, meanwhile, determined that Borley Rectory was no longer suitable accommodation for future rectors and their families.

Now, not only was the house vacant, but it was at last on the open market. Harry Price saw a unique opportunity. He could have the place to himself and finally get to the bottom of what was really happening at Borley Rectory.

This was the beginning of Price's full-scale paranormal investigation.

Harry Price came to Borley Rectory a self-proclaimed sceptic, writing early on in *Most Haunted*: 'I did *not* believe in the legend [of the nun] and did *not* believe in spirits.'

Somewhere along the line, this changed, but in the beginning, at least, he insisted that he was not convinced of the rectory's hauntedness, apparently once telling a local that, 'I used to think it was all 100 per cent bunkum, but now I think it is only 97 per cent bunkum.'

To be sure, he found the legends 'charming' and enjoyed the company of the worldly Reverend Smith and his wife Mabel. He considered them intelligent people who genuinely believed they were experiencing something unusual in their new home. It just wasn't enough to constitute proof of the paranormal. Nor was it enough to fill the pages of a bestselling book.

Price's scepticism only grew when the Foysters took over the dwelling. While he was a great deal more diplomatic in his published writings, his personal papers reveal his true beliefs: that Marianne was responsible for the phenomena and may have been suffering from hysteria.

Yet something convinced him not to turn his back on Borley. Though he placed little stock in the Foysters' claims, Price was nevertheless entertained by a copy of Lionel's personal journals he'd been given, which documented in dramatic detail the alleged paranormal events experienced by the couple during their eighteen-month tenancy. What's more, he was intrigued to discover that even after the Foysters' departure in the autumn of 1935, villagers continued to report strange lights, shadowy figures and the thunderous clatter of phantasmal coaches in the vacant rectory's general vicinity. Did the haunting persist even when there was no one left to haunt? Well, Harry would just have to find out.

In May 1937, Price made arrangements to lease the rectory for £30 a year (or about £1,500 in today's currency). Even for a tumbledown haunted house in the middle of nowhere, this seems like a bargain. Price immediately got to work setting out the parameters of his paranormal investigation. At last he had full jurisdiction over the case. He no longer needed to depend on the testimony of potentially unreliable witnesses and could now bring in scrupulous, serious-minded investigators and maintain a strictly controlled environment.

'I reiterate that I wanted as far as possible to eliminate myself and my friends, and all previous occupiers, from taking any active part in my proposed inquiry,' he explains. 'I wanted *independent evidence* from intelligent, competent and cultured strangers who were not spiritualists; and, if they knew nothing about psychical research, so much the better.'

On 25 May 1937, Price placed an advertisement in *The Times* calling for 'intelligent, intrepid, critical, unbiased' participants to take part in an investigation of a reputedly haunted house. A background in science was listed as an advantage, but basically anyone of sound mind and 'independent means' (there would be no renumeration) was invited to apply.

The response was overwhelming. Some 200 people applied, ranging from thrill-seeking society women to professional mediums; hack journalists to decorated army officers; exorcists to engineers. Of those 200, Price deemed that forty were of the 'right sort' – mainly science and medical professionals, university students and off-duty military personnel.

Successful candidates were given a small blue handbook outlining their duties and a declaration form to sign promising to abide by Price's rules, which included the strict instruction not to photograph, write about or lecture on the subject of the haunted rectory. This was, after all, Harry's investigation.

The 'official observers', as Price dubbed them, would be required to camp out overnight in the empty house, taking careful note of anything unusual they saw, heard, felt or smelled. Investigators would either work alone or in pairs, and no unauthorised visitors were permitted on the premises. When they arrived, they were instructed to draw circles in chalk around every portable item in the house; to lock and seal all doors and windows; and to fill in their observational reports as soon as they witnessed something out of the ordinary.

While intriguing, the investigators' findings were not exactly earth-shattering. Nearly all the participants related some sort of anomaly; however, much of what was witnessed was rather understated, especially when compared to the experiences of the Bulls, Smiths and Foysters. A matchbox moving a mere millimetre wasn't exactly the same as a full-bodied apparition, though Price would argue it was 'no less miraculous'.

Most of the observers' experiences were auditory (bumps, shuffles, footsteps), occasionally olfactory (lavender, sewage, incense), but very rarely visual. Only one participant reported seeing a figure – or rather 'a round, dark object', which Price inferred to be 'a short, stooping' person.

Perhaps the strangest phenomena was the sudden appearance of pencil marks on the walls. But again, this paled in comparison to the phantom inscriptions that materialised under the Foysters' tenure. They got actual words, sentence fragments, like 'Marianne Light Mass Prayers', whereas the observers just got illegible handwriting.

'The really exciting happenings that occurred at Borley invariably took place when the house *was occupied by a family*,' Price concedes, seeming to suggest that without a resident family, the haunted house had somehow lost its full power. Almost as though the ghosts had been deriving their energy from the living occupants. Maybe they could only muster so much strength from stoical strangers who stayed less than twenty-four hours.

In turn, the investigators could only get so much from the ghosts. With no connection to the property, no knowledge of its history or legends, and no reason to be particularly invested in what was happening within it, the official observers were left with all ghost and no story – senseless scribbles and meaningless noises.

But by now, Harry Price really *was* invested. Just as it had been for the Bulls, Smiths and Foysters, Borley Rectory had become the embodiment of Price's longing: his passionate desire to prove his mastery of psychical investigation. He emerged from the year-long investigation in 1938 confident about his findings, proclaiming that 'the evidence submitted by our witnesses for the haunting of Borley Rectory would be acceptable in a court of law in consideration of their number, their integrity, their unemotionalism, their disinterestedness and their skill.'

This unemotional reportage was of scientific value, Harry recognised, but perhaps not the stuff of bestselling books. To animate his cold, hard facts he would need to inject some sizzling human interest. So, he decided to enter some evidence of decidedly less scientific value – the results of a series of seances.

Of course, as a respected sceptic, Price felt it his duty to include a disclaimer, cautioning his readers about the 'notoriously unreliable' nature of such communications. 'I need hardly warn the reader not to take this seance information too seriously,' he writes, then goes on to devote three full chapters to the content of these spurious sessions...

The seances were conducted in the rectory between 23 and 25 October 1937 and were led by a Mr Sidney Glanville, a retired engineer and one of the official observers, whom Price describes as 'neither a spiritualist nor a "believer"'.

Together with his son Roger, a Mr A. J. Cuthbert and Mr Kerr-Pearse, Glanville made his first attempt to contact the spirits in a table-tilting session. This is a method of spiritualist communication wherein participants sit around a table, with their fingers placed lightly on the surface, while one of them recites the alphabet aloud. The table is meant to rotate or tip when the appropriate letter is said, in order to spell out a word. Exactly the sort of cheap parlour trick that Price previously sought to debunk.

In their first session, Glanville and his colleagues made contact with 'Harry Bull', who informed them that the legendary nun did indeed roam the rectory grounds and that her restless soul awaited a proper Christian burial. Her remains, he said, could be found buried beneath a fir tree in a corner of the garden.

Next, Glanville tried his hand at something called planchette writing, which involves a heart-shaped piece of wood affixed to rolling castors with a pencil inserted at the tip. Participants place their fingers on the planchette and ask the 'spirit' questions; the 'spirit' then provides written responses via the planchette.

At first, Glanville deemed the session a failure as he could make no sense of the responses. However, when he gave the scripts to his adult daughter, Helen – who purportedly had no prior knowledge of Borley or its legends – she was able to piece together a pretty scintillating narrative involving a nineteen-year-old French novice named Marie Lairre who, at some point in the mid-seventeenth century, travelled from her nunnery in Le Havre, Normandy to a similar sort of establishment at Bures near the rectory. She became involved with a local man who absconded with her, and later strangled her to death, disposing of her remains in an unmarked grave on the rectory grounds. Her murderer, she reveals, was not a monk, but a member of the Waldegrave family, the aristocratic owners of Borley Manor.

Buoyed by these dramatic results, Helen Glanville decided to try her hand at planchette writing. On 27 March 1938 at her home in Streatham, south London, some 75 miles from Borley, Miss Glanville received a still more astonishing missive regarding the rectory.

The large, scrawled words produced by the planchette read:

> *Sunex Amures and one of his men MEAN TO BURN THE RECTORY tonight at 9 o'clock end of the haunting go to the rectory [...] and under the ruins you will find the bone[s] of murdered wardens... [We] mean you to have proof of [the] haunting of the rectory at Borley, the understanding of which tells the story of murder which happened there.*

As it turns out, the rectory didn't burn down that night, as predicted, but it *did* burn down exactly eleven months later while under the care of a Captain W. H. Gregson, who had purchased the property shortly after Price's tenancy ended. Reportedly, Gregson was unpacking boxes when he knocked over an oil lamp in the hall, igniting a blaze that would end up gutting the entire house.

Was it really an accident? Was it an act of arson? Or was it the work of the mysterious 'Sunex Amures' and his men, carrying out the grim prediction foretold to Miss Glanville? The insurance company were of the opinion that it was definitely the deliberate act of a living person. But Harry Price was now erring strongly on the side of the supernatural. Or at least, he now *wanted* to believe – and, more importantly, he wanted others to believe, too.

At the end of his nearly ten-year study of Borley Rectory, when he finally sat down to collate his findings and write the first of his two books on the case, Price made the shrewd decision to downplay his earlier doubts about the Foysters; to stress the reliability of the Smiths and the Bulls; and to place the narrative of the murdered French novice, Marie Lairre, at the climax of his investigation. Because without a compelling backstory – a history for his haunted house – it would be nothing but banal bumps in the night recorded by a bunch of emotionless investigators. And who would want to read a book about that?

Harry's instincts were right. Released in October 1940, as the Battle of Britain raged and readers sought comfort, escape, and a sign that life persisted after death, *The Most Haunted House in England* was a great success. As many contemporary critics pointed out, the book had something for everyone, sceptics and believers alike. 'A thoroughly exciting but convincing book that will appeal to the lover of thrills and the serious student,' concluded one review.

The end of Borley Rectory

Soon after *Most Haunted* was released, Price was inundated with letters from enthusiastic readers all over the country, most of them wanting to give their own theories about the haunted rectory. Unsurprisingly, much of the attention was on the captivating figure of the murdered nun. Who was she? What was she doing in Borley? Why was she murdered? And, most importantly, what could be done to prove she really existed? This became the focus of Harry's second book.

The End of Borley Rectory was published in October 1946, just over a year after the end of the Second World War. As the dust settled, and the world came to terms with the staggering losses (there were some 75 million global casualties), the public was perhaps more desperate than ever for proof of the afterlife. With Borley, they could have that proof, Price promised.

'If six years ago, I came to the conclusion that I could find no other explanation for some of the Borley phenomena than the popular theory of survival after death,' Harry states, 'I unhesitatingly declare I am still of that same opinion … I would go so far as to state that the Borley case presents a better argument for "survival" than any case with which I am familiar.'

The End of Borley Rectory was also, apparently, the end of any incredulity on the author's part. If his first book loosely followed the format of a scientific paper, Price's second resembled a police detective's evidence board: a jumbled collage of potentially connected clues to an unsolved mystery. And effectively, that's what the whole affair had become – less scientific investigation, more murder investigation. Before, Harry had simply been searching for evidence of paranormal activity; now, he was searching for a body.

Inspired by the spiritualist communications received by the Glanville family, and the theories of his readers, Price began his hunt for the bones of the Borley nun in the summer of 1943. In particular, he was acting on the advice of the Reverend W. J. Phythian-Adams, canon of Carlisle, who, after reading Price's first book, came up with a new and cohesive narrative to explain the haunting of Borley Rectory once and for all.

The cleric's theory was this. During the English Civil War, one of the young progeny of the Catholic Waldegrave family travelled to France in order to escape the chaos of his homeland and surround himself with followers of his own religion. While there, he became infatuated with a young French novice with whom he eloped, returning with her to England, where he set her up in 'secrecy in the old, remote family manor of Borley'. The husband then departed, leaving his young French bride, 'a foreigner among strange faces, marooned, in an empty countryside and watching and waiting only for his return' (hence her perpetual pacing along the garden path). At long last he returned, thundering down the drive in an ominous black coach in the dead of night. But it was not a joyful reunion. The young lord had had a change of heart and wished to make a more advantageous marriage to someone of better social standing. He thus 'disposed' of his problem for good.

But where did he dispose of her? Phythian-Adams didn't think her remains were in the garden, as the Glanville table-tilting session maintained. 'This answer [was] too readily given to satisfy the questioner,' he argued, 'and it conflicts with the essential fact that the focus of the haunt was in the house.' He urged Price to look to the cryptic wall-writing, and especially at the message reading: 'Marianne, Get Help … Well … Tank … Bottom me.'

She was in the bottom of a well-tank.

Though Price was able to easily persuade Captain Gregson to allow him to excavate his fire-damaged property, the actual process was no mean feat. With the war still in full swing, there were few able-bodied workers to help with the dig, and those who were available were not exactly assured of their safety. 'Owing to enemy action, Essex was not a particularly healthy spot to linger in, though vital business might necessitate one's presence there,' Price recalls. In the end, it was the incumbent rector's gardener who did most of the hard work.

Then there was the matter of finding the well-tank. Price was under the impression that there were four wells on the estate: two in the courtyard and two in the cellar. For some reason, the investigator was convinced that the well he was looking for was in the cellar. Probably because it was not only *inside* the house, but in a dark and spooky part of it.

However, as Andrew Clarke points out, Price seems to have been confusing wells, sumps and tanks. The well-tank – the vessel that stores water and controls the water pressure – would have been a more modern addition to the house. It would have been located in the attic, which had been destroyed in the fire. The reservoirs in the cellar were sumps or troughs, shallow pits designed for draining flood water. And to complicate matters further, one of those troughs – the one Price believed to be the well-tank – had recently been filled in.

None of this would deter him. The dig commenced on 17 August (with Harry doing little of the actual digging, on account of his dicky heart). Price's small team – including the current rector, Jennings, and his wife; their gardener, Mr Jackson; and a pathologist, Dr Eric Bailey – began with the extant trough, which was in a narrow extension of the cellar that jutted out under the courtyard. Beneath a shallow layer of debris, they found bits of broken pottery, old wine bottles, 'ancient bricks' that were apparently from an earlier building, a milk jug and lots and lots of frogs. No nun.

Forced to press on, Price directed the team to a location under the kitchen passage where he believed the old 'well-tank' had once been. This time it was harder going, with Jackson requiring a large pickaxe to break through the brick floor that overlaid a thick layer of marl beneath.

'By 1.45 we had picked and shovelled and sifted some tons of marl, and had dug to a depth of three feet,' Price reports. Then, at last, they hit pay dirt. Out of the rough silty earth, Jackson produced the remains of a 'jaw bone of some animal (with five teeth in situ)'. While the gruff gardener dismissed it as being the mandible of a pig, the pathologist (according to Harry) immediately declared it to be human. Five minutes later, they unearthed a piece of skull. 'There was no mistaking to what animal this fragment belonged,' Price maintains. 'It was human.'

No further remains were found.

The jaw bone was subsequently sent to a London dental surgeon, who agreed with Dr Bailey, surmising that it was the left mandible of a young woman, probably no older than thirty, who had died at least 100 years earlier. Jackson, meanwhile, remained convinced that what he'd handed Price that day was part of a swine skeleton.

'Did we find truth at the bottom of a well?' Harry asks his readers. 'Were the human remains those of the ill-fated Marie Lairre?'

He certainly thought it possible. Others were less convinced. When it was proposed that the bones be reinterred in the Borley churchyard, the locals balked, questioning the sense in giving a proper Christian burial to what they believed to be the remains of a pig. Instead, the bones were placed in a 'well-made dovetail cedarwood casket measuring five inches by four' and laid to rest in the churchyard in nearby Liston. It's unclear if the grave was ever marked or if anything remains of the tiny casket and its contents. Like the rectory itself, the bones of Borley have long since disappeared.

The crumbling ruins of the rectory were finally demolished in 1944. Four years later, on 29 March 1948, Harry Price died of a heart attack at his home in West Sussex. In the decades that followed, the story of the 'most haunted house in England' almost completely fell apart, collapsing like a house of cards. Accusations of exaggeration, deception and fraud were rampant, with fingers pointing in nearly every direction. No one, it seems, was completely innocent, but no one was deemed to be more guilty than Price himself.

In 1951, three members of the Society for Psychical Research, Eric Dingwall, Kathleen Goldney and Trevor Hall, launched a reinvestigation of the Borley case, the results of which were published four years later in their book, *The Haunting of Borley Rectory: A Critical Survey of the Evidence*. In a damning indictment of the once lauded sceptic, the authors concluded that nearly all of the phenomena reported at the rectory were either manufactured or misrepresented by the lead investigator. Though later writers would attempt to exonerate him, it was a lasting blow to Price's posthumous reputation.

And yet, more than fifty years on, ghost hunters are still flocking to Borley. Writers (myself included) are still writing books about it. Filmmakers are making films, TV shows and documentaries; bloggers are blogging; podcasters are podding. Why? What is it that makes the story of Borley Rectory live on even when the house is gone, the stories seemingly discredited, and the storytellers exposed as spouters of fiction?

As we know, nothing of the infamous building survives. The property has long since been split into a number of individual plots, with modern bungalows erected in place of the Victorian rectory. Of the original nineteenth-century development, only a much-altered and expanded cottage remains on the site.

The sole physical reminders of Borley are those grainy black-and-white photos reproduced in Price's books. And in the decades since his book was published, the photos have taken on an even greater iconographic significance.

Years earlier, in the summer of 1938, Harry Price was approached by an artist, Margaret E. Wilson, who had read about Borley and was interested in visiting. Not to ghost-hunt, mind you, but to paint a picture of the house. Based on its reported hauntedness, the artist had simply assumed it *must* be old and picturesque.

'I pointed out to Mrs Wilson, as gently as I could, that Borley Rectory was *not* old,' explains Price, 'that it was ugly; that it reminded me of the red bricks of suburbia, and that it was as much unlike the typical old country rectory as chalk is to cheese.'

Mrs Wilson was naturally disappointed. But had she been alive today, and viewing the house through our modern lens, she might have found exactly what she was looking for. To our eyes, those decades-old photos of Borley capture a very old house. A rambling, rotting Victorian red-brick manor which, if not exactly picturesque, is definitely atmospheric. The classic haunted house. So quintessentially spooky that many of us struggle to accept that it might never have been haunted at all.

HAMPTON COURT

THE GHOSTS OF FAME

4

> Royal palaces should, by all the canons of the supernatural, be haunted. If convulsions of nature happen, according to old belief, when the great die … then it should be the merest commonplace to see ghosts in ancient palaces.
>
> *Charles G. Harper (1863–1943)*

The terrifying Tudors

On three consecutive days in October 2003, the security staff at Hampton Court Palace in Surrey were interrupted during their daily duties by the sporadic sounding of an alarm. The trigger for the alarm was a double-doored fire exit in a small exhibition space located to the south of the famed Clock Court, named for the sixteenth-century astronomical clock that towers over its entrance.

Because it was broad daylight – around lunchtime on a typically busy day at the popular visitor attraction – there was no immediate cause for concern. Though the gallery here was off the beaten path of the more heavily trafficked parts of the palace, a new display had recently been installed in the space. It was therefore perfectly plausible that a confused member of the public had unwittingly set off the alarm as they attempted to exit the exhibition.

And yet, each time staff went to investigate, they found the doors shut and the room empty.

A combination of curiosity and obligation encouraged the guards to review the CCTV footage of the area. The security camera that would help them identify the source of the nuisance was positioned high on a scaffolding pole adjacent to the fire exit. It had slipped from its original position, and now offered an off-kilter view of the gallery exterior. Footage showed the offending doors violently swinging open, seemingly of their own accord. The force of the mysterious action had actually caused physical damage to the doorframe.

On one occasion, the camera caught the culprit.

In the blurry black-and-white footage the doors were once again seen swinging open, but this time, a willowy figure in a hooded cloak emerged from the shadows to close them again. Though the image was fuzzy and distorted, it appeared to be a person in Tudor costume.

Hampton Court is one of a group of former royal residences that are currently operated by Historic Royal Palaces (HRP). The residences include Hampton Court, the Tower of London, Kensington Palace, the Banqueting House and Kew Palace, and they are major tourist attractions, catering to both adults and children. HRP is known for employing theatrical tactics to entertain and educate their guests, including the use of costumed tour guides. So it would be natural to assume that the figure in the video was merely an elaborately dressed member of staff helping to lock up for the day, or perhaps a mischievous employee pulling a prank on his colleagues in the weeks leading up to Halloween.

Not so, claimed Hampton Court staff member James Faukes when he was later interviewed. 'I thought someone was having a laugh, but none of our costumed guides own a costume like that,' he said. 'It is actually quite unnerving. It was incredibly spooky because the face just didn't look human.'

Somehow, the soon-to-be infamous footage of the shadowy figure with the inhuman face was leaked to the press, and by December the mainstream media had picked up the scoop, with stories appearing in *The Telegraph*, the *Evening Standard* and *The Times*, as well as on the BBC evening news. The story soon went global, gaining attention as far afield as Peru, Australia and China.

The Hampton Court ghost went viral. 'Skeletor', as he was nicknamed, would become the world's first digital-age spectral celebrity.

It's a cold grey morning, less than a week before Christmas, and my family and I are huddled under an archway at the West Gate of Hampton Court Palace, seeking shelter from the bitter wind whipping across the open courtyard before us. We're all shivering – me especially. I'm a terrible excuse for a Canadian.

From where we're standing, I have a clear view of the imposing red-brick edifice of the sixteenth-century palace. Chimneys, towers and pinnacles loom above me. From here, it's difficult to fully appreciate the sheer scale of the sprawling 1,300-room structure. At a whopping 509,000 square feet, Hampton Court ranks as the third largest royal residence in Britain, only just behind Windsor Castle. Meanwhile, Buckingham Palace, the official home of the British sovereign since 1837, is the largest by square footage, but still falls short of Hampton Court's 60 acres of formal gardens and 750 acres of royal parkland – a popular tourist attraction in warmer months.

I'm here to meet Ian Franklin, a retired State Apartment warder, who worked at the palace from 1997 to 2020. Of all the hundreds of employees who have passed through Hampton Court's halls over recent years, Ian is the one I most want to talk to. Not only was he here when the infamous 'Skeletor' footage was captured, but he also helped to launch the palace's ghost tours in October 2002. If anyone knows about Hampton Court's ghosts, it's Ian.

When he arrives, Ian quickly ushers us into a small vestibule, only marginally warmer than the frigid courtyard, where our tour begins. Although I'm here to talk ghosts, Ian has kindly agreed to show my family around before we get down to business. I've brought my parents, who are visiting from Canada for the holiday season, my husband and our youngest son. He's been learning about castles at school, and though he's very keen on the idea of visiting a real-life one, he seems a bit bewildered by all the names and dates that Ian is throwing at us. To simplify things, I point to a picture of Henry VIII: 'See, that's the king!'

Now, this he gets. Because even though my son hasn't reached the age where the school curriculum covers Tudor history, this guy *looks* like a king. Indeed, old King Hal is the most recognisable monarch in Britain, if not the world. What Elvis Presley (the 'king' of rock and roll) is to pop music, Henry is to actual kingship: his image an instant signifier of historic royalty. Ironically, the most familiar images of both men show them in midlife crisis – bloated, pompous, over the top.

While he was neither its first nor its last owner, Henry VIII is intrinsically linked with Hampton Court. The building itself has come to embody his sensational life and legacy: an enduring symbol of the Tudor monarch's absolute power. From the beginning, his acquisition of the property marked a pivotal moment in his life, as well as a turning point in British history: divorce, schism with Rome, the birth of the Church of England.

The construction of Hampton Court began in 1514 under the auspices of Cardinal Thomas Wolsey, Archbishop of York – and, at the time, Henry VIII's chief minister and right-hand man. Wolsey was one of the kingdom's richest and most influential figures, and he intended to build a magnificent home to reflect his position. A home modelled after those of his continental counterparts – the wealthy Italian cardinals who lived like princes in palaces designed by top Renaissance architects. Though Wolsey succeeded in this mission, it would soon prove to be part of his downfall.

Wolsey's fall from grace occurred less than fifteen years after Hampton Court's construction. It wasn't explicitly because his extravagant house was perceived as a threat to the king, as many earlier historians have suggested. But it certainly didn't help matters that he owned such an enviable property at a time when his star was waning.

The cardinal's downfall was a result of his having failed to secure a divorce (or rather, an annulment) for the king from his first wife, Catherine of Aragon, who had been unable to provide him with a male heir. In September 1528, Wolsey was ordered to vacate Hampton Court and surrender it to the crown. It quickly became the king's preferred rural retreat, serving simultaneously as a sumptuous family home and a symbolically charged bulwark of monarchical control.

Before guiding us out of the vestibule, Ian instructs my son to close his eyes. He's building up to something. For the fun of it, I close mine too. We step through the doorway and are directed to open our eyes again and look up. The Great Hall, where we now stand, is 106 feet long and 40 feet wide, draped in priceless tapestries, lit by glittering stained-glass windows and crowned by a gilded hammerbeam ceiling. It is without a doubt one of the grandest spaces in the palace.

The Great Hall was one of the earliest improvements to Hampton Court overseen by Henry VIII. Rebuilt in 1532, it was the first in a sequence of rooms leading to the king's apartments. Henry's designers, Christopher Dickenson and James Nedeham, based their work on previously existing royal residences and earlier medieval palaces, such as Westminster Hall, to evoke a sense of continuity, antiquity and chivalry. Even in the sixteenth century, visitors would have felt as though they were stepping back in time.

At the heart of what remains of the Tudor palace, the Great Hall of today isn't exactly the same space that Henry VIII would have experienced, but it's an impressive approximation of the original, brought back to life by Edward Jesse, the deputy surveyor responsible for its major refurbishment prior to opening to the public in 1844. When Jesse took up the reins, the room was relatively bare, as a result of earlier renovations undertaken by the austere Georgian court. The walls had been whitewashed and left unadorned; the windows were colourless and the ceiling unpainted. The only reminder of its former glory was the intricately carved hammerbeam ceiling. Thus, Jesse and his army of architects and artisans were presented with a blank canvas onto which to project all their own fanciful notions of a bygone era.

Over a six-year period, the Great Hall was fantastically transformed. A phalanx of mighty stags' heads were mounted to the walls; vibrantly coloured heraldic shields were installed in the windows; the timber ceiling was highlighted in dazzling splashes of blue, green, vermilion and gold paint; and the series of sixteenth-century Dutch silk tapestries depicting the life of Abraham, believed to have been commissioned by Henry VIII himself, were removed from the State Apartments and reinstalled in the Great Hall, where they are thought to have originally hung.

Part historical recreation, part romantic reimagining, no other part of the palace so effectively captures the grandiosity of King Henry's reign.

The Great Hall has been a firm favourite since it opened to the public in the mid-1800s, and by the turn of the century, visitors could purchase postcards of the hall as souvenirs from the hawkers who lined the Thames, greeting the day trippers travelling there by boat from central London. The most curious and collectable of these early postcards, though, are the sepia-toned photographs of the Great Hall superimposed with illustrations of white spectral figures (even though no ghost stories have ever been linked to this room). Clearly, more than a century ago, the palace was already firmly associated with two things: Tudor history and ghosts.

Today, Hampton Court attracts an estimated 500,000 visitors each year. Many (if not most) of these visitors come to the property expecting to hear about the scandalous lives of the Tudor monarchs, mixed in with a few ghost stories. Why is that? How did the palace become so strongly connected with this period in history, when it had served as a royal residence for the Stuart kings, William and Mary, Queen Anne, and two of the four Georgian monarchs? And how did particular historical figures, and their time of residence, become so strongly linked to the supernatural?

It seems that properties like this – buildings like the Tower of London, Windsor Castle and Edinburgh Castle; palaces that have served as the backdrop to pivotal moments in history and that have hosted the colourful figures who have helped shape that history – are inevitably assumed to be haunted. The structures, the stories and the key players become fused into one phantasmal diorama.

But as Ian points out, given the millions of people who have traversed the palace's corridors over time, why should it necessarily be the best-known figures – the kings and queens – who haunt it?

Referring to the palace's most famous ghostly residents – two of the six wives of Henry VIII, Jane Seymour and Catherine Howard – Ian points out that the assumption that these are not only Tudor ghosts, but the ghosts of the most exalted figures of the period seems a bit far-fetched. It's not like these ghosts come with a placard saying who they are, he adds.

In recent years, tourist attractions such as Hampton Court have actively embraced ghost stories as part of their immersive experience. They've used them as a way to bring their site's history alive. Scores of properties in the UK and around the world have opted to incorporate legends and folklore into the official canon, weaving real historic personalities into a ghostly cast of characters. Quite simply, it's a means of narrating the past in an exciting and potentially more universally appealing way.

When Ian helped to launch the ghost tours at Hampton Court in the autumn of 2002, it was a novel enterprise. However, it quite quickly became common practice. His first tours roughly coincided with the early noughties boom in ghost-themed television programming, including the pioneering paranormal reality series, *Most Haunted*, which premiered on the Living TV channel in 2002.

Featuring presenter Yvette Fielding nervously slinking through a slew of historic, reputedly haunted, and often very famous properties across the UK, *Most Haunted* became a cult hit. It lasted almost twenty years and launched a number of copycat shows on both sides of the Atlantic.

Thanks to the publicity of such shows, tourists soon descended on the historic properties featured on them, hoping to catch a glimpse of a ghost or two themselves. Most sites welcomed the ghost hunters with open arms – anything to get more people interested in their properties.

This might seem like an obvious reason as to why Hampton Court is famed for ghosts in the modern era, but as we've already established, paranormal tourism (or 'Gothic' tourism, as it has been dubbed by academics) began at Hampton Court more than 100 years earlier – albeit unofficially. The reason that, in the early twentieth century, ghost postcards were only sold at the riverside, not within the palace grounds, was because they were verboten. At this time, the Royal Family, who owned the property – and still do so today – did not wish to court such publicity. Haunted houses were then considered not particularly becoming of the monarchy. The warders were supposedly sworn to secrecy, but stories still managed to slip out: people wanted the ghosts and they wanted those postcards.

At some point, the royals must have turned a blind eye, allowing Ian and HRP's Live Interpretation Manager, Chris Gidlow, to start actively marketing the supernatural (although they might not use such a bold term as 'marketing'). For the first two or three years, Ian explains, he did the tours for free. These began as unticketed events held for the 'Friends of Hampton Court' – strictly limited to palace volunteers and season ticket-holders. The paid public tours wouldn't commence until 2005. And eventually, Ian says, the 'jump scare' element came in, with people in black cloaks lurching out of dark corners to startle people. 'That's not what I wanted,' he laments. 'It's not what I intended.'

Ian wanted to tell the *real* stories – the uncanny events that he and his colleagues had been experiencing on a regular basis for years. And quite often, those experiences had nothing to do with famous figures or the more gruesome episodes of Tudor history. But the public had come to expect blood, beheadings, sex and celebrity. The ghosts of fame – and infamy.

In what follows, we will be unpicking the curious connections between Tudor history, 'Gothic' tourism and the supernatural – all set against the backdrop of one of the most notoriously haunted buildings in the United Kingdom.

Part-way through our tour of Hampton Court, Ian abruptly halts before a doorway leading out of the Great Watching Chamber – the first room in Henry VIII's State Apartments, where warders once stood guard, controlling access to the most exclusive part of the palace.

We are about to enter the most famously haunted part of the palace – the aptly named Haunted Gallery, the setting for Hampton Court's best-known ghost story.

The legend is as follows. On 2 November 1541, Henry VIII received a note informing him of his fifth wife's alleged infidelity, during an All Saints' Day service in Hampton Court's Chapel Royal. That the news should come to him on this day – a day devoted to prayer for the dead suffering in purgatory – was ominously fitting. Immediately he placed Catherine Howard under house arrest, confined to her apartments under round-the-clock watch by the king's guards while she awaited trial for treason.

As the story goes, a few days into her confinement Catherine managed to break free and make a mad dash down the corridor that led to the chapel, where she hoped to find her husband and beg him for mercy. Before she could reach the chapel, however, the guards seized her, dragging her kicking and screaming back down the hall to her prison.

She would never see her husband (or her freedom) again. Three months later, on 13 February 1542, Catherine Howard was beheaded at the Tower of London. She was just nineteen years old.

Believe it or not, the Haunted Gallery is the corridor's official name: used in guidebooks, marked out on maps, and even used by the curators and historians who work here. Whether or not the ill-fated queen really did escape and make a mad dash down the hall (a subject of debate among scholars), the corridor is widely believed to be haunted. Over the years, countless residents, visitors and members of staff have reported experiencing something supernatural here. Fainting, dizziness, cold spells, sensing a presence – such experiences were so frequent that, in spring 2000 Hampton Court decided to invite a team of parapsychologists to conduct an investigation. Under the supervision of Dr Richard Wiseman, Professor of the Public Understanding of Psychology at the University of Hertfordshire, some 300 volunteer participants were instructed to make their way down the Haunted Gallery and to report any uncanny experiences.

The results of the study indicated that participants who had prior knowledge of the space or a pre-existing belief in the paranormal were more likely to attribute any unusual sensations to ghostly activity. But the investigation concluded that 'suggestion alone' could not account for the myriad events that were reported. There were 'hot spots' where participants consistently experienced supernatural experiences, even though they had not been made aware of these locations prior to the experiment.

With this in mind, my family and I prepare to make our way through the Haunted Gallery. Side by side, my son and I begin our solemn procession down the long, dimly lit hallway. As per Ian's instructions, I pay close attention to how I am feeling. Do I feel cold? Lightheaded? Tingly? Well, yes, all those things, because as it happens, I have a nasty cold and it is positively Baltic in this palace. Nevertheless, I'm acutely aware of my own physicality. So preoccupied am I with every little shiver and twitch that I fail to properly take in my surroundings. Only later, when I review photographs of the gallery, will I notice the walls draped in deep green damask curtains, the rows of gilt-framed portraits, the low-hanging brass chandeliers.

When we reach the end of the hall, Ian is there waiting for us. He wants to know if we felt anything unusual and, if so, where? We shrug, not really sure what – if anything – we experienced. Coming up behind us, my mother remarks, 'I guess we're not sensitives.'

'Well, don't worry,' Ian reassures us. 'Nothing happened to me today either, but on some days you come around that corner and you're literally cut in half at the midriff by a draught…'

Evidently, Ian believes that something strange is definitely afoot in the Haunted Gallery. He's just not so sure about the conventional explanation for it.

A beautiful young victim, a scene of extreme pathos, and a grisly end. It's no wonder this has become the basis for Hampton Court's most famous ghost story, and the suspected cause for all the odd occurrences in this part of the palace. Over the years, paranormal events in the Haunted Gallery have included the aforementioned physiological symptoms, the unearthly sound of a woman wailing, and the apparition of a female figure dressed in white tearing down the hallway in terror.

Is this a prime example of the 'stone tape' theory in action? The endless replaying of a historical event so intensely charged with emotional energy that it has imbedded itself into the fabric of the building in which it occurred?

Well, maybe. If the historical event in question actually happened.

Though it's been incorporated into Hampton Court's official narrative, the story of Catherine Howard's terror-stricken race down the Haunted Gallery may well be apocryphal. According to public historian Alison Weir, the event could never have happened the way it's been described. Even if the queen had managed to break free from her captors (which Weir believes is highly improbable), it is unlikely that she would have followed the path she's traditionally said to have taken. The only logical access point from the Queen's Chambers would have been a staircase situated on the opposite side of the gallery from the Great Watching Chamber. Thus, if the event really happened, Catherine would have run from the opposite direction towards the chapel, bypassing most of her legendary route. She then would have been dragged back the same way.

Today, most scholars maintain the story is fiction. Granted, Historic Royal Palaces' chief curator, Lucy Worsley, has found evidence that in Catherine's time, there may have been a smaller staircase that led directly to the Haunted Gallery, and the route the queen is said to have taken. But the fact remains that the story itself is a relatively modern one. There seems to be no record of Catherine Howard's mad dash down the Haunted Gallery – or any reference to it being called the Haunted Gallery – until the late nineteenth century. This is hardly surprising, given what we know about the Victorians and their penchant for all things paranormal. And so I find myself wondering if this story – maybe *all* the palace's ghost stories – are simply the invention of Victorian storytellers.

Hampton Court didn't properly develop a reputation for being haunted until the nineteenth century, after it opened to the public; however, there are a few ghostly anecdotes that predate the Victorians, including one that dates back to the mid-1600s, when Hampton Court was under the control of Oliver Cromwell's Commonwealth government. The account comes from the diary of George Fox, an English dissenter and founder of the Quaker movement, who wrote about his visit with Cromwell at the palace on 17 August 1658.

'I met him riding in Hampton Court Park and before I came to him, as he rode at the head of his life-guard, I saw and felt a waft or apparition of death go forth against him,' Fox recalled, 'and when I came to him he looked like a dead man.' Only a few weeks later, Cromwell died of sepsis as a result of an untreated urinary infection.

What this passage describes might be an example of what parapsychologists term a 'death warning' – a foreshadowing of the death of another person received in a manner that defies ordinary sensory channels. Or it might simply be Fox's colourful way of saying that Cromwell looked bloody awful. At any rate, it's very different from the better-known supernatural stories associated with the palace, all of which follow the more traditional ghost story model.

In addition to Catherine Howard, there is also Jane Seymour, Henry VIII's third wife, whose ghost has been spotted gliding down the Silverstick Stairs on the anniversary of the birth of her much-prayed-for son, the complications of which resulted in her early death.

Then there's Sybil Penn, Hampton Court's notorious Grey Lady, a prominent courtier and nurse to both Edward VI and Elizabeth I, who died of smallpox while caring for the gravely ill queen. Dame Sybil's shadowy spectre is said to haunt her former apartment, where she allegedly still uses her spinning wheel. There's even talk of a headless Anne Boleyn skulking around the Clock Court, though sightings of her are comparatively rare – probably because she's so busy traumatising tourists at the five other properties she's said to haunt (more on this later).

While there are plenty of other accounts of the supernatural, ranging from the innocuous (the faint smell of flowers in the Georgian wing) to the dramatic (phantom hands reaching out from the panelling in the Wolsey Closet), these are the best-known stories. All feature high-profile Tudor women who died in sudden or violent circumstances, and who survive in the cultural imagination as the tragic yet terrifying embodiments of the tumultuous age in which they lived.

Divorced, beheaded, died, divorced, beheaded, survived...

This is the handy mnemonic device that has long been taught to history students to help them recall the order of King Henry VIII's six wives: Catherine of Aragon, Anne Boleyn, Jane Seymour, Anne of Cleves, Catherine Howard and Katherine Parr.

Even if you know nothing else about Tudor history, chances are that you know this rhyme, or, at least, you are familiar with its general sentiment: that Henry VIII is best remembered for a court dominated by sexual intrigue and violence. You might have learned all about the Tudors in history classes at school. Or perhaps you picked up the basic plot points from steamy TV drama series, movies or novels. You might even have caught wind of it through a family-friendly comedy (*Horrible Histories*, anyone?). One way or another, you will surely be aware of the 'terrible Tudors' and their salacious reputation.

But how has the Tudor period become so synonymous with sex and death? And when exactly did it become an acceptable subject for popular entertainment? In no small part, it is Henry VIII who is to blame for this legacy. Though in popular culture he's become a larger-than-life caricature, most modern depictions of the king do not much exaggerate his lust for power (and women), or his propensity for violence. Henry well and truly earned his reputation as a despotic womaniser.

Here are the indisputable facts: he married six women and executed two of them, along with 57,000 subjects, including family members, noblemen, clergymen and former friends, as well as ordinary men, women and even children. A good number of these poor souls were put to death for some form of treason – usually trumped-up charges brought against them for daring to displease the king in any way.

Such was the fate of Henry's second wife, Anne Boleyn, who, like her predecessor, failed to conceive a male child. Sensing her imminent downfall and hoping to accelerate it, Anne's enemies at court – including Henry's closest confidant, Thomas Cromwell, who would later be executed himself – cooked up a sensational story of adultery and incest. A supposed witness claimed that Anne had persuaded her own brother, George Boleyn, 2nd Viscount Rochford, to 'violate her, alluring him with her tongue in the said George's mouth, and the said George's tongue in hers'.

The nation was shocked – and generally sceptical – of the

accusations levelled against the queen. But in those days, the court of public opinion was far less influential than it is now. Anne would not be saved from the chopping block.

On 19 May 1536, at the Tower of London, Anne Boleyn was beheaded by sword in front of an audience of 1,000. Intriguingly, most of the witness accounts emphasise the queen's beauty and poise in the face of her death. Even before the sword fell, Anne had been transformed into a glamorous martyr: a bloody, yet beautiful, sacrifice to the king's mercurial whims. She was already reborn as an iconic female personification of the horrors of the Henrician court.

In the years between Anne Boleyn's execution and the fictional version portrayed in HBO's *The Tudors* (2000–10) and the BBC's *Wolf Hall* (2015–24), attitudes towards Henry VIII's turbulent rule have fluctuated. While no one has ever denied that Henry was a tyrannical lunatic, the period during which he and his descendants ruled has, at times, been cast in a more positive light. Of course, it saw the birth of the Church of England, a seismic change that many Britons viewed as the triumph of Protestantism over Catholicism: an important step not only for religion but also for nationhood, signifying England's increasing autonomy and global strength.

Yet, for some straight-laced Georgian and Victorian historians, it was difficult to reconcile the violent disruptions of Henry's reign with their cherished view of British history as a narrative of progress and moral improvement. In his five-volume tome *The History of England* (1848), historian Thomas Babington Macaulay eschews hundreds of years of history in order to kick off the story with James II and the Glorious Revolution of 1688 – to his eyes, a much more respectable era than that of the Tudors. In other texts where Macaulay does acknowledge Henry and his successors, he chastises the 'despotic' Tudor rulers for their total disregard for 'those institutions which we have been accustomed to consider as the sole checks on the power of the sovereign'. Somewhat incongruously, he also seems to suggest that the Tudor period was a golden age of prosperity, discovery and creativity. After all, Henry VIII's daughter Elizabeth I *did* patronise Shakespeare (though she too was known to be a big fan of beheading her enemies).

There was no way around it. The British people could no more deny the importance of Tudor history than they could the violence that defined it. They would have to find a satisfactory way in which to reconcile these two facts. And with the rise of 'Gothic' tourism, they would.

Horror heritage: the birth of Gothic tourism

According to literary theorists, 'Gothic tourism' is defined as the recreational practice of visiting a location that is presented in the terms of the Gothic. This does not mean a location that possesses the physical characteristics of the Gothic architectural aesthetic, but rather an environment that evokes the atmosphere and thematic elements of Gothic literature. Those key ingredients that Horace Walpole introduced in *The Castle of Otranto* – history, horror and the supernatural.

Included under the umbrella of 'Gothic tourism' are a wide range of fear-inducing leisure activities such as urban ghost walking tours, tours of haunted castles and stately homes, and modern theme park 'horror' experiences such as the Pasaje del Terror at Blackpool and the Sanctuary at Alton Towers. Basically, any recreational activity that is designed to scare.

Although a Gothic tourist attraction need not take place in an old property, they typically incorporate famously macabre historical events and the associated characters from the past. The popular 'London Dungeon' attraction, for example, is held in County Hall, South Bank, a relatively modern structure first built in 1911, but which includes theatrical interpretations of the Gunpowder Plot (1605), the Great Fire of London (1666), and the serial murders of Jack the Ripper (1888). Notably, it also features an attraction called the Tyrant Boat Ride, in which visitors join 'Anne Boleyn' on her final journey along the Thames to the Tower of London to face 'the full force of Henry VIII's wrath'.

Here and elsewhere, history and horror go hand in hand.

The appeal of such an attraction is predicated on two basic factors. At a site like the London Dungeon, we can enjoy the adrenaline-inducing thrill of knowing that such events *actually* took place, coupled with the comfort of knowing that they pose no threat to us. We can therefore take pleasure in the horrors of history.

Gothic literary specialist Emma McEvoy argues that it goes even deeper than that. 'Gothic tourism has much to tell us about particular places,' she explains. 'It is bound up with the way in which we think about our past and our surroundings, and the ways in which we construct our identities.' So, what scares us most reveals who we are – and who we are not.

Far from being a recent phenomenon, Gothic tourism has existed for almost as long as the Gothic novel itself. Almost two centuries ago, the first visitors to Madame Tussaud's newly opened Chamber of Horrors waxwork exhibition at London's Lyceum Theatre would have felt the same rush of terror-tinged excitement as visitors do today at its modern incarnation. Shrinking back from the hideous visages of the most notorious players of the French Revolution – which wasn't *that* long ago, but was separated by just enough time, space and political distance – the people of Regency London undoubtedly experienced a familiar mixture of dread and delight.

While it's difficult to pinpoint the precise origins of Gothic tourism, its rise in popularity in the first half of the nineteenth century seems to have coincided with a greater public interest in history and heritage tourism more generally. Prior to this time, the practice of visiting sites of historical significance – castles, country houses and the like – was mostly limited to members of the upper classes: people who had the education to engender an interest in history, and who were respectable enough to gain entrance to such properties, most of which then remained in private hands. A well-to-do lady or gentleman could call in at an illustrious house such as Chatsworth or Blenheim Palace and request a tour of the property from a member of staff, who would obligingly show them around, pointing out details of historical or artistic interest in return for a tip. Naturally, the tour would not include any mention of murder, sex or spectres.

But with the explosion in popularity of Gothic and historical fiction, there was suddenly a whole new market for heritage tourism. Ordinary folk who had read romances set in historic palaces and ghost stories set in ancient castles now wanted to experience these enthralling environments for themselves. Books like William Harrison Ainsworth's bestselling novel *The Tower of London* (1840) fuelled popular interest in a heritage landmark, and helped to shape the way in which the general public thought about the past – especially the Tudor past.

An imaginative recounting of the life and death of Lady Jane Grey, great-niece of Henry VIII, the ill-fated 'Nine-Day Queen' who was imprisoned and executed at the Tower in 1554, Ainsworth's book offered readers a detailed guide to the grounds and interior of the historic palace-cum-prison, together with all the titillating trappings of the Gothic novel. An ancient castle, a tragic (Tudor) heroine, dynastic drama, dungeons, death, torture and ghosts. It was all par for the Gothic course, only this time the setting and characters were *real*, or at least partly based on historical reality, making it all the more thrilling.

Liberated from the confines of the history textbook, woven into the pages of popular fiction, the past became not only exciting, but more democratic in its reach. And at exactly the same time, the real-life settings for these fictional narratives were becoming accessible to a much wider public, extending far beyond the traditional audience of aristocrats and ambassadors. And the public were, perhaps, less interested in the 'official' history of these illustrious buildings and more interested in their 'Gothic' history.

In April 1838, in one of her first acts as monarch, Queen Victoria declared that Hampton Court 'should be thrown open to all [her] subjects, without restriction, and without fee or gratuity of any kind'. Granting members of the public access to her personal property – free of charge, no less – certainly seems to be a dramatic gesture of queenly benevolence and generosity. Perhaps she wanted to please her people, and allow even her lowliest subjects the edifying experience of touring a historically significant property. As charitable as the gesture was, however, the queen wasn't exactly going to be inconvenienced by it.

Long before Victoria threw open the doors to Hampton Court, it had fallen out of favour as the monarchy's preferred rural retreat, with Windsor Palace taking its place by the mid-eighteenth century. Although in the years after Henry VIII, several rulers had made lavish improvements and additions to it, by the later Georgian period Hampton Court had, perhaps, become a little outdated.

Maybe modern monarchs didn't want to be reminded of their

uncouth Tudor predecessors. Or perhaps they simply didn't share their tastes. The Hanoverians – the German-originating line that took over the English throne in 1714 – were more restrained in their approach to both architecture and rulership. Or perhaps the rumour that a young George III had been harshly disciplined at Hampton Court by his grandfather was true, tainting the place for the grown-up king.

In any event, it was under the rule of the Hanoverians that Hampton Court ceased to be used as a royal retreat and instead became a Grace and Favour residence – that is, a property used to house courtiers, aristocrats and various other members of high society, who had either fallen on hard times or had somehow earned the right to live rent-free in the king's unused property. It would remain a swanky home for the down-and-out elite until the 1990s.

Queen Victoria's decision to open the palace to a broader cross-section of society was, in the beginning, a somewhat contentious one. Naturally, the Grace and Favour residents were none too pleased to be sharing their previously privileged spaces with the plebian masses.

As one of the few attractions open at that time on a Sunday – the only day off for the working classes – the palace proved immensely popular. After only a few decades, Hampton Court had seen some 10 million visitors traipse through its grounds, making it one of the most popular tourist destinations in the country. The scene was, according to some contemporary commentators, decidedly chaotic.

In a letter to the editor of *The Times* in November 1852, one Reverend D. Wilson denounced Hampton Court as 'a hell on earth; people come intoxicated, and the scenes in these gardens on the Lord's day are beyond description'. But the more liberally minded members of the public saw the democratisation of Hampton Court as a largely positive change. After all, wasn't it a good thing that the working classes were spending their free time in the hallowed environs of a historic landmark, rather than, say, a tavern or gambling den?

In contrast to the Reverend Wilson's characterisation of Hampton Court tourism, the palace's resident historian, Ernest Law maintained that: 'What Hampton Court lost in repose and dignity, it gained in cheerfulness; and what was sacrificed by its popularisation, was compensated for by the greater interest taken in the Palace, and the care devoted to it.'

Even though Law himself was a Grace and Favour resident, he

seems to have had no qualms whatsoever about the influx of day trippers. In fact, through his work as an author and informal consultant on palace restoration work, Law did a great deal to facilitate and encourage popular tourism there. As we will discover, the historian had a keen instinct for what the public wanted out of a heritage attraction – and he knew it included elements of the Gothic.

When it first opened, Hampton Court was presented to the public not as a historic landmark, but as an art gallery where some of the finest pictures in the Royal Collection were displayed, hanging in the recently refurbished State Apartments, a relatively modern part of the palace designed by architect Christopher Wren in 1689 to replace large portions of the original Tudor palace, which had been demolished at the behest of William III and Mary II. While social reformers argued that this offering would go a long way towards educating the masses and improving public taste, it seems to have had limited appeal. The average punter was probably not that interested in dingy 'Old Master' paintings or fussy baroque architecture – but they were interested in the splendour (and scandal) of the Tudor court.

That the earliest visitors to Hampton Court were only permitted in Wren's apartments, the interior courtyards and the gardens was a source of popular frustration. A tour of the palace that avoided all parts of the building associated with its most famous residents felt strange and unsatisfying. As one journalist remarked, the exclusion of the Great Hall from the tour was 'an omission which reminds one of the performance of *Hamlet* without the principal character'. Here, it is notable that this space – the heart of the Tudor Palace – is likened to an indispensable character in a play.

In response to popular demand, the Great Hall was the first of the Tudor rooms to be restored and opened to the public in 1844, followed by the Great Watching Chamber in the same year and Wolsey's Closet in 1881. Though it would continue to display paintings from the Royal Collection, the palace was gradually transforming from public art gallery to Tudor heritage attraction. Its artistic and architectural features would always be part of Hampton Court's appeal, of course, but for most visitors, the backstory of the building was just as compelling as its fabric and furnishings, if not more so. And Ernest Law, the man responsible for putting Hampton Court on the Gothic tourism map, understood this perfectly.

*

Ernest Law was born on 26 August 1854 to the Honourable William Towry and Matilda Law, members of the Westmorland lower gentry from the north of England, who at some point moved to the south, where they were provided accommodation as Grace and Favour residents at Hampton Court. In turn, Ernest would eventually earn his own place at the palace – the Pavilion, a seventeenth-century house situated on Barge Walk in the palace park – which he occupied for some thirty years with his wife Katherine.

The young Law was educated at Oscott College, a Catholic seminary school in Birmingham, followed by University College London, where he graduated with a Bachelor of Arts degree in 1874. He went on to have a successful career as a barrister. However, his true passion was history, especially Tudor history.

Thanks to his lifelong connection to Hampton Court, his intimate knowledge of the property and his acquaintance with its modern occupants, Law was uniquely equipped to write about the palace in a way that no other historian – amateur or otherwise – could. His publications are full of evocative historical anecdotes, detailed descriptions of parts of the building that were then inaccessible to the public and, most importantly for our purposes, titbits of ghostly folklore, which he seems to have picked up from his fellow Grace and Favour residents, several of whom claimed to have had ghostly encounters of their own.

Law maintained that he did not believe in ghosts himself. Nevertheless, he wrote about them, and later admitted to Charles G. Harper, author of *Haunted Houses* (1907), that he was at least partly responsible for Hampton Court's haunted reputation. 'I am often accused of having originated the ghosts,' he said. 'Certainly, when I first began, scarcely anyone knew of their existence, and they were not recognised with the unanimity they deserve – as they are now.'

While he might not actually have been the 'originator' of the ghost stories, he certainly popularised them, and there is strong evidence to support the idea that Law was responsible for coining the term 'Haunted Gallery'. It does not seem to appear anywhere in print before the publication of his book *The New Guide to the Royal Palace and Gardens of Hampton Court* in 1882. A floor plan reproduced in the book is perhaps the first ever to label the hallway in question with its now-standard moniker. No explanation is given for why he has labelled it in such a way.

A few years later, in his *History of Hampton Court in Tudor Times*, Law finally offered up a reason, writing: 'The old mysterious "Haunted Gallery", the door of which is on the right hand as you go down the Queen's Great Staircase, has its name from being supposed to be haunted by the shrieking ghost of Queen Catherine Howard.' He then goes on to recount the classic legend, exactly as it is told today. For added excitement, he also includes some first-hand accounts of the royal revenant as relayed to him by his palace neighbours.

The first testimonial comes from a Mrs Cavendish – almost certainly Rose Cavendish Boyle, the Grace and Favour resident who occupied the apartment adjacent to the Haunted Gallery from 1873 to 1901. She told Law that: 'Once, in the middle of the night, some years ago, [I] was suddenly startled out of a profound sleep by a loud and unearthly shriek proceeding from that quarter, followed immediately by perfect stillness.' This account was corroborated by Elizabeth Rigby, Lady Eastlake, a highly respected author and art critic, who recalled that while staying with her friend Rose, she was similarly shaken awake by the same unnerving noise.

At the time Law was writing, the hallway was inaccessible to the public, having long since fallen into disrepair and been relegated to a lumber store used by the palace residents. But thanks to the amateur historian's efforts – both through the publicity generated by his guidebooks and his proposal schemes for the renovation of the space – the Haunted Gallery would eventually earn its place on the Hampton Court tour route, opening to the public in 1918. In the same year, Law published *The Haunted Gallery of Hampton Court and its Associations with Shakespeare*, a 26-page booklet ostensibly focusing on Shakespeare's connection with the Elizabethan court, but which doubles as the author's manifesto, perfectly distilling his overarching vision of the palace, its past and its modern presentation.

Law writes:

> *It is not only for such archaeological features, and the air of antiquity, which this Haunted Gallery is redolent of that gives it its chief claim*

> *on our attention. Much more is the mystic 'aura' that penetrates and transfuses it all, owing to its association with so many famous historical incidents, and so many illustrious historical characters. For not in stones nor in its gold is the greatest glory of a building – nor even in its antiquity – but in the subtle charm that invests it, by its associations with those who, in the past, lived and moved within its walls.*

More than a century later, this sentiment has been kept alive at Hampton Court through Historic Royal Palaces' mandate to put 'Stories over Stones' – or in other words, to place emphasis on social history over architectural. The modern stewards of the palace seem to understand, as Law did before them, that it has always been the stories – including the ghost stories – that the public have cherished most.

'I'm Henry the Eighth, I am ... or am I?'

At the end of our guided tour, I send my family off to explore the Tudor kitchens and gift shop while Ian and I retire to a quiet corner of the palace to talk. We settle ourselves on a bench in the Wolsey Closet, an intimate space measuring about 14 × 12 feet wide, but which feels even smaller thanks to its elaborate décor. The massive stone fireplace, the wall-to-wall wooden panelling and the imposing frieze of sixteenth-century paintings depicting scenes from the 'Passion of the Christ' makes the room feel simultaneously cosy and claustrophobic.

This room is one of the oldest in the palace, dating to its original period of construction under Cardinal Thomas Wolsey, hence its name. Its initial use remains a mystery, but historians speculate that it might have been purpose-built as a private nook for Wolsey and Henry VIII to discuss important personal and political matters out of earshot of the rest of the court. It may very well have been the space in which Henry VIII first confessed his desire for a divorce from Catherine of Aragon. Today it's not nearly so conducive to clandestine conversation, but it seems as good a spot as any for us to have a chat about the Hampton Court hauntings. So, does Ian actually believe in the ghosts?

'Ah, the $64,000 question,' he muses. 'As someone who spent twenty-odd years collecting testaments from palace employees and visitors, I would be disrespectful – borderline ignorant – if I said I didn't believe.' Then he pauses, adding a caveat. 'Perhaps the question is wrongly put. Do I believe in phenomena that make people believe in ghosts? Yes, most certainly!'

When it comes down to it, though, Ian isn't convinced that Hampton Court is haunted by the ghosts of Tudor kings and queens. In fact, when I suggest to him that these are the most commonly reported sightings at the palace, he stops me. 'Ah, that's actually not true, but it's interesting, isn't it?' Instead, he insists, the most frequently described supernatural events are decidedly more mundane. Strange feelings, funny odours, doors inexplicably opening or closing – even locking – of their own accord. But there's hardly ever any explicit evidence to link these events to human agency, let alone to dead monarchs.

'I mean, there's always been that tendency to attribute hauntings to famous people,' Ian agrees. 'In King Henry VIII's palace, who would you expect to find haunting it?'

Well, what about Henry himself? The infamous 'Skeletor' footage?' I ask.

'No one at Hampton Court ever said it was Henry VIII,' Ian replies emphatically. 'I think it was the *Sun* newspaper, on the advice of supposed experts, that said it was Henry VIII.'

It must've been someone else in sixteenth-century clothing, then. The ghost of another member of the Tudor court, perhaps, or, as many have suggested, a modern employee in fancy dress. Not necessarily, Ian argues. Because the video quality is so poor, it's impossible to say for sure, but he thinks it might be a perfectly ordinary living person, wearing a long Afghan coat.

I must admit this boggles my mind. I've watched this footage dozens of times and never once entertained the possibility that it could be anything other than a figure in Tudor costume. It's slowly dawning on me that, in spite of my avowed scepticism, I might have been the unwitting victim of pareidolia.

A commonly offered explanation for supposed supernatural experiences, pareidolia is the human tendency to impose significance on random visual or auditory stimuli. It is the perceptual function that makes us see the shapes of animals in clouds, or the face of a man in the moon, or the figure of the Virgin Mary on a piece of burnt toast. Our brains simply can't handle meaninglessness, so they attempt to rearrange information and present it in a way we can recognise and understand.

Obviously, the 'Skeletor' video is hardly abstract in the way a cumulous cloud is – it plainly captures a human being – but a person in an Afghan coat lurking in the shadows of a Tudor palace seems a little random. I mean, who wears an Afghan coat in this day and age? This isn't the 1970s. Screw that, my brain says, and reinvents the figure as a sixteenth-century courtier in an ermine-lined cloak. Staffers at the *Sun* took this one step further and determined the figure to be Henry VIII himself.

But as Ian says, no one at Hampton Court – staff or visitor – has ever actually claimed to have seen the spectre of the famed Tudor king. What's more, though the Wolsey Closet is said to be haunted by someone – or something – there's little evidence to suggest that it's the cardinal himself. That the two men most famously connected with Hampton Court are conspicuously absent from the ghostly folklore leads me to another revelation. All the ghost sightings – bar 'Skeletor' – are of women.

Head curator Lucy Worsley attempts to explain the preponderance of female phantoms as being a product of the popularity of spiritualism in the Victorian period. 'The services of a professional medium – someone who is paid to communicate with the dead – became more popular with the bereaved. And with the rise of these (often female) mediums, came what their clients wanted: a rise in sightings of female ghosts and spirits.'

There's no denying that the emergence of one of Hampton Court's best-known ghost stories (Catherine Howard in the Haunted Gallery) coincided with the ascent of spiritualism and the female medium. And as Ian tells me, the area was a centre for spiritualism in the late nineteenth century. 'There's this background here,' he says. 'One of the gardeners was involved in spiritualism and in publishing one of those spiritualist newspapers. So, it attracted people of a certain type.'

But I think there's more to it than that. As we saw with Chillingham Castle, an ancient fortress that was likewise used and occupied by countless men, it also became populated by the ghosts of women and children. The haunted house (or castle or palace) of our modern understanding is inevitably tied up with notions of the 'domestic' and of 'family' – ideal or otherwise – which is traditionally defined by the presence of women.

On top of this, there has long been a tendency to hold up famous women of the past – particularly those who died tragically – as amorphous symbols of time and place; their ghosts symbolising the social and political dynamics of their period in history.

In England, the most famous example of this is unquestionably Anne Boleyn. Her key role in the events that led to the birth of the Church of England make her interesting and important in her own right. But it was her precipitous rise from provincial gentry to Queen of England, followed by her swift downfall and gruesome execution, that turned her into an icon. Today, she is said to haunt Blickling Hall (her birthplace), Hever Castle (her childhood home), Rochford Hall (where she first met Henry VIII), Windsor Castle and Hampton Court (her marital homes) and the Tower of London (the site of her death), making her one of the most well-travelled ghosts in the nation, if not the world.

She is surpassed only by the Scottish monarch Mary Stuart – or Mary, Queen of Scots – who was executed for treason by her cousin, Elizabeth I, in 1587. Mary is said to haunt a staggering ten properties around Scotland and the north of England, suggesting that the eternal queen was somehow able to leave her mark on nearly every residence she ever lived in.

It is not just British monarchs who possess this uncanny ability. On the other side of the Atlantic, there is the restless spirit of famed film actress Marilyn Monroe, who, like her UK counterparts, died a sudden and unnatural death (a self-induced barbiturate overdose), but who lives on in popular imagination as a symbol of Old Hollywood: beautiful, yet empty and broken. The blonde bombshell's ghost has been spotted at three of her favourite 'haunts' in life (a bar, a coffee shop and a restaurant), two former residences, two hotels, an amusement park and a cemetery. She is often seen in reflective surfaces, such as the full-length mirror that once hung in her favourite suite at the Hollywood Roosevelt Hotel, where she lived for two years at the beginning of her career in the 1940s. Perhaps her beauty was so timeless and unforgettable that even the mirror couldn't let go of her image.

But are staff and guests at the Roosevelt really seeing Marilyn Monroe? Or are they, as Ian puts it, 'dot-connecting'? Does a fleeting glimpse of blonde hair cause the brain to immediately conjure up the image of the most famous blonde of all time? Who knows? Maybe Marilyn really *is* the hardest-working ghost in Hollywood.

Years ago, long before Ian's tenure and before the ghost tours began, I visited Hampton Court for the first time on a childhood family holiday. Though I wasn't much older than my son is now, I have vivid memories of the experience and the impact it had on me. After the visit, I returned home to Canada with a new-found passion for Tudor history and an obsession with my favourite figure of the Henrician court – Anne Boleyn.

I'm still not entirely sure what the fascination was – whether it was because she was a seductive woman with the power to bring the King of England to his knees, causing him to alter the course of British history simply for the chance to have her as his bride, or whether it was more to do with the grim circumstances of her death (even at a young age, I clearly had a slightly morbid bent). It was probably a mixture of both.

Maybe in my pre-teen mind, Anne Boleyn represented a kind of real-world fairy-tale princess: a damsel in distress, emotionally imprisoned in the gilded cage that was Hampton Court, her tyrannical husband's oppressive headquarters, and later, physically imprisoned in a tower just like Rapunzel. But Anne would lose more than just her hair.

At any rate, I'm certainly not the only person to have projected my fears and fantasies onto this historical figure. The dozens of books, plays and films (not to mention ghost stories) featuring the tragic queen are a testament to her enduring allure.

That year, I decided to dress as my Tudor-era idol for Halloween, enlisting the help of my mother – a talented seamstress – to whip up a sixteenth-century inspired gown made of vibrant violet faux silk. Though the standard Tudor headdress – known as a gable hood – was beyond my mum's capabilities, I managed to achieve the effect by wearing a long dark wig tied back under a swatch of cloth. To complete the look, I powdered my face deathly white and splashed my neck with ribbons of fake blood.

Not unexpectedly, my North American neighbours doling out the sweets that October night had no idea who I was meant to be. Their best guess was Marie Antoinette, France's own beautiful, beguiling and ultimately beheaded queen (naturally, Marie's ghost is said to haunt the grounds of the Palace of Versailles, the French equivalent of Hampton Court).

Even though nobody knew who I was, I loved that costume.

It was this childhood trip to Hampton Court – and the fancy dress inspired by it – that inspired my lifelong interest in social history; in the stories of the past and the people who shaped it. In the end, perhaps it doesn't matter if the palace really is haunted by the ghosts of Tudor queens. Even if it's not literally haunted, it is certainly imbued with that 'mystic aura' Ernest Law spoke of – the haunting atmosphere that will forever remind us of the 'illustrious historical characters' who once wandered its halls.

THE MYRTLES PLANTATION

ENSLAVED BY A HAUNTED HISTORY

5

There are no ghosts, white folks, and I can prove it. If there were ghosts, slaves would come back and f*** you up, and you do know that.

Paul Mooney (1941–2021)

Southern Gothic: the most haunted (plantation) house in America

It was the witching hour. At around 3 a.m. on a moonless night in March 1980, Frances Kermeen, the proud new owner of the Myrtles Plantation in St Francisville, Louisiana, was wide awake. It was becoming a frustratingly regular occurrence.

Each evening for the past several nights – the first nights she had spent in the 200-year-old mansion – Frances would drift off into a peaceful slumber, only to be woken by the sound of heavy footsteps shuffling up and down the staircase and in the hallway just outside her first-floor suite. At first, she assumed it was one of the house's other living occupants; the former owner, John, had remained in residence to help Frances settle in, and sometimes hosted friends. But when Frances politely confronted her temporary housemates about the nocturnal noises, they assured her that they had never left their rooms, all of which were in a separate wing of the house.

It had been a little over six months since Frances, a vivacious twenty-eight-year-old, had made the decision to uproot herself from her native California and move some 2,000 miles south-east to start afresh as a bed-and-breakfast operator in rural Louisiana. Already she was beginning to think she might have made a mistake. To be sure, Frances adored the house, and felt it was somehow her calling to return this faded old Southern dame to her former glory. But she had a niggling feeling that this property was going to give her a great deal more grief than the historic houses she had restored back home in San Jose.

Frances Kermeen was no coward, though. She was a strong, independent young woman, determined to live out her girlhood dream of owning a historic inn. She wasn't about to let some restless spirits stand in her way, any more than she had allowed a bunch of conservative small-town Southerners prevent her from buying the house of her dreams on account of her marital status. The solution to that had been fairly straightforward: she had simply married her long-term boyfriend, Jim, to seal the deal.

Had her new husband not still been back in California, tying up the loose ends of their old life, she might have felt a little less uneasy about the spectral footsteps, but because she was alone in a strange new environment, Frances opted to abandon her bedroom for the night and move downstairs, closer to the company of the living. She set up camp in a sitting room just outside the suite where her predecessor, John, was staying.

What would soon prove to be a false sense of security allowed Frances to fall back to sleep, though it wasn't long before she was abruptly awoken once again.

'I had the eeriest feeling that someone was watching me,' she later wrote in *The Myrtles Plantation: The True Story of America's Most Haunted House*, a book about her paranormal experiences at the Myrtles. 'I had been sleeping on my stomach, and as I rolled over to look around, in the dim light in the room I could see a figure standing next to the couch looking down at me. The woman was dressed in a long, flowing, dark green gown, [and was] holding a round tin with a candle in it.'

It was this light source, she soon realised, that was illuminating the previously pitch-dark room. In the flickering light, Frances could barely make out the mysterious figure's distinctive appearance: 'Her face was dark and very square, and a green turban was wrapped around her head, concealing her hair.' Understandably terrified by this unexpected stranger, Frances squeezed her eyes shut and began to scream as loudly as she could, assuming that the occupant of the adjacent room would quickly come to her rescue.

He didn't.

'After what seemed like an eternity, I finally opened my eyes and gathered enough courage to reach out and touch the long, flowing gown,' Frances claimed. 'As my hand passed right through the gown, through her body, she slowly disappeared.'

Frances had just been accosted by the ghost that would go on to become the plantation's best-known spectral celebrity: Chloe, the green-turbaned slave.

The Myrtles Plantation is a historic home located on the outskirts of St Francisville, the parish seat of West Feliciana in south-central Louisiana, a fertile upland region running along the banks of the Mississippi River, 30 miles north of the state capital, Baton Rouge, and some 110 miles more from the vibrant cultural capital, New Orleans. Built for General David Bradford in 1796, the 22-room mansion once sat at the centre of a 4,000-acre cotton farm, which, prior to the abolition of slavery in 1865, was worked by as many as 500 enslaved African American labourers.

Over the years, the property has seen a long succession of owners, all of whom enjoyed a luxurious lifestyle financed by the cotton industry. Since the 1950s, however, the house and grounds have been open to the public, laying claim to a reputation for being one of the most haunted homes in America.

There is no denying that the Myrtles is haunted, in its own kind of way. Whether by the literal ghosts of former slaves and slave-owners, or simply by the echoes of the terrible past to which it silently bore witness, the mansion is forever marred. If walls could talk, they would betray all kinds of dark secrets: stories of revenge, pain and suffering; tales of terror experienced not only by those in bondage, but also by those wealthy white landowners who lived in perpetual fear that the people they had enslaved might one day rise up against them. Their glittering Baccarat crystal chandeliers, Carrara marble fireplaces and gilt-framed rococo mirrors must have been but a small comfort when the precarious foundations of their privileged way of life was constantly under threat.

For all its fanciful fittings, the Myrtles cannot have been a happy home, and in this respect, it was typical of the Southern American plantation house.

First of all, what exactly is a plantation house? It is the residence of a plantation owner – or, in other words, the homestead belonging to the proprietor of a large-scale agricultural operation. In addition to being, quite literally, a 'planter's home', the plantation house was – and continues to be – a simulacrum for a historical lifestyle specific to south-eastern America, where, from the late seventeenth to the early twentieth century, fields of cotton, indigo, sugar and tobacco covered a vast expanse of territory stretching west from the South Carolina lowlands all the way to the border of East Texas. In the antebellum era (the period prior to the outbreak of the Civil War), each plantation was like a small but powerful empire. And at the heart of each plantation was the plantation house, a stately home that presided over a major agricultural complex made profitable through the use of slave labour.

For almost as far back as I can remember, such paradoxical properties, at once opulent and odious, have held a unique fascination for me. Ever since I took that first memorable trip to the Southern states as a young child and spent the night in a former plantation house in Charleston, South Carolina (once the nation's largest port and marketplace for selling enslaved Africans), I was bewitched. For reasons I didn't yet fully understand, I instinctively felt that the house was haunted. Granted, the innkeeper didn't market it in this way – back in the mid-1990s 'haunted hotel' experiences were few and far between – and perhaps it wasn't haunted at all. But like all grand old Southern homes of its ilk, it would surely have seen its fair share of tumult and tragedy.

Now, their property's dark past doesn't seem like something the proprietor of a historic hotel or heritage site would want to advertise to paying customers. And certainly, when I first visited the South nearly a quarter of a century ago, the grim spectre of slavery was still being conveniently ignored; the proprietors of historic hotels and heritage sites preferred not to advertise topics such as bondage and torture. Instead, the dark and shameful past lurked in the shadowy corners of nearly every historic visitor attraction south of the Mason–Dixon line, kept at bay by a system of curatorial rhetoric designed to minimise the horror and highlight the supposed harmony and romance of antebellum society.

Until fairly recently, visitors to any plantation house would be encouraged to direct their attention towards the architecture, the fine art, the antique furnishings. In narratives that almost exclusively focused on the lives of the white homeowners, slaves would be routinely referred to as 'servants' or 'staff'; victims of rape and sexual abuse were called 'lovers' or 'mistresses'; and plantation owners were often described as being 'kind and benevolent', allegedly treating their slaves like 'members of the family'. In this way, the subject of slavery was effectively minimised, skirted around or sugar-coated.

In the wake of recent seismic sociopolitical events, however, it has become increasingly difficult for Southern heritage sites to side-step slavery. While many of these properties still desperately cling to traditional narratives, continuing to emphasise the grandeur of the buildings and the extravagance of their past owners' lifestyles, it is now no longer possible to ignore the elephant in the room.

In the words of Tiya Miles, a bestselling author and Harvard history professor specialising in African American studies: 'Without slavery there is no South, as a region or an idea. But if vacationing tourists must somehow confront the ugliness that repels as well as attracts their notice, they would probably rather do so from a safe emotional distance.' So, how do the proprietors of Southern heritage attractions manage to facilitate such an experience? How do they acknowledge the horrors of slavery without alienating their casual, pleasure-seeking customer base? The solution was the ghost tour.

The Myrtles Plantation was something of a trailblazer in the business of ghost tours. In the 1980s, nearly two decades before most other Southern American heritage sites were attempting to cash in on the supernatural and morbid, the Myrtles was already advertising candlelit evening tours, 'murder mystery' events, and overnight stays in its rumoured-to-be-haunted rooms. By the early 2000s, with the precipitous rise of 'Gothic tourism' – and its more sinister cousin 'dark tourism', the practice of visiting historical locations linked with death and tragedy – the Myrtles was primed to reap the benefits of a now booming industry.

Among historians and scholars of tourism, ghost tours are a controversial topic. Quite aside from the blatantly commercial aspect of it, scholars question whether ghost tours improve the public understanding of the past or help people to develop empathy for victims of historical injustices. Professor Miles argues that Southern American ghost tours work to reduce the history of slavery to a grisly horror show that lacks any critical engagement with actual events or the personal experiences of enslaved peoples. Richard Sharpley, the Associate Director of the Institute of Dark Tourism Research at the University of Central Lancashire in the UK, assumes that at least some of those who seek out 'dark tourism' destinations such as haunted plantations do so out of morbid or voyeuristic impulses; this implies that sites that cater to this type of clientele must be in some way exploitative or disrespectful of the history they harbour. And Erika Robb Larkins, a Professor of Anthropology at San Diego State University, maintains that: 'When [a site of] atrocity becomes a recreational attraction, visitors are themselves inflicting further violence as they search out unique and "authentic" experiences.'

Judith Richardson, senior lecturer in English at Stanford University, believes, on the other hand, that ghost stories have the power to reveal hidden histories and forgotten lives. Similarly, UC Santa Barbara sociology professor Avery Gordon argues that: 'The ghost is not simply a dead or missing person, but a social figure, and investigating it can lead to that dense site where history and subjectivity make social life.' Her research has demonstrated that ghost stories can give marginalised groups – such as African Americans, Native Americans and women – a voice that is seldom heard on the traditional heritage property tour.

It should come as no surprise that I believe ghost tours and ghost stories can be effective alternative tools of communicating historical narratives to a wider audience. But of course they can also be problematic – particularly in the context of the plantation house, where stories are typically told by white narrators to a predominantly white audience. What's more, like all legends, plantation house ghost stories are invariably exaggerated and are rarely based on archival evidence, making them potentially misleading.

However, if we go into the ghost tour with the full knowledge and awareness of the limitations and biases of these stories, we can still glean important meanings and messages. Even though plantation house ghost stories might be understood as racially insensitive forms of entertainment, they are significant for what they reveal about the people who tell them. They expose society's greatest fears, deepest regrets and most carefully guarded fantasies. Even a ghost story with almost no basis in historical reality can still manage to reveal broader social truths.

Such is the case of the story of Chloe, the green-turbaned slave, the Myrtles' most familiar legend. As we will learn, the ghost of Chloe (or 'Cleo' or 'the French governess' as she is also referred to) is a simultaneously tragic and terrifying figure: a multifaceted, ever-evolving symbolic character whose malleable identity seems to mirror our own changing attitudes towards race relations, past and present.

As we prepare to cross the threshold of the Myrtles Plantation, we must be cautious and aware of the dangers that lie within. Exploitation, misinformation, and the commercialisation of the darkest chapter in American history are all hazards we will be forced to face. But with a good measure of critical awareness, we will be able to successfully (and responsibly) navigate its haunted halls.

Luxury, luridness and little white lies: the business of plantation house tourism

One blisteringly hot mid-August, my husband and I make our own pilgrimage to the Myrtles Plantation. In summer in the American South, there is a certain quality in the air. It is a still, sticky closeness, broken by the occasional warm breeze, which feels like the heat expelled from an open oven or the dying exhaust of a car whose engine has recently been switched off. There is a kind of electricity in the air, making one feel strangely sensitive to every living (or not so living) thing around them. The trees are shrouded in Spanish moss, the floral equivalent to massive strands of spider webs, which look deliberately grown to dress the set of a real-life ghost story. The natural environment alone lends itself to tales of the supernatural, and that's before you begin to consider the region's macabre history and evocative architectural heritage.

Our journey to the Myrtles has taken us through the heart of the Southern states. When we finally reach the plantation gates and make our way down the oak-lined drive, we are more than a little relieved to find that the property doesn't exactly live up to the stereotypical haunted house of nightmares. Rather than an abandoned, derelict wreck, the Myrtles Plantation is a lively tourist enterprise and the place is teeming with visitors. Some have come for a celebratory meal at the 1796, the plantation's high-end restaurant; some for a night-time house tour; and some to stay in the boutique bed and breakfast.

The main house is not nearly as imposing as you might expect. Though decidedly elegant in an understated sort of way, the Myrtles is a far cry from the glimmering white neoclassical behemoths one generally envisions when picturing a Southern plantation house. A relatively compact one-and-a-half-storey clapboard structure adorned with seafoam-green shutters and delicate ironwork railings, the house seems less 'haunted mansion' and more 'country cottage'. And that's effectively exactly what it is – a larger, grander version of the vernacular workers' cottage or 'Creole Cottage'.

Appearances can be deceiving, I suppose, but there is nothing immediately scary about the Myrtles. Still, I feel that Southern electricity in the air and a tingle of anticipation for what the night might have in store. After checking in and depositing our luggage, we decide to unwind after our long car journey (and before a potentially sleepless night) with some libations.

Because it's still a little too steamy to enjoy cocktail hour outside in the quaint little courtyard or on the mansion's wraparound porch, we make our way into the air-conditioned lounge, where we are served drinks by bartenders with syrupy Southern accents. Our decadent dinner of Gulf shrimp and grits (a local delicacy) is taken in the main dining room, a converted carriage house fitted with funky, modern light fixtures, rustic furniture and a floor-to-ceiling wood store that supplies the restaurant's wood-fired oven. All around us are couples enjoying romantic candlelit dinners. Like us, they seem reluctant to bring their evening to an end. By the time we eventually step back outside, the sun has dipped below the horizon and the lush live oak trees and crepe myrtles that encircle the property are lit up with tiny twinkling fairy lights.

I must admit, I'm so thoroughly seduced by the Myrtles' charms that I've almost forgotten why we've come here. It's only when the temperature finally drops and we decide to take a stroll through the plantation grounds that I am reminded. Beyond the main house, the restaurant, café, gift shop and an attractively landscaped pond, there is a smattering of cabins dotted between the trees. These are modern replicas, intentionally built in a similar style and in the approximate location of the humble dwellings once inhabited by the many enslaved people who lived, worked and died here. It seems bizarre, even perverse, that these rustic abodes, adorned by charming signs reading 'Cypress Cottage', 'Willow Cottage' and 'Live Oak Cottage', can all be hired as holiday accommodation.

Away from the other tourists, engulfed in darkness and accompanied by a symphony of cicadas, the Myrtles doesn't feel so much frightening as unsettling.

For those who are not familiar with it, the area popularly referred to as the 'Deep South' is a geographic and cultural region generally considered to encompass the states of Georgia, Alabama, South Carolina, Tennessee, Mississippi and Louisiana. These were among the eleven states that seceded from the United States in 1861, prior to the Battle of Fort Sumter, which signalled the start of the Civil War. Today, the area is commonly associated with devout religion, Republican politics, steamy weather, Southern fried cuisine and, of course, slavery. It is also home to the highest proliferation of plantation houses in the nation. In St Francisville alone – a town covering just 1.8 square miles, with a population of less than 2,000 – there are six.

Just like the castles and stately homes of Britain, scores of plantation houses are open to the public as visitor attractions. But unlike Britain, where most of the major heritage tourism sites are operated by charitable or educational trusts or government agencies, plantation houses remain, for the most part, privately owned, for-profit businesses that cannot survive on heritage tourism alone. As such, they typically rely on multiple revenue streams, including retail, entertainment and hospitality ventures – and therein lies the ethical quandary. That places where enslaved African Americans were imprisoned and tortured have been transformed into luxury bed and breakfasts and wedding venues is inarguably insensitive and offensive to their descendants. And yet, without these revenue streams, what would become of these architecturally and historically significant, and often incredibly beautiful, buildings?

The ghost tour has been put forward recently as a fresh form of income generation available to the plantation house, one that more directly confronts the dark history of these properties, shakily bridging the gap between entertainment, leisure and uncomfortable historical truth. In the American South where, perhaps inevitably, the spirits of slaves have assumed centre stage, ghost tours have become the linchpin of the 'dark tourism' industry. It wasn't always so, though: according to former owner Frances Kermeen, when she took up the reins at the Myrtles over forty years ago, ghosts were not considered the subject of polite conversation, let alone the basis for a lucrative business venture. 'In the 1980s, people didn't talk about them,' she tells me. 'And most places didn't want to be known for having ghosts, even as late as the 1990s.'

While rumours had been circulating for years that the Myrtles was haunted, it was not something that Frances claims she ever actively promoted or monetised – though she did apparently allow the tabloid newspaper the *National Inquirer* to run a story about the Myrtles, entitled 'Inside America's Most Haunted House'. She also hosted candlelit evening tours every year on Halloween, but the proceeds from these events, she says, went entirely to charity.

'I told my staff not to talk about the ghosts,' Frances insists. Only if visitors broached the subject in private were tour guides permitted to speak freely about the Myrtles' supposed spectral inhabitants.

However, for Frances's successors, John and Teeta Moss, who purchased the plantation in 1992 and still own and operate the property today, its ghosts are their bread and butter. 'Explore one of America's Most Haunted Homes' reads the strapline on their company website. A large black-and-white photograph – purportedly depicting the ghost of an enslaved girl that the Mosses claim to have captured while taking pictures of the property for insurance purposes – is displayed on a placard just outside the main visitor entrance. The evening 'mystery tours' run seven nights a week, with multiple slots available at weekends, suggesting that most of the 60,000 visitors to the house each year come in search of spirits.

At $25 a head, these tours are major money-makers – and not just for the Myrtles. Ghost hunters in the American South can also visit the Ferry Plantation in Virginia, the Poplar Grove Plantation in North Carolina, the Hofwyl-Broadfield Plantation in Georgia and the Oak Alley Plantation in Louisiana, among others, for a similar experience.

Clearly, the ghost tours at the Myrtles (and elsewhere) are mercenary in nature. And yet, they seem to have been conceived of in good faith. The Mosses – and Kermeen before them – likely never intentionally set out to exploit the suffering of the enslaved people who once toiled on the Myrtles' fields, nor did they intend to deliberately spread historical misinformation. Rather, they simply recognised that there is a large and captive audience for ghost stories. And it is an incredibly diverse one.

Some visitors to the Myrtles come to hear scary stories; some come in the hope of having a supernatural experience of their own; some come seeking novelty and an alternative perspective; and some come in search of a better understanding of the brutal reality of life on the Southern plantation, and believe that the ghost tour is the best way to access the dissonant knowledge that is ordinarily off-limits on the conventional heritage house tour. Some, like me, hope to accomplish all of the above.

The next morning, perhaps predictably, my husband and I do not wake feeling well rested. Exhaustion from jet lag and long days of travelling should have carried us through the night effortlessly, but the mansion had other ideas. The room we were staying in, Kermeen later tells me, was part of the nursery wing, and one of the most haunted rooms in the house. But we didn't have ghosts to blame for our restless night; unsurprisingly, the 200-year-old walls are far from soundproof, while warped and uneven floorboards betray the movements of even the lightest of foot. What's more, our room's antique four-poster bed, while attractive and perfectly in keeping with its period setting, proved creaky and a great deal smaller than the beds we're used to.

When we make our way downstairs for our house tour, we learn that the small single-storey structure adjacent to the main house, which serves as a reception area, is actually the oldest building on the property. The original homestead of the plantation's first owner, General David Bradford, it was built in 1794, two years before the construction of the mansion – though you'd never guess it in its current form: a brightly lit commercial space comprising a café, gift shop and check-in desk.

Here, there is an array of Myrtles-branded merchandise on offer – fridge magnets, Christmas ornaments, coffee mugs and more. One wonders what old General Bradford would make of it all – or what the men, women and children he enslaved would think of the many products emblazoned with the image of the mansion they were forced to build and maintain.

Prompted by the ringing of a bell, a dozen other tourists (mostly middle-aged white couples like us) gather on the veranda outside the main visitor entrance. A petite silver-haired woman introduces herself as Connie, our tour guide. 'Welcome to the Myrtles Plantation, one of the most haunted homes in America,' she begins, setting the tone for what will be a unique hybrid of a traditional plantation house tour and a contemporary ghost tour. After laying out a few ground rules (no food or drink; no flash photography; no sitting on the furniture, etc.), Connie unlocks the door and beckons us inside.

'Here in Louisiana, we take all our friends and family through the back door,' she explains, suggesting that, because we are entering through what would once have been the family's private entrance, we should now be positioning ourselves in the role of the privileged guest, perhaps imagining that we are members of the antebellum elite.

As Connie waits for everyone to file in, I glance around the entry hall for the first time. Every inch screams wealth, from the hand-painted floral wallpaper to the intricate friezework moulding to the colossal crystal chandelier (which apparently weighs over 300 pounds and was purchased from a castle in France).

Like most heritage property tours, Connie begins her narrative with a rundown of the key historical players – the men and women who helped shape the opulent environment in which we are now standing. We hear a bit about General Bradford, or 'Whiskey Dave' as he has been nicknamed, a Pennsylvania-born Revolutionary War officer and lawyer who acquired the land in 1794 from the governors of what was then known as Spanish West Florida. At the time, Bradford was on the lam, dodging charges for his involvement in the Whiskey Rebellion (1791–4), a violent protest against a tax levied on grain mixtures used in the production of whiskey. But even after he was pardoned by President John Adams in 1799, Bradford elected to stay in the South, finding that he was earning a tidy profit from the cultivation of indigo, and later cotton, on the verdant plantation he called Laurel Grove.

Next up was Judge Clarke Woodruff, Bradford's former law student and son-in-law, who married his eldest daughter, Sarah Matilda, and took over the plantation in 1817. Following the untimely deaths of his wife and two children, Woodruff abandoned the plantation in 1831, taking his only surviving daughter to live in the larger settlement of Covington, Louisiana.

Then came Ruffin Gray Stirling, who purchased the property in 1834 and financed the major expansion and remodelling of the home, transforming it from an eight-room farmhouse into the twenty-two-room mansion it is today. His wife Mary was reportedly responsible for the home's lavish interiors, and for its changed moniker 'The Myrtles'; the locally growing crepe myrtle was one of her favourite plants.

After a protracted discussion of the original layout of the eighteenth-century house – a configuration called saddlebag construction, a form of architecture native to the South, featuring a central chimney or hall, flanked by two rooms on either side – the focus of the tour abruptly shifts. There is a change in the atmosphere, and we draw closer together. This is the part I've been waiting for: the story behind Chloe.

As Connie tells it, one day, Judge Clarke Woodruff was out on horseback in the cotton fields. He spotted an absolutely *gorgeous* slave girl (emphasis Connie's) and immediately asked her to come to work at the house and take care of his wife and three children. Of course, Woodruff's true intention was for the young woman to move into his home as his mistress, or concubine. The slave – the famous Chloe – would have had no choice in the matter, but apparently felt some measure of relief in trading her life in the fields for a more comfortable existence inside the manor house in what was, effectively, a promotion. Sarah, the judge's wife, was no fool. As the story goes, she became jealous and began plotting against Chloe. Fearful of losing her new position, Chloe began skulking around the house, listening in on her master's private conversations in the hope of gleaning some useful information that might help her to stay in his good graces.

One day, Woodruff discovered Chloe with her ear pressed to the keyhole of his office door. Furious, he grabbed Chloe by the hair, yanked her outside and sliced off her left ear as punishment. It was this deformity that she would later conceal with her signature green turban. To add insult to injury, she was banished from the house to work in the kitchen, which was located in a small outbuilding, where for ten hours a day, seven days a week, she was forced to stand over an open fire in the sweltering heat of the Louisiana summer.

Desperate to regain her privileged position in the main house, Chloe hatched an ill-conceived plan, reasoning that if the children fell sick, surely she would be asked back into the house to nurse them to health. It just so happened that two of the children had upcoming birthdays, and who better to bake a cake for them than the newly appointed cook? Not realising that just one leaf of oleander could be deadly, Chloe laced the cake with sixteen leaves. Reportedly, Sarah Woodruff and two of her children died within the hour.

Wild with fear and remorse, Chloe ran to the other slaves, pleading for them to listen to her side of the story and protect her. But, remembering her cushy job in the house which she had enjoyed while they were still out picking cotton in the hot sun, they were unsympathetic, and swiftly put her on trial and found her guilty. She was hanged from a branch of one of the plantation's many live oak trees. It does not escape my attention that the same name adorns one of the rebuilt cottages I saw the previous evening.

As Connie finishes her story, there is a long pregnant pause. The hall is so quiet you could hear a pin drop. And then, she lets out a deep sigh before declaring: 'Well, the story of Chloe is just that – a story. Take what you want and leave the rest.' And with that, we're on to the next room.

The rest of the tour is a bit of a blur. There are more names and dates, more architectural details, and even a few more ghost stories. But all of it kind of blends together in my mind with the myriad other heritage house tours I have taken. None of what I subsequently see or hear can compare with Chloe. Real or not, she's clearly the star of the show.

Towards the end of our tour, Connie asks us to gather around her in the centre of what is called the Ladies' Parlour. As its name suggests, it is a distinctly feminine space: light and airy, with pale peach walls and a suite of white upholstered furniture. Nothing about it suggests it is haunted, but according to Connie, it is the 'psychic centre of the house', with some kind of supernatural vortex that extends from the settee in the middle of the room, straight up through the chandelier and into the guest room above – the guest room where my husband and I have just spent the night.

'I've been working here for nine years,' Connie confides in us, 'and have I ever seen Chloe?' She smiles and shakes her head. 'No, but I have seen plenty of other ghosts.' She goes on to tell us that there are at least fourteen spirits believed to be in residence at the Myrtles, including men, women and children.

'I think they're all over Louisiana,' she continues. 'I think it's in the dirt. The poor slaves, the people who lived in these houses, the soldiers who have fallen all around here… For some reason, they didn't make a complete transition to the other side. And I don't know if they want to stay here or if they're expecting us to help them move on. I just don't know.'

Another dramatic pause. 'But I do know that the Myrtles is haunted. It's not just a gimmick to get you to spend your money.'

Shapeshifter: the origins and evolution of the Chloe legend

As it turns out, Sarah Woodruff and her two children died of yellow fever, not poisoning. There is no record of a slave called Chloe, nor any evidence of a hanging taking place on the property. Of course, it's entirely possible that some elements of the tale are true, but there's nothing whatsoever to substantiate it.

So, who is Chloe? If, as the historical record indicates, she never actually existed as a living, breathing person, how did she get here? Did she appear out of thin air? Or was she created for a purpose? While it's difficult to answer these questions definitively, the evidence would suggest that Chloe materialised slowly and organically over time. At first hazy and undefined, as the years wore on, Chloe gradually became more solid, eventually developing a fully formed backstory. Rather than being the invention of one person, Chloe and her story appear to be a long-running collaborative project. With each new generation, new pieces of the Chloe puzzle are added, to form an intricate picture of American society's complicated relationship with its own past.

As we will see, the ghost of Chloe began as little more than a faint reminder of a bygone era, one without a clear message of any kind, let alone a critique of the age from whence she came. Over time, however, she evolved into a much more potent symbol of the antebellum South, shifting from a benevolent entity to a malevolent one, and finally to a richly nuanced anti-heroine.

The current iteration of Chloe as described on the Myrtles' tour is a relatively recent development. This version of Chloe – the young, beautiful sex slave turned accidental killer – has only been around for a couple of decades. However, certain elements of her story can be traced back almost a century.

One of the earliest recorded references to ghosts at the Myrtles Plantation can be found in the book *Louisiana: A Guide to the State* (1941), one of a series of travel guides produced by the Federal Writers' Project, an initiative of the American government that gave work to unemployed writers during the Great Depression. The entry on the Myrtles reads as follows:

> *[The plantation] is a one-and-a-half-storey house with wide verandas and ornate iron grillwork. The house is set in a grove of live oaks. Several ghost stories are centred around the Myrtles. One concerns a little French lady in a green bonnet. She is reputed to make nocturnal visits to the guest rooms, lifting the mosquito net and peering at the occupant of the bed.*

Here, we have the germ of the Chloe story, in its most rudimentary form: the ghost has no name, no backstory, no individual identity. She's also described as a 'French lady', not an African American slave. And yet she wears a green headdress and apparently has a penchant for sneaking up on sleeping house guests.

Some have credited this early version of the story to the Williams family, the last owners to oversee the Myrtles as a working plantation, who lived there from 1891 until the early 1950s. According to their descendants, the family spoke of seeing the ghost of a woman wearing a green bonnet. The same spirit was supposedly seen by the next owner of the Myrtles, Marjorie Munson, a wealthy widow and amateur musician from Oklahoma who purchased the plantation in 1953. Shortly after, she wrote a song called 'The Ghost in the French Bedroom', referencing a room in the house that is furnished with a suite of French-manufactured gilt furniture – which could have led to the confused assumption that the ghost was French.

This was the version of the story that circulated for the first few decades. Throughout the 1960s and 1970s, several variations appeared in periodicals and papers. The ghost started out as simply a 'French lady in a green bonnet'. She then became a 'French governess in a black dress and green bonnet'. And by the late 1970s she was 'a French governess hired in 1825 to care for the owner's daughter'.

While in some of these early accounts the governess is described as missing one or both of her ears, it is said that a previous employer was responsible for her disfigurement. What's more, she was an employee, not a slave; she was not the judge's lover; and she was not accused of murdering his wife and children. Instead, she was missing (and presumably mourning) a child of her own. In this version, the ghostly figure poses no threat to those in the present nor those in the past and, in turn, she was not harmed by anyone in the Myrtles household.

Like most ghost stories, the 'French governess' tale can be seen as a reflection of the prevailing social attitudes of its day. It seems to have first surfaced at some point between 1890 and 1940, a period that witnessed the Colonial Revival movement, a kind of national celebration of early American history and culture. At this time, there were widespread efforts to restore and preserve Southern heritage sites, many of which were subsequently opened to the public as tourist attractions. The narratives that were promoted at these sites (including the ghostly ones) reflected a desire to reconnect with the past – a past that was commonly felt to be a lost 'golden age' of the American South.

This was an era that long preceded the Civil Rights movement of the 1960s – a time when it was still eminently possible to paint slavery out of the picture of the colonial past. Evidently, plantation house ghost stories have been around for a lot longer than 'dark tourism' has. However, it seems that they initially served a distinctly different purpose; not to draw attention to past horrors, or even necessarily to frighten, but much more simply to demonstrate a house's historical pedigree. These types of tales could be melancholy, wistful even, but very rarely were they truly scary.

The transformation of the Chloe myth from an unnamed French governess in a green bonnet to a slave woman in a green turban seems to have occurred in the 1980s, coinciding with the tenure of Frances Kermeen. In her book *The Myrtles Plantation: The True Story of America's Most Haunted House* (2005), Kermeen claims to have heard from her neighbours the story of an (as yet unnamed) slave who poisoned her mistress and her children. Through her own research, however, Francis learned that the story had some pretty considerable holes in it – namely, that Sarah Matilda Woodruff and her two children died of yellow fever.

Yet the story evidently struck a chord with her. Throughout her book, Kermeen repeatedly references a feeling of affinity with Sarah Matilda. When Kermeen discovers that one of her young employees at her B&B is having an affair with her husband, she even goes so far as to intimate that her own experiences at the Myrtles might be mirroring those of Sarah – although Judge Woodruff's infidelity seems to have been a useful plot point in Chloe's story, rather than a historically documented fact.

For Frances, the legend had not only taken on personal significance, but it had also completely changed in tone and meaning. Where before, the green-bonneted (white) servant was a sad, but ultimately benevolent, presence, the green-turbaned (black) slave was an insidious interloper who threated the sanctity of her mistress's marriage, as well as her very life. Could this be read as a reflection of the deeply rooted anxieties of all plantation house owners, past and present? The spectre of the slave – in particular, the house slave – representing a disruptive and potentially deadly threat to the privileged white household? Or might it represent a modern-day anxiety superimposed over an element of residual historical guilt?

It is from Kermeen that we first get a name for our ghost, which she says came from one of her customers, a tourist who claimed to be psychic and reported hearing 'a woman crying in the French bedroom, so she went to investigate'. Here, she said she stumbled upon 'a mulatto slave dressed in a green frock with a green turban wrapped around her head, whimpering in the corner'. The tourist went to comfort the woman, asking her name and how she could help. 'The slave told her that her name was Chloe and that she had just learned that her father was white.'

This encounter is significant for a few reasons. First, the tourist's description of the ghost matched Frances's own early spectral encounter exactly. Second, the ghost was said to be 'mulatto', a term that is now deemed offensive, but which was traditionally used to identify a mixed-race person with one black parent and one white parent. Historically, people of colour who had even a little European blood were viewed as racially superior and more attractive, and Southern literature and folklore abounds with mulatto and quadroon (one-quarter black) heroines. Even to this day, it is frequently stated that the 'beautiful' Chloe is mulatto.

Notably, however, the ghost seen by both the tourist and by Kermeen does not seem to fit the now-standard description of Chloe. The figure they claimed to have seen was a 'large, homely woman with a very square jaw'. She was older and matronly – more in keeping with the stereotypical black 'Mammy' figure – thus, not a logical love match for Judge Woodruff. It seems, then, that at the beginning of Kermeen's tenure, Chloe and the younger, more attractive, poison-wielding slave were two separate entities. But they would soon meld together.

By the mid-1980s, the story had solidified. Appearing in a number of magazine and newspaper articles around this time, the Chloe (sometimes misprinted as Cleo) narrative read as follows: Judge Woodruff had an affair with one of his slaves and the trouble began when he broke it off… Chloe reacted by telling the owner's wife, and one of her ears was cut off as punishment. Chloe then poisoned the household food for revenge, and the result was that she killed three of the residents, including two children.

At this point, we have all the main beats of the modern story. We're just missing some of its colour and specificity. This would come in Joan Bingham and Dolores Riccio's 1989 true ghost story anthology, *Haunted Houses USA*, which was apparently the first publication to cite poisonous oleander in a birthday cake as Chloe's method of murder. The authors describe Chloe as 'exquisite'; her relationship with Woodruff as 'a torrid affair'; and the ear-severing punishment as Chloe's 'final humiliation', leading her to exact revenge on the judge's wife and 'two adorable towheaded daughters' (in fact, it was a boy and a girl who died in 1824).

For the next decade or so, this would be the canonical narrative. Throughout most of the 1990s, Chloe remained the beautiful temptress, the willing homewrecker, the spurned lover turned spiteful killer. But then, somewhere around the year 2000, her story evolved once more.

The popular true ghost story anthologies of the early 2000s proffered a new modus operandi for Chloe. In books like Barbara Sillery's *The Haunting of Louisiana* (2001) and Alan Brown's *Haunted Places in the American South* (2002), it is suggested for the first time that Chloe might not have deliberately murdered Sarah Matilda and her children, but instead had simply wanted to make them ill. How and why Chloe came to lose her ear also becomes a much more central part of the narrative. She didn't simply confront Mrs Woodruff about her husband's infidelity, nor was she eavesdropping out of sheer nosiness. She was desperately trying to gather information that might somehow help her maintain her position. And when caught, she was viciously disfigured for what would seem to the modern reader to be a fairly minor infraction. Thus, it was now possible to view Chloe as the victim rather than the villain.

Present-day visitors to the Myrtles are presumably far more attuned to the fact that Chloe, if she did exist, could never have been the duplicitous homewrecker she was previously made out to be. As a slave – and in some versions of the story, a fourteen-year-old girl – she could have neither refused nor consented to her owner's sexual advances. She could only have endured them.

This latest revision of the Chloe narrative suggests a greater societal awareness of the harsh realities of slavery. And while the story might be entirely fictional and told within the context of a commercial recreational activity, it nevertheless addresses some hard truths, however indirectly.

The story of Chloe can never really be considered a 'true story' in the strictest sense. Unless some intrepid sleuth succeeds where others have failed and definitively proves her existence, Chloe, the green-turbaned slave, will remain a myth. But even if she isn't real, her described experience is *very* real. Every element of her modern narrative is backed up by the historical record.

Let's begin with a seemingly superficial detail: the green turban. It is known that among African Americans in the antebellum South, the turban served a practical, as well as a decorative, and even symbolic, purpose. According to costume historians and scholars of material culture, the turban or headwrap was initially worn by both enslaved black men and women. For those toiling in the fields, it helped to protect their heads from the elements, whisked sweat away from the face, and helped to reduce the spread of head lice.

Over time, however, it became the standard headwear for African American women, especially those who worked in privileged positions in the plantation household. Whereas female field slaves would don kerchiefs – and in some jurisdictions were legally mandated to wear them, both to signify their enslaved status and to conceal their hair, thus diffusing their alluring femininity – house slaves (as well as free women of colour) would wear more decorative headwraps called 'tignons'. These were scarves in luxurious fabrics and deep colours, often ornamented with ribbons, brooches or beads.

Chloe's turban signified her elevated station: as a house slave (and a possible favourite of her master), she was afforded a headdress dyed with a richer, more expensive pigment. In a fictional context, the hue could symbolise her jealous nature, or may even be a tacit reference to her method of murder – 'arsenic green' was a popular pigment in the nineteenth century and the poisonous oleander plant was known to have similar properties to arsenic. At any rate, it's perfectly plausible that a female house slave at the Myrtles might have worn a green turban.

It's equally plausible, perhaps even probable, that said slave might have been subjected to the sexual advances of her owner. Even the much hallowed Founding Father Thomas Jefferson – who once described slavery as a 'hideous blot' on the history of mankind – had sexual relations with his slaves, resulting in his siring as many as six illegitimate children. It's commonly believed that Jefferson was in a long-term romantic relationship with one of his female house slaves, Sally Hemmings, and it's possible that their bond was based on mutual affection. But because she remained a slave for the entirety of his life, she could never have fully consented to the arrangement.

Such relationships were, at best, unbalanced and coercive – and at worst, abusive.

One of the most harrowing first-hand accounts of sexual abuse experienced by a female slave comes from Harriet Jacobs in her memoir *Incidents in the Life of a Slave Girl* (1861). Jacobs was born into slavery in 1813 in Edenton, North Carolina, where she spent her childhood in the service of a fairly progressive white woman, who treated her humanely and even taught her to read and write. However, when Jacobs was twelve her 'kind mistress sickened and died', and she was soon sent to work for the household of one of her late owner's relatives, a wealthy physician and plantation owner, referred to in the memoir as 'Dr Flint' (a pseudonym for one Dr James Norcom). In a few short years, Jacobs' life changed irrevocably.

'I now entered my fifteenth year – a sad epoch in the life of a slave girl,' she writes. 'My master began to whisper foul words in my ear ... I turned from him with disgust and hatred. But he was my master.'

Though she was young, Jacobs evidently knew that she had no power to refuse the doctor. 'I was compelled to live under the same roof with him – where I saw a man forty years my senior daily violating the most sacred commandments of nature. He told me I was his property, that I must be subject to his will in all things.'

Jacobs never explicitly describes these 'things', but her trauma is palpable. Her most poignant passage, reflecting on the shared experience of sexually exploited female slaves, reads as follows:

> *[Every slave girl] will learn before she is twelve years old why it is that her mistress hates such-and-such among the slaves ... She will become prematurely knowing in evil things and soon she will tremble when she hears her master's footfall. She will be compelled to realise that she is no longer a child. If God has bestowed beauty upon her, it will prove her greatest curse.*

The women who found themselves in this unenviable position had only a few options. They could attempt an escape (as Jacobs managed successfully in 1842); they could accept their fate and try to make the most of their ostensibly more comfortable lives in the plantation household (as it is often suggested that the fictional Chloe did);

or they could take matters into their own hands (again, something that has been attributed to Chloe). The latter was obviously the most extreme and least common course of action, but it did happen. There are several well-documented cases of female slaves violently retaliating against their masters and mistresses.

The best-known example is the case of Celia, a nineteen-year-old slave living on a cattle farm in Calloway County, Missouri. On the night of 23 June 1855, she bludgeoned her master to death with a stick. On her arrest, she claimed that she had acted out of self-defence: that her owner, Robert Newsom, had been assaulting her for years, and that, on this night, she had repeatedly implored him to stop on account of her pregnancy. Her trial became a national *cause célèbre* – not because such incidents were all that unusual, but because it was one of the first times in American history that an enslaved black woman had attempted to mount a defence based on rape. Ultimately, however, she was found guilty and sentenced to hang on 10 October 1855.

Sexual abuse wasn't the only thing that drove female slaves to violence. Fear of physical punishment was probably the most common motive for both enslaved men and women. Weary from daily drudgery, worn down by regular insults, humiliation and torment, exasperated by the sheer injustice of it all – an enslaved woman might snap for any number of reasons. This could manifest in an outburst of physical violence, or it might take the form of a more quietly destructive act – arson, perhaps, or the use of poison.

One of the more sensational criminal trials on record in the American South is the case of Jenny, an enslaved woman from Johnston County, North Carolina, who in November 1780 was charged in the poisoning deaths of four members of the Bryan family. Where the fictional Chloe stood trial before her peers and was put to death in the far more conventional manner of hanging, Jenny was tried and convicted by the county and was sentenced to death by burning. On 18 November 1780, just two weeks after her trial commenced, Jenny became the penultimate American convict to be burned at the stake.

Though they are historically verifiable, the above examples of crime and punishment in the antebellum South are not exactly indicative of the norm. Most slaves didn't bludgeon, strangle or poison their owners, and very few met an end quite so grisly as Jenny's. But that certainly doesn't mean their lives were free from violence.

This brings us to Chloe's disfigurement. Was the severing of an ear a normal form of punishment for a slave? Would slave-owners routinely perform acts of mutilation for disciplinary or power-asserting purposes? Unfortunately, yes. Records indicate that this was depressingly common. With varying degrees of severity, enslaved African Americans throughout the South were subjected to what can best be described as 'human branding' – bodily defacement designed to make a mark, send a message, or sometimes just to inflict pain.

At the extreme end of the scale, there were the sadistic practices of slave-owners like Delphine LaLaurie, a wealthy socialite from New Orleans. If ever you travel to the city and go on one of the many ghost walks on offer, you will inevitably hear about the infamous Madame LaLaurie and her house of horrors (now reputed to be exceptionally haunted). It's a three-storey French Empire-style townhouse located on Royal Street in the heart of the historic French Quarter, the city's main tourist district. On 10 April 1834 the house caught fire, attracting a large crowd of curious onlookers. At the time, the LaLaurie Mansion was renowned for its decadent interiors, lavish parties – and something more insidious. Rumours swirled that LaLaurie treated her slaves exceptionally cruelly (which is saying a lot given that, at the time, most slave-owners thought nothing of whipping their workers). These rumours would soon prove true.

News reports that appeared in local papers the following day stated that bystanders who tried to help extinguish the fire had attempted to access the slave quarters in the attic to ensure that everyone had been evacuated safely. When LaLaurie refused to hand over the key to the locked room, the bystanders broke down the door and found 'seven slaves more or less horribly mutilated ... suspended by the neck, with their limbs apparently stretched and torn from one extremity to the other'. It seems that LaLaurie hadn't intended to simply kill the slaves; instead, she meant to keep them 'in existence to prolong their suffering'.

Madame LaLaurie was driven out of New Orleans by an angry mob, suggesting that her actions were considered beyond the pale. In contemporary accounts, as well as in modern history textbooks and popular ghost stories, LaLaurie is portrayed as a monstrous aberration. But her acts of cruelty were not unprecedented; they just usually happened behind closed doors. The only thing that might have made her conduct truly extraordinary was the fact that she was a woman – and even then, it might not.

In a chapter in Harriet Jacobs' memoir entitled 'Sketches of Neighbouring Slaveholders', the author describes the various ways in which a slave-owner might torture their slaves. Though she was never subjected to such treatment, she was perfectly aware that it was going on all around her.

'There was a planter in the country, not far from us, whom I will call Mr Litch,' Jacobs recalls. 'He was an ill-bred, uneducated man, but very wealthy. He had 600 slaves, many of whom he did not know by sight.' According to Jacobs, on account of Litch's wealth and powerful connections, he had no fear of being held accountable for his actions, and in consequence, habitually acted with callous impunity.

'Various were the punishments he resorted to,' she says. 'A favourite one was to tie a rope round a man's body and suspend him from the ground. A fire was kindled over him, from which was suspended a piece of fat pork. As this cooked, the scalding drops of fat continually fell on his bare flesh.'

Then there was Mrs Wade, another neighbour. 'At no hour of the day was there cessation of the lash on her premises,' Jacobs reports. 'Her labours began with the dawn, and did not cease till long after nightfall. The barn was her particular place of torture. There she lashed the slaves with the might of a man.'

At other nearby properties, slaves were reportedly branded, flayed, attacked by bloodthirsty dogs, and left naked and tied to trees overnight in inclement weather. Jacobs admits that this type of treatment was publicly frowned upon and that slave-owners would usually conceal their conduct from the community. But enslaved people talked, and thus, Jacobs knew of these dark deeds, and lived to tell about them.

In other contexts, however, injuring slaves was not only openly acknowledged but also discussed in remarkably casual terms.

When slaves went on the run, their owners would often place 'missing persons' reports in local and regional newspapers. In these notices, descriptions including clothing, personality traits and distinguishing physical features would be listed. Jacobs' report read as follows:

> *A $100 reward will be given for the apprehension and delivery of my servant girl, Harriet. She is a light mulatto, 21 years of age, about five feet four inches... She speaks easily and fluently and has an agreeable carriage and address. Being a good seamstress, she has been accustomed to dress well and has a variety of fine clothes made in the prevailing fashions...*

This was a fairly lengthy and flattering description of a missing slave. Most others read like this: 'Ran away, a black girl named Mary. Has a scar on her cheek, and the end of one of her toes cut off' or 'Ran away, Anthony. One of his ears cut off, and his left hand cut with an axe' or 'Ran away, the following negroes: Randal, has one ear cropped; Bob, has lost one eye; Kentucky Tom, has one jaw broken'. In notices like these, the disfigurement of slaves is treated as an objective, common, physical descriptor.

From these accounts, the mythical Chloe emerges as a figure very much grounded in historical reality. Everything – from her appearance to her experience of physical and sexual abuse to her reactionary course of action – rings true. Perhaps the most intriguingly authentic element of it all is the fact that she is now said to take the form of a ghost.

Though it wasn't something that slave-owners openly admitted, there are numerous reports from freed black men and women that plantation owners lived in perpetual fear of the avenging spirits of their deceased slaves. One evocative account comes from Sophia Word, a formerly enslaved woman from Clay County, Kentucky, who remembers a slave-owner from a neighbouring plantation who was exceptionally cruel: he whipped one slave 'most to death for forgetting to put onions in the stew'. Several days after the whipping, the woman was reportedly found drowned in the river in an apparent act of suicide. 'The master could never live in that house again,' Word claimed, as each night he would wake to see his victim standing over his bed. 'He then moved to Richmond, where he stayed a while until he later hanged himself.'

So maybe Chloe never really existed, but clearly, plenty of others like her did, some of whom might have stuck around to remind us of their horrific mistreatment.

The waking nightmare

We began this chapter with Frances Kermeen's alleged paranormal encounter at the Myrtles. She describes being asleep in her bedroom when she suddenly hears the footsteps of an unknown presence in the hallway outside her door. Finding that she can't sleep, she goes to a different room, mistakenly assuming that this environment will be more conducive to peaceful slumber. Kermeen is then accosted by the green turban-sporting spectre. This would seem to be a truly extraordinary event. Something, one would imagine, that few others could claim to have experienced. Yet it's actually a fairly regular occurrence – and not just at the Myrtles Plantation, but at scores of other haunted houses across America and beyond. Why is this? Why do ghosts most commonly come to us in our bedrooms? Well, aside from any paranormal causes, there may be neurological, psychological or even evolutionary explanations for such phenomena.

Before delving into these potential causes, let's first review a few of the numerous reports of nocturnal visitations at the Myrtles. Right from the beginning, in the earliest published account of ghostly activity at the plantation in the 1940s, it is said that an apparition (the 'French lady') approaches visitors in their beds. Similar encounters were reported over the following decades, right up to the present day.

Contemporary accounts include a female guest who awoke several times throughout the night feeling 'like someone was bent over me … watching me while I slept'; a male guest who described the feeling of something 'sitting on his chest', pinning him to the bed, making it impossible for him to move; a female guest who 'couldn't sleep all night because she kept hearing heart-wrenching sobs coming from the walls'; and most dramatically, a male guest who awoke from a nightmare to find 'a black lady in old-time clothing sitting at the foot of his bed, washing his foot [in] a water bowl'.

They're all slightly different, varying in degrees of frightfulness, but they all roughly correspond with a classic form of paranormal encounter that has been related throughout the ages and across the globe. The entity who appears (or makes their presence known) at the foot of a person's bed or in their bedchamber, often causing feelings of dread, sadness or powerlessness.

In medieval and post-Reformation England, these entities were known as 'night hags' – demonic creatures who immobilised their victims by sitting on their chests, much like the ancient mythical creature the 'incubus' or 'succubus', who did so for sexual purposes. In Germanic and Scandinavian folklore, the being is referred to as a 'mare' (from which we get the English term 'nightmare'), a malevolent female spirit who is said to visit people's bedrooms at night to 'ride' their chests, causing them to experience frightening dreams. In Islam, the entities are traditionally believed to be evil 'jinns', or spirits, who are usually invisible, but who can take the form of humans, animals or beasts. And in Thai folklore, it is a ghost called Phi Am who has the power to injure, and even suffocate, his sleeping victims.

The list goes on. These spectral night visitors are literally universal. And while their ubiquity might suggest that they are very real and omnipresent around the world, modern medical professionals tend to think there's a neurological rather than a supernatural cause: that those who experience these entities are actually suffering from some form of parasomnia or sleep disorder.

One of the most common explanations for nocturnal supernatural experiences offered by sceptics is sleep paralysis – a common (and generally harmless) event that can occur when a person is in the process of falling asleep or waking up. For a brief period, the mind will be conscious, while the body remains in a state of full paralysis. The person may experience pressure on the chest, difficulty breathing and generalised feelings of anxiety.

If you don't know what is happening to you, this debilitating sensation would naturally frighten you. But why would it cause you to hallucinate a ghost or demon? According to psychologist Ciaren O'Keeffe, a lecturer at Buckinghamshire New University, this could be your brain's way of trying to make sense of something it doesn't understand.

'It provides you with a scary outcome or interpretation,' he explains. 'Why? Because you are vulnerable and helpless and your brain is trying to determine why.' As a form of self-protection, your brain decides that there is an imminent threat. Depending on your cultural background, personal circumstances or environment, your brain will create an individualised form of threat or distress.

Studies show that certain factors might increase your chances of having an episode of sleep paralysis – or a similar parasomnia, such as night terrors or sleep-related hallucinations. Chronic sleep deprivation, jet lag, the consumption of alcohol or caffeine prior to bedtime, underlying anxiety or an unsuitable sleeping environment can all lead to episodes of parasomnia.

When you stop to think about it, there are few settings where one might be more likely to experience this than a place like the Myrtles: a tourist destination where rich food is plentiful and liquor flows freely in the adjacent restaurant; an atmospheric old home alleged to be haunted, with creaky floors, (somewhat) uncomfortable beds and the constant din of fellow ghost-hunting guests and staff, who are more than likely working to reinforce the expectation of a supernatural experience, rather than diminish it.

But not all nocturnal ghostly encounters can be explained away by the effects of a sleep-related neurological misfiring. There may be an even more basic explanation. As humans – and mammals – we are conditioned to believe that in order to sleep we must be in a safe environment free from predators. For pack animals like wolves, this means safety in numbers. And indeed, for much of human history, people have also slept communally. Even today, in many parts of the world, it is far more common than sleeping alone. But for the past few centuries in the West, most people – or at least, most middle- and upper-class people – have slept alone, apart from a singular bed partner, thus making them both literally and psychologically vulnerable. So again, as a form of self-protection, a person's brain might conjure imagined threats in order to keep them alert to danger.

At the plantation house, the sleeping occupant is especially susceptible. Historically, even when plantation owners were alone in their bedchambers, they were never completely alone in their homes. There would always have been an interloping 'other' lurking somewhere inside: the house slave. Perhaps this was simply a benevolent living presence, or maybe it was an embittered one who presented more of a threat. Or maybe, just maybe, it was a dead one – a vengeful spirit who remained forever tethered to the house to wreak havoc on its sleeping occupants.

In any event, the plantation owner would have to remain vigilant, regularly searching the murky shadows of their bedroom for signs of danger. And while the modern owner or overnight guest of a plantation house would have no rational cause for concern, they may still feel a certain level of anxiety when the lights go out and they can't quite see what may or may not be hiding in the darkness.

When it comes down to it, the haunted plantation house – like so many other iterations of the haunted house – is a manifestation of our collective fear of 'the enemy within'. And in this case, the 'enemy' has every reason to be hostile.

RAYNHAM HALL

THE DEATH OF THE ENGLISH COUNTRY HOUSE

6

> The paradox of the English country house is that its state of permanent decline, the fact that its heyday is always behind it, is part of the seduction.
>
> *Lev Grossman (1969–)*

The Brown Lady of Raynham Hall

It was late in the afternoon on 19 September 1936, and Indre Shira, a London-based photographer, and his art director, Hubert C. Provand, were setting up one of their final shots of the day. They were at Raynham Hall in Norfolk on an assignment for *Country Life* magazine, a forty-year-old weekly periodical devoted to rural leisure pursuits and upmarket properties. Richly illustrated editorials focusing on aristocratic estates were a staple of the publication, and Shira and Provand had been tasked with taking the photos for their feature on Raynham, the country seat of the Townshend family for the past 300 years.

Though consummate professionals who wouldn't dream of rushing their task, the two men were beginning to pick up their pace. It had been a long day that had started around 8 a.m. Now it was around 4 p.m. and the optimal light for photography in an already dim space was fast beginning to fade. If they were going to get their shot of the hall's grand oak staircase, this was the time.

They positioned themselves at the bottom of the stairs and began preparing the camera – what they would later describe as 'an old stand camera' with a possibly 'faulty bellows' and a lens with a six-second exposure time, supplemented by a flash bulb. Whether or not the device was defective in any way, it had allowed the men to work productively for the previous eight hours, so they had no reason to believe it would fail them now.

With Provand behind the camera and Shira operating the flash, they took their first shot. No problem; nothing out of the ordinary.

Provand then began setting up for another exposure, when suddenly Shira saw something. 'All at once, I detected an ethereal, veiled form coming slowly down the stairs,' he would later allege. 'Rather excitedly I called out sharply "Quick! Quick! There's something there … take the photo!"'

On an ordinary autumn day in the early twentieth century, two photographers for a glossy lifestyle magazine had unwittingly captured what many believe to be the fabled Brown Lady of Raynham Hall, one of the most famous ghosts in Britain.

At its apogee in the eighteenth century, the stately red-brick manor house, Raynham Hall in north Norfolk, was renowned for its innovative architecture, expansive art collection and powerful owner. Constructed in the early 1600s, the house was expanded a century later by famed Palladian architect William Kent, under the direction of Charles, 2nd Viscount Townshend. At the time, Lord Townshend was one of the most influential men in the country; a former prominent Tory turned Whig statesman, he served as the leader of the House of Lords under his brother-in-law, Prime Minister Robert Walpole. Only 7 miles down the road from Walpole's extravagant family seat of Houghton, Townshend's own 62-room mansion was a clear testament to his immense wealth and power.

But by the end of the nineteenth century, Raynham Hall and the Townshend family had fallen on hard times. A major agricultural depression, combined with a series of personal misfortunes, had led to Raynham's *fin-de-siècle* downfall.

In 1899 John, 6th Marquess Townshend, inherited a bankrupt estate, and was forced to sell off much of the family's priceless art collection, rent out the hall, and find a rich wife – which he did in August 1905, marrying Gwladys Sutherst, the daughter of a London lawyer. It wouldn't be until after the 6th Marquess's death in 1921 that the Townshend family would return to its once glittering family seat, and the Dowager Marchioness would take on the onerous task of returning Raynham to its former glory.

Raynham wasn't the only country house to fall into decline during this period. The combined effects of war, increased taxation, financial mismanagement and a declining aristocratic class saw hundreds of such houses either sold off or abandoned. As a result, far more ghost stories about these houses began to circulate. After all, what better recipe was there for a haunting than a history of greatness descended into obscurity: grand old houses, once home to lustre and finery, pomp and power, now standing derelict and empty?

Somewhat miraculously, Raynham Hall managed to survive these challenges with Gwladys, Marchioness Townshend, at the helm. Prudent sales and the gradual easing of the effects of the depression were largely to thank for the avoidance of foreclosure, but Gwladys added to this by actively endorsing the ghostly folklore of the manor, effectively bringing the house back to life. Gwladys's determination to stick it out in dark times and prove that the seat still had a strong connection with its illustrious past would be a saving grace.

As well as allowing *Country Life* to publish the image of the so-called Brown Lady, the marchioness had also penned her own account of the Brown Lady, published less than a year before the release of Shira and Provand's photograph.

So named for her brown silk brocade dress, the apparition made famous by *Country Life* was said to be Lady Dorothy Townshend, the eighteenth-century mistress of the manor, who purportedly died under mysterious circumstances. Reports of her ghost had first emerged in the nineteenth century, and at least a few of the early witnesses were respectable, well-educated visitors to the house who had no reason to make things up.

Today, unlike most heritage properties with well-known ghostly inhabitants, Raynham Hall does not promote the paranormal. It remains privately owned, still inhabited by the Townshend family, headed by the 8th Marquess Townshend. The family earns their keep by means of a vast residential portfolio, agricultural holdings, and a wedding and event business. On the handful of days a year that the manor house is open to the public, visitors are encouraged to explore its architectural wonders, rather than its supernatural ones.

Despite earlier sales, Raynham Hall still retains a significant art collection. And this is how I came to know about the house and its haunting. In 2019, I was a contributor to a scholarly research project called Art in the Country House. Funded by Yale University's Paul Mellon Centre, an educational charity devoted to promoting research in British art history, the Country House project was a collaboration between researchers working at eight stately homes, which would result in an online resource for students interested in country house art collections. As a curator working at Mount Stuart in Scotland, I was among the researchers responsible for supplying information about the Bute Collection, a trove of art treasures added to by various generations of the Bute family, the Earls and Marquesses of Bute. Meanwhile, a group of art and architectural historians working at Raynham Hall were covering the patronage and collecting practices of the Townshend family. For a historian, it was a unique glimpse into the history and general goings-on in British stately homes.

While our research didn't cover any aspects of the paranormal, as the project wore on, our conversation turned, occasionally, to the less highbrow stuff of gossip and intrigue. Stories of eccentric home-owners emerged; cantankerous staff members who presided jealously over archives and art collections as if they were their own; and, of course, ghost stories.

As far as country house ghost stories go, Raynham Hall's Brown Lady is a pretty compelling and well-documented one. The Brown Lady stuck with me long after the country house project had ended – so much so that, when I found myself still thinking about her a couple of years later, I decided to put my scholarly work aside and write an essay about her. This essay subsequently appeared in *Country Life* magazine – the same publication that had printed her ethereal portrait over seventy years earlier.

It was through my research for this article that I realised the most interesting thing about the story was not necessarily the ghost herself (though she *is* delightfully romantic in that classic English country house ghost sort of way). Nor was it the famous photograph, now widely considered to be a fake. Rather, it was the scandalous, almost soap-opera-like rise and fall of the Townshend family, and what I would call the 'afterlife' of their original ghost story – the resurgence in interest in the Brown Lady some 200 years after the death of the actual woman, and a century since her ghost was first sighted.

The Brown Lady's comeback coincided not only with the peak of the spiritualism movement, but also with a period in history that witnessed the slow 'death' of the English country house. A time when, across the nation, formerly great estates were being broken up, sold off, donated and, sometimes, left to crumble. Some of those that clung on looked to their ghosts to get them through.

As with the American plantation houses, English country house ghost stories from the first half of the twentieth century were used to illustrate a home's heritage and to harken back to a previous golden age. These ghost stories were their swansong – a last-ditch effort to keep the past alive.

Dorothy Townshend, later known as the Brown Lady, was the thirteenth child of Robert and Mary Walpole of Houghton Hall, aunt of Horace Walpole and wife of Charles, 2nd Viscount Townshend. Relatively little is known about Dorothy's life but that she was born on 18 September 1686 at Houghton and that at some point in the summer of 1717 she married Lord Townshend and moved into their marital home of Raynham Hall, where she remained until her death in March 1726.

How she died is a matter of conjecture. Her official cause of death is listed as smallpox, but it has long been rumoured that this was a cover-up; that she was actually the victim of foul play at the hands of her hot-tempered husband who, in the context of his political career, was described as being 'abrasive, stubborn, impatient, and overbearing'. Historians have characterised him as a 'passionate man who loved and hated quickly and rarely changed his mind once an opinion had been formed'.

Some say it was Lady Townshend's extravagant spending that incurred his wrath. According to her twentieth-century successor, Gwladys, Marchioness Townshend, '[Dorothy] was a charming and frivolous spendthrift, with a pardonable love for pretty clothes, judging from a lengthy bill for chiffons which is kept among our family papers.'

Others believe that Lady Townshend had discovered her husband's infidelity. But the most common version of the story by far is that it was Charles who discovered Dorothy's unfaithfulness. That he learned of her affair with the Duke of Wharton, a notorious rake and philanderer, and in the ultimate act of revenge, sent away their children and locked her in a bedchamber until she starved to death.

The fact that Dorothy's children were removed from the house and that she was locked in her room arguably gives more credence to death by a contagious disease, marked by social distancing and quarantine, rather than death by revenge. At any rate, this is the now-standard iteration of the legend.

Based on her alleged manner of death, it was perhaps inevitable that Lady Townshend would go on to haunt Raynham Hall. As we know from previous haunted house narratives, immurement (the act of confining someone in enclosed quarters until death) is a sure-fire way to create a ghost.

One of the earliest recorded sightings of Lady Townshend was by Colonel Charles Loftus, a naval officer and relation of the Townshends. Sources differ on when exactly his encounter occurred, with some claiming it was as early as 1835 and others as late as 1849. But in any case, it was on a December night at some point in the first half of the nineteenth century, when Loftus was staying at Raynham Hall following a family Christmas party. After a long game of chess that lasted into the wee hours of the morning, he and his friendly competitor decided to retire to bed. As they mounted the main staircase together, they spotted a lady in an old-fashioned brown silk dress standing on the upper landing. She mysteriously vanished upon their approach.

Being a hardened veteran, Colonel Loftus wasn't frightened. Rather, he was curious and determined to get to the bottom of the mystery. The following night, he held watch in a position in the upstairs corridor, where he was relatively certain that the figure – should she make another appearance – could not make an easy retreat. His military-like stakeout proved successful and after a short while, he caught sight of her again: 'A handsome woman, dressed in brown – but to his horror, [she] had two empty eye sockets representing the place where her eyes should have been.'

Loftus later made a sketch of the woman, which was said to look remarkably similar to a portrait of Lady Dorothy Townshend in a brown dress, then still in the family art collection. Unfortunately, neither the original portrait nor the spectral sketch survive.

The next notable sighting of Lady Townshend – now dubbed the Brown Lady – occurred in the early 1840s. The witness was another family friend, and as it happens, also a military veteran: Captain

Frederick Marryat, a former naval officer turned novelist, whose accomplishments included service in the Napoleonic War and the War of 1812, and a lifelong friendship with Charles Dickens (a known sceptic with an ironic love for ghost stories).

Marryat had heard of Raynham's ghost, and for a lark, he asked to sleep in the house's most haunted room. He intended to prove that the 'ghost' was simply a disgruntled ex-employee or some other intruder playing tricks on the Townshends. His hosts obliged and put him in Lady Townshend's former quarters, where the portrait of her in her trademark brown dress hung above the bed. He stayed for two nights without incident, sleeping with a pistol under his pillow. On the third night, however, a couple of the young Townshend boys knocked on Marryat's door to inform him of a disturbance in the corridor.

According to a later recounting of the event penned by Marryat's daughter, Florence, her father came out into the hall in his night-clothes, armed with his pistol. 'The corridor was long and dark, for the lights had been extinguished, but as they reached the middle of it, they saw the glimmer of a lamp coming towards them from the other end. My father was in shirt and trousers only, and his native modesty made him feel uncomfortable, so he slipped within one of the outer doors in order to conceal himself until the lady should have passed by,' she wrote, in a slightly bizarre elucidation of Victorian decorum that placed propriety over fear of home invaders.

'He watched her approaching nearer and nearer until, as she was close enough for him to distinguish the colour and style of her costume, he recognised the figure as the facsimile of the portrait of the Brown Lady.' Just as Marryat was about to demand that the mysterious figure stop and explain themselves, the presence 'halted of its own accord and, holding the lighted lamp to her features, grinned in a malicious and diabolical manner at him'. Alarmed by this reaction, the trigger-happy Marryat 'discharged the revolver right in her face and the figure instantly disappeared … the bullet passing through the door and lodging in the panel of the door opposite'.

Evidently, no mortal weapon could impede the Brown Lady.

A decade went by before the next witness came forward: Lady Anne Sherson, the eldest daughter of the future 4th Marquess of Townshend, was attending a New Year's Eve ball at Raynham on 31

December 1855, when she and several other attendees were 'surprised to see a small lady dressed in an antique costume passing through the throng without apparently knowing anybody'. While this sighting wasn't nearly as unsettling as the previous ones, it did bring with it some disturbing news as, by this point, it was commonly believed that the appearance of the Brown Lady was a portent of death. Lo and behold, the following day, the household was informed of the unexpected passing of Lord George Townshend, the disgraced 3rd Marquess, then in exile in Genoa (more on him later).

There are a handful of other nineteenth-century reports, though none that come with verifiable dates or witnesses. There is said to have been a pair of unnamed gentlemen visitors who caught sight of the Brown Lady walking away from them down a corridor.

'I say, look! There's a pretty figure in her evening dress,' one of the men supposedly remarked to the other.

'Who can she be?' the second man pondered.

'She certainly has an exquisite figure; I wish she would give us a glimpse of her face,' said the first.

Hardly had he finished speaking when the lady turned and looked at them. But the eyes were void of all speculation. The beautiful Brown Lady had only a death's head.

Serves them right for leering, I say.

Following Lady Sherson's (somewhat more) verifiable account of 1855, the Brown Lady lay dormant for more than half a century. Or at least, she didn't crop up in personal correspondence, memoirs or the society pages of newspapers and periodicals. It's possible that she was still making her presence known to the living occupants of Raynham Hall, but as we will learn, the Townshends had, by then, far bigger concerns than a sporadically appearing spectre.

When she did finally make her re-entry into ghostly high society, the Brown Lady had had a makeover. Where before she had been a menacing figure with a death-like visage, who often brought ill tidings and seemed to delight in tormenting male house guests (perhaps proxies for her 'abusive' husband), by the twentieth century, she was utterly benign: ethereal, graceful and demure, rarely, if ever, interacting with those who encountered her.

This probably had much to do with the fact that the Brown Lady's main champion – and *de facto* publicist – Gwladys, Marchioness

Townshend, felt sympathy for the historical personage she viewed as a 'charming' yet ultimately tragic figure. Marchioness Townshend didn't put much stock in the classic story of Dorothy Townshend's immurement, although she could imagine a scenario in which her predecessor was in a loveless marriage, and had possibly endured a bleak, isolated existence in the Norfolk countryside, devoid of contact with her children and much of the outside world.

In her essay in *True Ghost Stories* (a 1936 anthology edited by Townshend and one Maude Ffoulkes, Townshend remarks: 'I have accepted the story of [Dorothy's] starvation as being symbolical of [her] tragedy of starved affections, which always represents such a terrible death-in-life.'

Gwladys clearly felt sorry for Dorothy. But she also knew how to put her to good use. 'The unhappy wife and mother has now become the Family Ghost,' the Marchioness writes, implying both a sense of ownership and familial connection with the apparition. 'She chiefly confines her appearances to the principal staircase and some of the corridors at Raynham Hall.'

The former location was a serendipitous one, given that this was where the *Country Life* photographers later captured her image. It was also on a staircase that Lady Townshend's nephew, Horace Walpole, caught sight of the 'ghost' that would inspire him to write the first ever Gothic novel. However tenuous, the Brown Lady's purported manifestation on the staircase worked as a subtle reminder of her illustrious lineage and, in turn, the living Townshends' link to historic greatness.

It had long been considered an asset for an aristocratic household to have a resident family ghost. After all, having a ghost meant having a history. And now more than ever, having a ghost was invaluable to once great families desperately clinging to their ancestral homes. So, the Brown Lady of Raynham Hall ceased to be scary and instead became a comforting reminder of happier times. Not that it was all that happy for poor old Dorothy, of course, but her epoch did represent the Townshend family's heyday.

*

Family (mis)fortune: the rise and fall of Raynham Hall

Writing in 1658, Sir Thomas Browne, a Norfolk-based physician, esoteric author and general polymath, described Raynham Hall as 'the noblest pyle among us'. Its reputation was not just due to its sheer size or modish architectural style, but also because of the prominence of the family that lived in and owned it. Prior to the eighteenth-century ascendency of the Walpoles at nearby Houghton Hall, the Townshends were situated at the top of the local hierarchy, and their seat at Raynham was the most important centre of politics and patronage in Norfolk for nearly a century.

How and why some families in Britain were able to rise above their provincial neighbours to become regional powerheads – and often political leaders with national influence – is complex, and there was no one set path for the pursuit of familial greatness. Shrewd spending and investment, charismatic politicking, military victory, intelligence, good looks and royal favour could all help. Generally speaking, however, it came down to being in the right place at the right time – and perhaps most crucially, forming alliances with the right people. This was how many men, including the Townshend patriarchs, got their families to the top. Once they got there, though, their position was by no means secure. At every turn, their enemies were poised to topple them. But if they played their cards right, they might be able to hold on just long enough to secure a comfortable legacy for their descendants.

The Townshend family has owned land in northern Norfolk since the twelfth century. For a good portion of the family's early dynastic history, they were minor country squires, living comfortably yet modestly, seldom venturing outside their own county for several generations. And while there was no obvious indication of their future greatness, there were glimmering signs of possibility. They already possessed a key ingredient for success: land in exactly the right place.

Prior to the Norman Conquest of 1066, much of the marshy lowlands of East Anglia had been converted into productive farmland, making it a desirable area for settlement. According to the Domesday survey conducted at the behest of William the Conqueror in the 1080s, Norfolk and the neighbouring East Anglian counties of Suffolk and Cambridgeshire were the wealthiest and most densely populated regions in the nation. As we saw in Chapter 3 on Borley Rectory, this resulted in a proliferation of urban centres, ecclesiastical communities, and a thriving wool and textile industry that dominated the British economy for much of the medieval and early modern period.

The medieval Townshends were sheep farmers, but by the fifteenth century they had become titled members of the landed gentry: knights and baronets of Raynham, giving them the honorific title of Sir (or Dame) Townshend. This title wasn't nearly as good as, say, an earldom or viscountcy, which would have given them access to the peerage (lifting them above the official status of commoner) and a hereditary title that could be passed down through the generations. But at least it set them apart from their sheep-farming neighbours.

Over the centuries, the Townshend patriarchs gradually turned their attention away from land management towards careers in law and politics. The founder of the family fortune was Sir Roger Townshend, a prominent lawyer who sat as MP for Bramber in West Sussex in 1467 and, around that time, began to expand his lucrative Norfolk estate. Sir Roger got the ball rolling, but it wasn't until the mid-1600s that his great-great-great-grandson Horatio took things to the next level.

Young Horatio grew up in strange and exciting times. He came of age during the interregnum – the period between the English Civil War and the Restoration – and while he was serving as MP for Norfolk in Oliver Cromwell's Protectorate Parliament, he felt the winds of change. He and others knew that opinion now swayed in favour of the return of the monarchy. Because Horatio was in his mid-twenties and only a country squire with little importance in the grand scheme of things, he wasn't viewed as a serious threat to potential political enemies, so he was able to slip under the radar. The strategic importance of Horatio's home county of Norfolk, with its industrial wealth and major North Sea ports, coupled with his overlooked political savvy, made him a key ally for the restoration of Charles II.

For his service to the crown, Horatio was made 1st Baron Townshend in 1661, then 1st Viscount Townshend in 1682 – at long last raising his family from provincial plebes to members of the nobility.

The house that the future 1st Viscount Townshend inherited in 1648 lacked a certain something. Raynham Hall was large, yes, and it was said to have been designed by Inigo Jones, the architect widely credited with bringing classicism to England. However, when Horatio got his hands on it, the house was bare and incomplete. Something had to be done to transform it into a house befitting of a nobleman. Though the 1st Viscount made few structural changes to the existing house – a three-storey brick structure with stone accents and Dutch gables, set in an H-plan design – he spent a considerable sum on interior decoration. He commissioned monumental full-length portraits of himself, resplendent in his peer's robes, and his wife, Mary, draped in swathes of satin, from Sir Peter Lely, the leading portraitist of the day. He dressed the walls of the state rooms with tapestries and expensive textiles such as damask. And he splashed out on an array of luxury items, including a set of silver plates engraved with his newly created coat of arms; a dozen spoons 'of the Italian fashion'; a suite of silk-upholstered chairs custom-made for a royal visit from Charles II; and a pair of pricey 'screw turne Damaske' pistols (guns made from Damascus steel, a metal prized for its strength and intricate patterning).

What might have seemed like conspicuous consumption actually served a practical purpose. The 1st Viscount was planning for the future – laying the foundations for a collection of family heirlooms. That he placed importance on passing down the family seat fully intact is evidenced by a line in his will which stipulated that 'all jewells, plate, household stuffs ... armes and other my goods ... should not be sold or severed from Raynham Hall upon any occasion or pretence whatsoever'. He would have surely been most displeased by the contradictory course of action taken by his late-nineteenth-century descendants.

Thanks to Horatio's careful management of his property and his political connections, his son, Charles, was able to take over a stable, lucrative estate when he ascended to the viscountcy in 1687. Like his father before him, the 2nd Viscount pursued a career in politics, but he was not satisfied with the limited power that came with being a local MP; he sought a position with national – even international – influence.

In 1709, Queen Anne appointed Townshend the ambassador to the Dutch States-General, an important diplomatic post in the Hague, where, during the War of Spanish Succession, Townshend was responsible for brokering peace talks between the warring nations.

On his return to England in 1711, he quickly won the favour of the new King George I, who, in 1714, elected him Secretary of State for the Northern Department. While in this role, Townshend and his colleagues successfully quashed the Scottish revolt known as the Jacobite Rising of 1715. And though, a few years later, he unwittingly earned the displeasure of the king, who had been temporarily led to believe that the viscount and others were involved in a plot to overthrow him in favour of his son, Townshend had by now forged the most powerful alliance of his career. In 1717 he married Dorothy Walpole, the younger sister of his childhood friend and neighbour, Robert, a rising star in the House of Commons.

For nearly a decade, between 1721 and 1730, the British government was firmly in the control of two ambitious upstarts from northern Norfolk. The Walpole–Townshend ministry saw the former serving as Chief Minister in the House of Commons and the latter the leader of the House of Lords. But it wasn't always a harmonious pairing. Bitterness and jealousy often reared their ugly heads – particularly on the part of Townshend, who was forced to stand by and watch as his old boyhood mate, a social inferior, eclipsed him in terms of wealth and influence. Yet Townshend could still take comfort in the knowledge that his political career had helped to raise his family's profile.

When he finally retired from office in 1730 and returned to Raynham Hall, the viscount found that, while his seat was perhaps no longer the 'noblest pyle' in the county (that honour now went to Walpole's Houghton), it was still inarguably grand. In fact, it was grander than it had been when his father had left it to him, thanks to the expansion and remodelling work he had commissioned architect William Kent to carry out in the latest Palladian style.

Charles shared his father's prudence and his hope that the Raynham estate would remain grand (and lucrative) for generations to come, and devoted his retirement to agricultural improvements. His main claim to fame was his invention of the four-crop rotation method, involving the alternation of wheat, barley, clover and turnip, earning him the nickname 'Turnip Townshend'. It wasn't a glamorous legacy, but it ensured that his tenant farmers were able to keep their fields productive, year in, year out, without a fallow period, guaranteeing them a steady stream of income. And so, for a time anyway, the Townshends would remain at (or near) the top. The same, however, could not be said of their neighbours, the Walpoles. When he died in 1745, Robert, by then 1st Earl of Orford, left an estate that was heavily mortgaged. As a result, his heirs were forced to dispose of his renowned art collection, which was eventually sold to Empress Catherine the Great of Russia in 1778.

For the next several generations, the Townshends of Raynham steered a fairly steady course, though there were peaks and troughs. A high point was the creation of the Townshend marquisate in 1787, when George, 4th Viscount and 1st Marquess Townshend, was rewarded with an elevated title for his military prowess in America during the Seven Years' War and later as Lord Lieutenant of Ireland. A low point was the very public outing and disgrace of George, 3rd Marquess Townshend, whose estranged wife Sarah petitioned the courts for an annulment in 1809 on the grounds that her husband was 'impotent', incapable of producing an heir, and engaged in an affair with his male 'Italian secretary'.

Still, the Townshend family limped on, managing to retain their country seat and all its opulent contents until the close of the nineteenth century, when financial crisis finally hit.

The Townshends' downfall was gradual but largely predictable. They weren't profligate spenders, but they certainly liked nice things, and by the early nineteenth century, they owned four country estates – in Staffordshire, Warwickshire, Hertfordshire and Norfolk. At least two of these boasted grand manor houses, Raynham and Balls Park in Hertford, which were known to contain valuable collections of fine art, furniture, china and other luxury items.

A combination of untimely deaths, scandal and surprisingly liberal values from the 5th Marquess, who was known as 'the beggar's friend', meant that scarcely a century later, the Townshends would be down to just one estate and country house – and they could ill afford even that.

To top it all off, the Raynham estate was forced to endure the agricultural depression that hammered the English countryside throughout the 1880s and 1890s. Poor harvests caused by bad weather; outbreaks of bovine disease; foreign competition that drastically undercut the domestic value of crops such as wheat and corn; rural depopulation – these factors had a devastating impact on landed estates up and down the country. The Townshends were not alone. However, they might have been better equipped to weather the storm if it had not been for their own internal struggles.

On 26 October 1899 John, 6th Marquess Townshend, inherited his family's crumbling estate. He was something of a sorry figure, and not just because of his disastrous financial situation. Frail and sickly, with a diminished capacity for recognising when he was being taken advantage of, the new marquess almost immediately fell into the clutches of a conman who attempted to fleece him under the guise of offering financial advice. The would-be hustler was one Arthur Gregory Robins, the son of a respected cleric and grandson of a prominent London art dealer, whose best-known sale was the 1842 auction of the contents of Horace Walpole's Strawberry Hill House.

Evidently Robins had inherited his grandfather's passion for art, for soon after meeting Townshend and gaining employment as his personal chaplain, he began to develop an unusually intense fascination with his employer's art collection. As the marquess's future wife would later recall, Robins 'displayed one marked characteristic – a frenzied interest in the treasures at Raynham Hall'.

In his capacity as chaplain and advisor, it was Robins who first convinced the marquess to sell items from his family collection. Whether Townshend was strong-armed or genuinely thought it a good idea, he initially permitted Robins to arrange the sale of smaller items, such as china and silver, to private dealers and collectors. This was a somewhat shady undertaking for a couple of reasons. First, Robins had begun to remove items from the house without prior consent. He took these items to London and Brighton to sell on his own, in all likelihood pocketing some of the profits. Second, regardless of whether or not he had Townshend's permission, Robins was technically stealing. Like most aristocratic households – then and now – much of the contents of the Townshend country seat did not literally belong to the incumbent patriarch. Many of the more valuable items (especially those with historical or dynastic significance) would have been placed in a family trust and declared heirlooms. Individual beneficiaries could use and enjoy these objects within their lifetime, but they could not sell them without the consent of 'interested parties' (other family members) and their appointed trustees.

To sell bigger and better items, Robins and the marquess would endeavour to play by the books. The first step for Robins was to convince the marquess to appoint him executor of the Townshend family trust. The next was to draw up a new deed of settlement for Raynham Hall.

According to the terms set out in the Settled Land Act of 1882, as a life tenant, Lord Townshend might be permitted to sell the contents of Raynham if he had no other means of raising capital. By law, however, he'd have to apply to the court for permission, at which point other beneficiaries could raise objections. Robins would still have to persuade the rest of the family to go along with his plan, but he was confident that he could work on that – and, if necessary, convince the court to compel them to do so.

In the meantime, low on liquid assets, Robins attempted to find his employer some fast cash. To accomplish this, he would follow the course that so many other hard-up aristocrats at the turn of the century had taken. He would endeavour to find Townshend a rich American heiress to marry. In the spring of 1902, Townshend and Robins set sail for America on a wife-finding mission – which also apparently involved some ancillary activities on the latter's part, including visits to mesmerists, purportedly in a bid to learn how to exert mind control over the marquess. But the main focus of their sojourn was finding a millionaire bride.

Between 1870 and 1914, 430 American women married into families of the English landed gentry. The Yankee daughters of oil barons, railway tycoons and publishing magnates, in many cases, managed to save the dying dynasties of Great Britain. These included Leonora Bennet, who we met in Chapter 2, the wealthy socialite from Washington state who became the 7th Countess Tankerville of Chillingham Castle. Meanwhile, wealthy Americans also helped by buying up insolvent estates for themselves. The Carnegies of Pennsylvania bought Skibo Castle in Scotland; the Astors of New York bought Hever Castle in Kent; and the Burns family of New Jersey bought North Mymms in Hertfordshire.

While 'Gilded Age' Americans had the money, they evidently felt they lacked the noble lineage of the English landed gentry and all the trappings that came with it. Intriguingly, according to contemporary reports, American tourists and prospective house-buyers were particularly interested in any old pile with a haunting. 'A really well-authenticated ghost fetches a big price,' reckoned one commentator.

It's not clear whether Robins, on behalf of Townshend, talked up the Brown Lady of Raynham Hall in a bid to attract a bride. Perhaps not, as Robins and Townshend ultimately failed in their mission, returning from America empty-handed. Robins subsequently arranged a marriage with Eniza Sheffield, an exotic widow with allegedly noble Spanish ancestry; however, when it was discovered that the future bride was really a penniless barmaid from Southampton, the wedding was called off.

Instead, the 6th Marquess married Gwladys Sutherst, whose barrister father, Thomas, offered to pay Townshend £30,000 in exchange for a title for his only daughter. As it turned out, it was a good choice. Not a love match, perhaps, but a solid selection for the role of marchioness. For although Gwladys lacked a dowry large enough to solve the marquess's money problems indefinitely, she was an intelligent, creative and compassionate woman, dedicated to restoring the Townshends' fortune and reputation.

Gwladys also brought some glamour to Raynham Hall. While she couldn't boast of being a millionaire American heiress or the progeny of Spanish royalty, she could claim to be 'the first peeress to write for cinema'. The marchioness wrote scripts for eight silent films, as well as penning a play, a novel, a book of poetry, an autobiography and, of course, an anthology of 'true' ghost stories. What's more, in 1928 she was elected the first female mayor of King's Lynn, Norfolk. Possibly punching a bit above his weight, Lord Townshend had clearly landed a good catch.

But it wasn't time for them to live 'happily ever after' just yet. The marquess still had to rid himself of the insidious influence of Arthur Robins, who, in December 1903, had successfully petitioned the court for permission to sell much of the contents of Raynham Hall.

The sale held the following March generated approximately £40,000 (or the equivalent of £3 million today), as well as a great deal of public interest. It allowed members of the press and the general population a glimpse into the once opulent lives of a fallen family. A mixture of sympathy and subtle disdain coloured many newspaper reports on the sale, with *The Times* remarking:

> *The predominant feeling, as one looks at this interesting assemblage of historical portraits, is one of regret that they are to leave their old home and to be scattered all over the world. At Raynham, they meant a great deal; they were the authentic illustrations of a great historic past, of the men of one family who through many generations had done noteworthy services to their country.*

If a reporter for *The Times* felt regret, imagine how the Townshends must have felt!

Robins may have been right in recommending the sale of the Raynham heirlooms; it probably was the fastest and easiest way for the family to get out of debt. Yet it doesn't seem that Robins was genuinely acting in his employer's best interests.

Following the successful sale, Robins managed to get himself written into the marquess's will, and appointed as his agent on a ten-year contract with a large salary. Even after Townshend's 1905 marriage to Gwladys, the agent was still skulking around, wielding undue influence – so much so, that, only a few months after returning from honeymoon in Paris, the marquess vacated his marital home in London (Raynham having been previously rented out) in order to move in with Robins and his family in Brighton, for reasons that have never been made clear.

Something had to be done. Perhaps out of parental concern for his daughter – though more likely out of his own selfish financial motives – Thomas Sutherst took drastic (if not criminal) action. He orchestrated a plot to lure the marquess back to London, where he would be locked in a bedroom in his Mayfair mansion until Sutherst could have him declared legally insane. By having him sectioned, Sutherst hoped to keep Robins away and ensure that the marquess didn't give away any more of his money.

In July 1906, an inquest into the mental health of the marquess was held at Lincoln's Inn Old Hall. Following a fortnight of evidence and cross-examination, a verdict was reached: it was determined that, while he was clearly incapable of managing his money, the marquess was not actually insane. A sympathetic judge recognised the manipulative conduct of both Robins and Sutherst, the latter of whom was subsequently struck off the bar for effectively kidnapping his noble son-in-law.

Remarkably, despite the public scandal, the marquess and marchioness reconciled. Together, they would endeavour to set the Townshend estate to rights.

Two years later, in the spring of 1908, they returned to court, seeking to have Robins removed as a trustee on the 'grounds of misappropriating the Townshend heirlooms and financial misconduct'. Again, the judge ruled in the marquess's favour, ordering that the duplicitous former advisor be stripped of his role and pay back the cost of the heirlooms he had sold without consent.

Alas, they would never see a penny. In May 1908 Robins fled the country aboard the SS *Marathon* to Melbourne, Australia, never to return, thus marking an end to a strange and turbulent chapter in the Townshend family's history.

Ruin, reinvention, revival: the fate of the twentieth-century country house

On 13 May 1937, a grand reception was held at Raynham Hall in honour of John, 7th Marquess Townshend's twenty-first birthday. With some 3,000 guests in attendance, including friends, family members, local dignitaries, tenants and various well-wishers, the event marked a momentous occasion. More than just a 'coming of age' party for the young marquess, it was a celebration of Raynham Hall's triumphant (and somewhat unexpected) return to greatness. Newspaper reports on the event – which appeared as far afield as Canada and Australia – ran with the headline *Mother Works Years to Save Estate for Son.*

As it turns out, Gwladys was not just a talented writer; she was also a shrewd businesswoman, who took care to 'make sure every little thing' on her family's estate paid. Thanks to her efforts, the marchioness had somehow been able to turn Raynham around. In the spring of 1937, she and her party guests celebrated with beer, bonfires and fireworks. It was a jubilant affair on a scale the hall hadn't seen for over a generation.

When she had first crossed the threshold of her late husband's ancestral seat sixteen years earlier, the dowager marchioness probably could not have imagined the gaiety of her future fete. The hall had never been her home during the marquess's lifetime, having been rented out on a twenty-one-year lease to a family friend, Sir Edmund Lacon, who had promised to help save the Townshends' ancestral seat from sale. Because Lacon had a Norfolk seat of his own, Ormesby House in Ormesby-St-Michael, and business interests in London, it's unlikely he spent much time at Raynham. And so, by the time the dowager took up residence, Raynham Hall must have been a dreary, desolate place indeed. While not quite empty, it was greatly depleted of the treasures that had once been packed to its rafters. Cobweb-filled corners and layers of dust atop the remaining pieces of art and antique furniture would have been a poignant reminder of Raynham's noble heritage and now faded glory. But at least it was still standing and continuing to serve its originally intended purpose.

Owing to the long-lasting impact of the agricultural depression of the 1880s, the subsequent depression of the 1930s, and a 50 per cent inheritance tax introduced in 1934, owners of stately homes across the country were being forced to part with their family seats en masse. Scores were demolished. Countless others were donated to the newly established National Trust. Some, like Stowe in Buckinghamshire and Prior Park in Somerset, were turned into boarding schools. Others, like Tayworth Castle in Perthshire and Shaw Hill in Lancashire, were transformed into luxury hotels or golf clubs. Many more, like Leeds Castle in Kent and Cholmondeley Castle in Cheshire, were repurposed as wartime hospitals. And some, like Witley Court in Worcestershire and Woodchester Mansion in Gloucestershire, were simply abandoned.

Comparatively speaking, Raynham Hall – which remained intact and had never been wholly abandoned or stripped of all its treasures – had fared pretty well. Still, the journey towards restoration would be a long and arduous one.

Feeling sad, lonely and overwhelmed with the task at hand, one can imagine the dowager marchioness wandering aimlessly through Raynham's sparsely furnished rooms, perhaps pausing for a moment in front of the one remaining portrait of Lady Dorothy Townshend. Gazing at her predecessor's pale, stoic visage, the marchioness might have felt a pang of sympathy – camaraderie, even. Maybe she wouldn't feel quite so alone if she could convince herself that the Brown Lady was still there, keeping her company. Maybe the ghost could help her.

That the dowager marchioness took solace – pleasure even – in the notion of ghosts at Raynham Hall is evident in her writing. In *True Ghost Stories*, Gwladys speaks of the Brown Lady and her fellow spectral housemates in resoundingly positive terms. They are variously described as being peaceful, playful, friendly and even chivalrous. What's more, they are no ordinary ghosts; they are the ghosts of greatness. Gwladys explains:

> *Raynham Hall, known throughout Norfolk as the Great House, the home of the Townshends for successive generations, is haunted not only by the historic Brown Lady (mentioned in all important literature on the subject of the supernatural) but also by a tragic Duke and the harmless phantoms of animals and children.*

Here, the marchioness elides past and present, house and haunting, in an effort to illustrate the holistic and enduring importance of Raynham and its inhabitants. At the time of her writing, the 'Great House', while perhaps still a shadow of its former self, was on its way back to greatness, and in an eccentric stroke of genius, the dowager marchioness harnessed the medium of the ghost story as a promotional tool.

Consider her use of the legend of the 'Red Cavalier' – the 'tragic Duke' mentioned above. While he's an obscure figure today, John, 1st Duke of Monmouth, was a prominent player in the lead-up to the Glorious Revolution of 1688, at a time when the Townshend family were at their zenith. The natural-born son of Charles II and his mistress Lucy Walter, Monmouth was put forward as a potential Protestant claimant to the English throne when the late king's controversial Catholic heir, James II, came to power. Following an unsuccessful uprising (the Monmouth Rebellion), the duke was captured and executed for treason at Tower Hill on 15 July 1685. Prior to that, however, he evidently spent some time at Raynham Hall.

'The Monmouth Room at Raynham (so-called on account of the ill-fated Duke of Monmouth having slept there when he stayed at the Great House with his royal father) is haunted by the ghost of the Duke,' Gwladys writes. 'At one of my house parties, the Monmouth Room was occupied by the loveliest debutante of her year, who begged to sleep there, as she wanted, beyond all things, to meet the Red Cavalier.'

Though this anecdote yields no ghostly result, it does, nevertheless, give Gwladys the opportunity to advertise the fact that she was hosting gatherings at Raynham attended by society's best and most beautiful.

The next guest to stay the night in the Monmouth Room had a more memorable experience. The marchioness does not name her, but describes her as 'a spinster of a certain age'. Said 'spinster' purportedly lived a life 'devoid of romance and its possibilities' until her chance meeting with the duke. According to Gwladys, her guest was afforded 'one glamorous night, when she suddenly awoke to see the Red Cavalier standing at the foot of her bed, smiling in a most encouraging manner'.

As unnerving as this grinning spectre might sound, the 'spinster' reportedly loved it. 'She told us afterwards that she was not in the least frightened,' says the marchioness. She was 'only happily interested; and when, as befitted a courtier, the duke paid her the homage due to a Princess of the Blood, and bowed himself into the shadows of the wall, he became the happiest memory of a drab life'.

Gwladys's ghosts were gallant and glamorous. They regularly manifested on the nights she was hosting decadent soirees. Sometimes the soirees themselves were supernatural. Indeed, she claims that in the 'royal bedroom' at Raynham, the suite of chairs, ordinarily 'set overnight against the wall', were quite often found in the morning rearranged around a card table.

'The ghostly card-players remind me of other occurrences,' she remarks. 'Strange noises heard on the landing, whisperings and the swish of skirts, testify that the picture gallery is alive with the "Quality" who ruffled it in the days when the splendour of the Great House was undiminished.'

Evidently, these fun-loving spirits of 'Quality' were helping to bring Raynham back to life.

In the end, fortune was kind to Raynham Hall. Other country houses, however, were not so lucky. Their ghosts would not be afforded such cushy accommodation.

In an article appearing in the November 1897 issue of *Country Life*, entitled 'Deserted Houses', columnist Lucy Hardy remarks upon the abundance of abandoned properties then to be found dotted across the English countryside. 'There is always something melancholy-looking about an empty house, even if it be situated in a crowded and commonplace street,' Hardy observes. 'But this appearance is intensified in the case of one of those lonely abodes which the tourist or cyclist so often passes in the course of [their] country rambles.'

Hardy goes on to ponder the various possible reasons for desertion. Perhaps the homeowner was abroad, the house was too remote, or a tragic event such as a murder or suicide had recently taken place there. Strangely, Hardy makes no mention of the most likely explanation: that the homeowner simply couldn't afford the house's upkeep and had failed to find an interested buyer. It's possible she felt her readership – largely comprising members of the landed gentry and those who aspired to be – did not wish to be reminded of rural England's grim economic climate. But she had no qualms about tackling topics such as violent death and the supernatural. These subjects were evidently far less frightening to the cash-strapped upper classes.

'Sometimes local tradition gives its own account of why a house remained so long untended,' Hardy says. 'Certainly, there is no more fitting locale for a ghost ... than one of those old seventeenth- or eighteenth-century country houses.'

The derelict old wreck that has been deserted on account of its hauntedness is a ghost story trope that has existed for almost as long as the ghost story itself. While it's inarguably timeless and universal in concept, I wonder whether we might challenge the fundamental premise of such stories. Are these houses abandoned because they're haunted? Or are they haunted because they're abandoned?

Let's take a look at one of the many English country houses left empty at the end of the nineteenth century: Woodchester Mansion in Nympsfield, Gloucestershire. This Grade I listed neo-Gothic manor house was built between 1858 and 1870 for William Leigh, the scion of a Liverpool merchant dynasty. A fervent convert to Catholicism, Leigh spent most of his £100,000 inheritance (about £11,000,000 today) on various causes related to his faith. He had intended to create a Catholic community in the Cotswolds countryside, complete with church, monastery and almshouses. His new home, Woodchester, would be located at its heart. However, Leigh died in 1873, before it was finished. In fact, it would never be completed.

Today, the unfinished mansion is believed to be haunted. *Very* haunted, if its many appearances on paranormal-themed TV shows are anything to go by. But how did a house that was never actually lived in come to be known as one of Britain's most haunted homes? Aside from its stereotypically 'haunted' aesthetic (high Victorian Gothic), the fact that it is located in a remote wooded area down a mile-long track, and that a large colony of greater horseshoe bats live in its attic, Woodchester has a legend attached to it.

The story goes that, one day, construction on the mansion suddenly and inexplicably stopped. Some say it was on account of a brutal murder. Others suggest it was because of the portentous appearance of the 1st Earl of Ducie, the long-deceased owner of the house that had once sat on the land where Woodchester was being built. Still others believe the property is cursed. At any rate, for whatever reason, in 1870, the house was abandoned partially finished, with only the drawing room completed a few decades later in honour of a visit from the Roman Catholic Archbishop of Westminster.

Yvette Fielding, presenter of Living TV's *Most Haunted*, describes the Woodchester Mansion as:

> *An incomplete Victorian Gothic masterpiece, abandoned by the very builders that promised it life, ignored by the people who pledged to nurture it; an aborted mistake that should never have happened... Twenty-seven rooms, twelve years of blood, sweat and tears, and an unexplained mysterious end.*

But that's not really true. We do know, more or less, exactly why construction halted. In the late 1860s, William Leigh grew ill, suffering from a weak heart and chest ailments. By this point, his finances were already stretched thin. Augustus Pugin, the celebrated neo-Gothic architect who had provided the original designs for Woodchester, had warned Leigh that what he wanted for his extravagant home could not be achieved within the budget he had at his disposal. Ignoring Pugin's warning, Leigh proceeded with the project under the supervision of a far less experienced architect, and soon his coffers ran dry.

Prior to his death in 1873, he may have secured assurances from his heirs that the house would be completed, but this wasn't a promise that could be kept.

Leigh's eldest son, Willie, had allegedly procured two separate quotes: one for the cost to complete Woodchester; another for the cost of its demolition – neither of which the family could afford. And so the mansion sat empty and incomplete for the next 150 years, open to the elements and only protected from vandalism thanks to its isolated location. Finally, in 1992 it was purchased by Stroud District Council and placed under the management of the Woodchester Mansion Trust. However, even with the income generated from hiring the house out as a filming location for such high-profile productions as *The Crown*, the trust has only ever managed to afford the cost of preservation and upkeep, not further construction, thereby keeping Woodchester in a perpetual state of desolate incompletion.

Why do so many people believe Woodchester Mansion to be haunted? And why is it that all abandoned houses are popularly assumed to harbour ghosts? Partly, it comes down to that 'melancholy' look that columnist Lucy Hardy spoke of. A home bearing signs of years of neglect results in a tangible image of decay, evidencing the decline of the house itself – and of the people who once lived there.

Long before the modern 'death' of the English country house, ruin and decay were standard motifs of Gothic fiction. Horace Walpole's *The Castle of Otranto* was literally falling apart, mirroring the fractured state of the family that lived there. His young protégé, Ann Radcliffe, described a similarly crumbling castle and its decaying dynasty in *Mysteries of Udolpho* (1794). And across the pond, Edgar Allan Poe wrote of a dying New England dynasty in his classic horror story, *The Fall of the House of Usher* (1839).

But it's more than that. It's not just that we are pre-programmed to view such houses in a certain fashion because of the influence of Gothic novelists. As people accustomed to living in homes with our nuclear family, we simply can't stand the idea that a structure that was designed as a dwelling lacks the one thing that makes a house a home. We must, therefore, populate these empty houses with the inhabitants that we believe should rightly be there.

To Gwladys, Marchioness Townshend, those inhabitants were members of the beau monde – a debonair duke and charming viscountess: the 'family ghosts' of Raynham Hall, perfectly fitting for this once-grand country house.

THE AMITYVILLE HORROR

GHOSTS ON FILM

7

The Amityville Horror is the primal haunted house story ... and haunted houses are a concept which even the dullest mind has surely turned over at one time or another, if only around a childhood campfire or two.

Stephen King (1947–)

An American horror story: the Amityville phenomenon

On 24 July 1979, *The Amityville Horror*, a supernatural thriller film based on an allegedly real-life haunting, premiered at the Museum of Modern Art (MoMA) in New York. It was an oddly erudite setting for the screening of what was subsequently referred to by one film critic as 'pure B-movie schlock from beginning to end'. 'High' art it was not, but at the very least, the opening scenes would have packed a visceral punch for viewers at MoMA that summer evening. Within seconds of the theatre darkening and the projector whirring into life, the film's first audience was introduced to what would become modern cinema's most famous haunted house.

112 Ocean Avenue, Amityville, New York is the former home of the Lutz family, George, Kathy and their three children. In the winter of 1975, they claimed to have experienced a series of increasingly escalating paranormal events which led them to abandon the property and all their worldly possessions after less than a month in their would-be dream home. Though the veracity of their story has long been debated, the house itself is very real and still stands: a private family home nestled in an affluent little enclave on the southern shore of Long Island where, much to the chagrin of its current inhabitants, it continues to attract paranormal tourists.

But this is not the house that is seen in the Hollywood blockbuster. The house that actually appears in the film is 18 Brooks Road, Toms River, New Jersey – a stand-in for the notorious structure that was the setting for the Lutz family's twenty-eight days of terror.

Director Stuart Rosenberg had initially hoped to film on location in Amityville, but local authorities denied him permission. Neither the homeowner nor the village residents wished to court such publicity. Instead, Rosenberg would task set designers with building an elaborate temporary structure around the New Jersey home to make it look virtually identical to the Amityville original.

The opening credits of the film roll across a static shot of the dimly lit silhouette of the stand-in house, set against a crimson sky and flanked by gnarled bare trees. It is so dark that we can barely make out any detail, apart from the distinctive quarter-round windows on the top storey, which are aglow with a similarly ominous shade of red. As the credits continue, the bloody hue slowly fades to a washed-out greyscale, gradually revealing more of the house as it emerges from the shadows.

It is a three-storey suburban home featuring a symmetrical two-sided roof with two slopes on each side – what is known as a 'gambrel' roof, a defining feature of Dutch Colonial Revival architecture, a style popular in the north-eastern states in the early twentieth century.

The house is old but not ancient. Large but not grand. Smart but not flashy. For all intents and purposes, it looks like a fairly standard upper-middle-class family home. And yet, something doesn't feel right about it. Thanks to those unusual upper-storey windows, it feels like the house is watching us.

As the final credit line fades from the screen, the music – an unnerving chorus of children singing – abruptly stops and the house disappears behind a wall of torrential rain. A pause, then the camera pans up to a slightly different shot of the house, a fraction closer, albeit still at a wary distance. This time, flashes of lightning sporadically illuminate the façade. Though we can't see inside, it is clear that a gunman is making his way through the house. The windows light up with the flash of gunfire as the assailant passes from room to room, the shotgun blasts echoing the claps of thunder.

Suddenly we're in the house, the camera initially placing us in the position of the gunman's victims – prostrate in bed, peering out between the slats of the footboard to the open door beyond. We don't see the killer's face as he enters the room, only the muzzle of his raised rifle.

Boom. Cut to the exterior, the camera zooming in closer and closer, until we're gazing right into the infernal 'eyes' of the house. The house is watching us; we are watching the house; we are both watching the horror unfolding inside.

Finally, our perspective changes once again and we see the scene through the eyes of the killer – a slow panning shot of blood-spattered bedding and two dead bodies.

This is the prologue to *The Amityville Horror* which, in a few brief shots, recreates the real-life murder spree of Ronald DeFeo Jr, who shot and killed his family of six in the house just thirteen months before the Lutz family took up residence. This is the reason, we are later told, that the Lutzes were able to purchase the property for a song. But is this the source of the subsequent haunting?

In these opening scenes – easily the most effective and memorable moments in an otherwise largely forgettable film – it is subtly intimated that, even before the murders took place, there was already something seriously wrong with 112 Ocean Avenue. And in the aftermath of the event, the question on everyone's lips was 'Did the devil make DeFeo do it, as he later claimed? Or did the house?'

It's hard to explain why this story, and this house, caught public attention in the way it did. But the fact is, that evocative opening sequence of the film remains one of the most memorable of the haunted house subgenre, and it is perhaps for this reason that today, the word 'Amityville' exists as a virtual byword for the modern American 'haunted house'. Despite its critical reception, the 1979 film went on to bank $80 million at the box office (the equivalent of $331 million today), making it one of the most profitable films of that year, opening the door for a sequel, a 2005 reboot, and no fewer than thirty spin-offs and copycats with 'Amityville' in their titles.

It's a bizarre phenomenon that, at first glance, seems almost as mysterious as the incidents the Lutzes described happening in their 'haunted' home. However, as we probe deeper, it will become clear that Amityville's fame was, perhaps, foreseeable.

At the most basic level, there is the tantalising appeal of any terrifying tale that's branded with the label 'based on a true story', as evidenced by some of the best of the genre: *The Exorcist* (1973), *The*

Changeling (1980), *The Haunting in Connecticut* (2009), *The Conjuring* (2013) ... the list goes on. Audiences can't get enough of the real scary stuff. Nor is this unfamiliar; the ghosts we've met in earlier chapters are bolstered by their 'real' histories, whether they are the Tudor queen Catherine Howard, the eighteenth-century Viscountess Dorothy Townshend, or the historically authentic (if not literally real) antebellum slave, Chloe.

This 'authentic account' element was almost certainly what lured many viewers to the cinema in the first place in the 1970s, when the Lutzes' supposedly true story was making national headlines and Jay Anson's 'non-fiction' book describing their experiences – on which the film was based – topped the bestseller charts. And yet, in Stephen King's survey of modern horror fiction, *Danse Macabre* (1981), the author argues that, when it comes to the *Amityville* film, the 'true story' aspect of it is a red herring. 'Whether the Lutzes' house was really haunted or whether the whole thing was a put-up job matters very little. All movies are, after all, pure fiction, even the true ones,' he writes. 'Movies produce fiction as a by-product in the same way that boiling water produces steam ... or as horror movies produce art.' Not 'high' art, as we've established, but 'art' in the sense that the film functions as a mirror being held up to society, reflecting all our greatest fears and desires, as well as our more ephemeral preoccupations.

According to King, this is how all horror fiction works, not just *Amityville* and the haunted house subgenre. There is always what he describes as the 'text' and the 'subtext' of scary. For example, in the classic demonic possession film *The Exorcist*, the fear operates on two levels: the surface level (a formerly sweet twelve-year-old girl has been transformed into a ghastly, pus-covered, vomit- and expletive-spewing demon) and the subsurface level (as children transform from adolescents to teenagers and eventually adults, their parents fear that they will lose them forever).

In *The Exorcist*, this subsurface fear was simultaneously ageless and of the age. Of course, parents have always felt anxious about their children, but the parents of baby boomers in 1960s and 1970s America faced what was probably the most dramatic generational culture clash in history. The Civil Rights movement, second-wave feminism, heavy metal music, marijuana – it was all deeply foreign and unsettling to the generation who had lived through the Second World War. They found their kids positively terrifying.

Though it may not have been as expertly executed as *The Exorcist* (which received rave reviews and continues to top 'best horror movie' lists to this day), *The Amityville Horror* offers the same dual level of fear, the same balance of universality and period-/location-rooted specificity.

It is the story of a normal nuclear family who move into a house: a house they hope will be the answer to all their hopes and dreams; a house that ultimately lets them down in a number of devastating ways. It's set against the backdrop of the fuel crisis of the 1970s, but it could just as easily have taken place in the post-9/11 period (as the 2005 remake was) or during the 2008 financial collapse, or during the Covid-19 crisis of 2020 – virtually any moment in history when ordinary families felt under threat in their own homes.

The Amityville Horror is, at its root, a fairly simple and relatable story. This is why it has withstood the test of time. Although, as we will see, other films and other stories have accomplished significantly more with the same basic set of ingredients, *Amityville* persists for precisely the same reasons it was once dismissed by the critics – its familiarity and faithful adherence to an established formula.

And though the popular Hollywood film, through its visual format and wide reach, has undeniably strengthened haunted house iconography, has it actually done anything to fundamentally change or improve the existing model? Is the Hollywood film merely a repackaging of the haunted house of Gothic literature, admittedly in shiny new celluloid wrapping? To be sure, there are a few fresh twists, but in many ways, *Amityville* is the same old ghost story.

Based on a true story?

Although the 'true story' behind *Amityville* has been muddied by accusations of misrepresentation, exaggeration and full-on fraud, there *is* a real history here, coloured by many of the same themes that dominate the film it inspired. Familial dysfunction, financial insecurity, religious (and occult-ish) overtones were all at play in this real-life domestic drama.

The Amityville Horror is essentially the tale of two families: the

Lutzes and the DeFeos. Both were one-time owners of 112 Ocean Avenue; both were outwardly average middle-class American families of the 1970s (white, Christian, heterosexual, affluent). We might view them as exemplars of the 'American dream' come true. They were upwardly mobile folk who, through their apparent grit and determination, had been able to trade in smaller homes in less desirable areas for the suburban jewel that was 112 Ocean Avenue – a 4,000 ft^2, five-bedroom home located on prime waterfront property, complete with in-ground swimming pool, boat house and private dock.

Hidden beneath this veneer of superficial success, however, all was not quite what it seemed. Both families harboured secrets that would later show them not to be so idyllically ordinary after all.

The DeFeo clan – Ronald Sr, Louise and their five children – moved into the Ocean Avenue home on 28 June 1965. Their expectations were high for this move from the gritty tenements of Brooklyn to the Long Island suburbs, and this is shown in the sign they erected on the front lawn, which read 'High Hopes'. In naming their new home, the DeFeos were not only expressing their optimism, but also their vague pretensions at playing aristocratic landowners in the vein of the European Old World (modern American houses do not typically have names).

Ostensibly, the DeFeos had every reason to feel proud and confident. Ronald Sr ran a successful Buick car dealership, Louise was a glamorous society hostess, and the bountiful DeFeo brood were seemingly happy, healthy kids, on track to becoming just as comfortable and conventional in adulthood as their bourgeois parents.

But this was all a façade. In reality, Ronald Sr was a brutish, stereotypically testosterone-fuelled Italian-American patriarch, even though he was not actually the true alpha male of the family. It was his father-in-law, Michael Brigante Sr, who set up his job at the car dealership, who forked out the cash for the down-payment on the dream home, and who regularly showered his beloved daughter with lavish gifts of jewellery, perfume and provisions for the children. Ronald Sr was decidedly not the 'king' of his own castle and, unfortunately, he took his frustrations out on his wife and children. His eldest son, Ronnie Jr, was the frequent target of his father's violent rages.

Suffice to say, 112 Ocean Avenue was not a happy home under the tenure of the DeFeos.

We will never know precisely what happened at 112 Ocean Avenue on the night of 13 November 1974. The only surviving witness was Ronald DeFeo Jr, whose story changed so many times over the course of his thirty-year incarceration that it is virtually impossible to discern fact from fiction.

This much we do know: six of the seven members of the DeFeo family were found face-down in their beds, killed by gunshot. None showed any sign of struggle; none were found with sedatives in their systems. What's more, neighbours claimed not to have heard a single gunshot, even though the houses on the street were close together. Since it had not been fitted with a silencer, the thundering death blows of the .35 Marlin rifle used to commit the murders should have been clearly audible throughout the neighbourhood. Instead, the only thing neighbours recalled hearing that night was the incessant barking of the DeFeo family dog.

How did a single assailant manage to subdue and kill six victims without drawing any outside attention? It's a mystery only the murderer could explain. And indeed, Ronnie *did* attempt to explain it. Many times. First, he claimed it was a set-up by the Mafia, with whom his family allegedly had loose ties. Then the story morphed: it was the unintended consequence of a domestic dispute. He would tell detectives after his arrest that, 'Once I started, I just couldn't stop.'

At his trial in autumn 1975, DeFeo changed his story once again, this time claiming he had no memory of the murders, and therefore wished to enter a plea of 'not guilty by reason of insanity'. The jury didn't buy it, and declared him guilty of second-degree murder on all six counts. On 6 December 1975, he was sentenced to twenty-five years to life in prison.

Following his conviction, DeFeo came up with still more versions of the night's events, each one more elaborate and outlandish than the last. In one scenario, his sister Dawn had killed their father, their distraught mother had killed the children, and Ronnie had killed his mother in retaliation. In another, Dawn and an accomplice had killed the parents, Dawn alone had killed the children, and this time, Ronnie had killed Dawn in retaliation.

But his most dramatic account was this: on the night of the murders, Ronnie was relaxing on the sofa, minding his own business, when a shadowy form materialised out of nowhere, approaching him with the Marlin rifle in its outstretched hands. It was this dark figure – a ghost? A demon? His sister Dawn? – that he claimed had compelled him to murder his entire family.

A feeble attempt at getting his murder conviction overturned, perhaps, but a colourful yarn that would dovetail quite nicely with the next chapter in the Amityville saga.

In winter 1975, George and Kathy Lutz purchased the former DeFeo home for a mere $80,000 – a pittance for a home of this size in this location. The Lutzes had landed a pretty good deal, and they knew why, but it was a bargain they felt they couldn't pass up. Besides, the couple weren't really the superstitious sort (or so they claimed). George would later tell reporters, 'It felt like a dream come true.'

In truth, they really couldn't afford the house, even at its massively discounted rate. It was well over the Lutzes' originally agreed maximum budget of $50,000, and it was going to be a stretch, to say the least; although George ran a relatively successful land-surveying company, the economic winds were changing and business was drying up fast. They hoped they could make up the difference with the money they'd save on rent by converting the summerhouse into a home office for George. However, the plan doesn't seem to have panned out. The Lutzes never made a single mortgage payment on the property, suggesting that the true horror they experienced at 112 Ocean Avenue was financial rather than supernatural.

When they arrived at their new home on 18 December 1975, the Lutzes must have looked to their neighbours like the quintessential all-American family. George, a medium-built, sandy-haired man in his late twenties, with a fashionably full beard. Kathy, a petite blonde of a similar age, with her hair styled in the modish feather cut of the mid-1970s. And their '2.5 kids' – Daniel (nine), Christopher (seven) and Missy (five).

But, just as with the DeFeos, all was not as it initially appeared. For one thing, George Lutz was not the children's birth father, but rather their new stepfather, having married their mother earlier that year. And while he presented himself to the world as a loving and devoted parental figure, even going so far as insisting that he legally adopt the children before his marriage to Kathy, his stepsons later claimed that nothing could have been further from the truth. As an adult looking back, eldest brother Daniel described George as 'this guy who [beat] the shit out of me and Mum, who [was] no longer the mum I used to know'. Younger brother Christopher backed up his sibling's recollections, stating that, 'George was a former Marine and a black belt in jujitsu. I had no defence against him...'

According to his stepchildren, not only was George physically abusive, he was also a master manipulator. Though George claimed in the press that neither he nor his wife had any previous belief or interest in the supernatural prior to moving into 112 Ocean Avenue, the children maintained that he had an entire bookcase devoted to the subject of the occult. Intriguingly, neither Daniel nor Christopher deny that the family experienced paranormal events in their childhood home; they just think that, somehow, George had something to do with it.

Once again, it's hard to say what really occurred behind closed doors at the Amityville house. It does appear to be true that the family only occupied the house for a little under a month, as they claimed, leaving behind most of their belongings when they left (they were sold at auction after the bank foreclosed on the property). However, their actual motivation for abandoning 'High Hopes' has been hotly debated.

Many argue it was down to dollars and cents – the family simply couldn't afford to make ends meet in the increasingly bleak economic climate of the late 1970s. Others point out that, having only lived in the house for twenty-eight days, the Lutzes could not possibly have fallen so far behind on payments, though this isn't necessarily proof of their sincerity – or the supernatural. Perhaps the Lutzes knew all along that they couldn't afford the house, and hatched a plan to sell their story right from the start. Yet the fact remains that Kathy and George remained publicly steadfast in their claims right up until the day they died (in 2004 and 2006, respectively). Even after the couple divorced in 1988, they upheld a united front.

Within months of their departure, George and Kathy were holding press conferences, granting interviews and inviting television crews into their allegedly haunted former home. The lengthy list of reported paranormal events included cold spots; unseen presences;

disembodied voices; malodorous smells; mysterious black stains in the toilets; green slime dripping from the walls; and, perhaps most bizarrely, a menacing red-eyed pig called Jody, who was usually only seen by their youngest child, Missy. All of this certainly made for a remarkable story. A haunted house – maybe even a demonically possessed house – which had recently played host to a notorious mass murderer, who was now sitting in prison, prattling on to anyone who would listen about the dark forces that had compelled him to kill..

It wasn't long before they scored a book deal with publisher Prentice Hall, who gave jobbing writer Jay Anson the responsibility of putting the Lutz family's incredible ordeal down on paper. Published in the autumn of 1977, *The Amityville Horror* would go on to sell an estimated 10 million copies over the course of its four decades in print. That the phrase 'A True Story' was splashed upon its cover in bold red text almost as big as the title itself was surely a major factor in its success.

Despite its popularity, however, the book and its subjects almost immediately came under intense public scrutiny. For many, the whole thing seemed a little too convenient – not to mention lucrative – to be true. In an effort to clear their names, George and Kathy submitted to polygraph tests, which they reportedly passed, but this did little to disperse the swirling clouds of doubt.

Among the chorus of voices calling out 'Hoax!' was William Weber, a New York-based criminal attorney who, in May 1977, filed a $2 million lawsuit against the Lutzes for fraud and breach of contract. According to his testimony, Weber – who wasn't just any old lawyer, but Ronald DeFeo Jr's defence attorney – claimed to have approached the couple about developing a book together prior to their partnership with Anson and Prentice Hall. Apparently the lawyer had devised a plan that would benefit both the cash-strapped couple and Weber's troubled client. They'd cook up a sensational story that would suggest that the DeFeo murders had been supernaturally influenced, and sell it for big bucks. And that's exactly what the Lutzes did – only, instead of pursuing their partnership with Weber, the couple took the story and ran, leaving the lawyer in the dust with no profits of his own.

'I know this book is a hoax,' Weber later told the press. 'We created it over many bottles of wine.'

On 17 September 1979, the presiding judge, Jack B. Weinstein, ruled in Weber's favour, stating that, 'Based on what I have heard, it appears to me that to a large extent the book is a work of fiction, relying in a large part upon the suggestions of Mr Weber.'

Another revelation that emerged at trial was that the Catholic priest, Father Ralph Pecoraro (Father Mancuso in the book and Father Delaney in the film), who had previously claimed to have experienced paranormal events while blessing the house, never actually set foot on the property, making it impossible for him to have heard the guttural disembodied voice instructing him to 'GET OUT!', as depicted in both book and film. Without their star witness, George and Kathy's credibility was rapidly crumbling.

Perhaps the most damning blow of all came years later when Ronald DeFeo Jr himself spoke out on the matter. Though he may have at one point played along with the supernatural stuff when it suited him, Ronnie was now setting the record straight. In a handwritten prison letter dated 1 May 2000, DeFeo stated: 'As for *Amityville*, the only thing that's real were the murders... No ghosts. No demons. Just three people, of which I was one' (here, referring to himself, his sister Dawn and another accomplice).

But none of this would deter George and Kathy Lutz. It was, they insisted, a 'true story', and they stood by it for life.

Whether fact or faked, *The Amityville Horror* is an undeniably familiar story that closely conforms to an established formula. By this point, we should be well aware of the basic building blocks of the classic haunted house narrative. First and foremost, we have the setting. It must be a domestic structure (preferably big and old), and it must possess a troubled past to which we can attribute all subsequent supernatural (and inevitably negative) events.

Then there are the central characters. These are almost always newcomers – new owners, new tenants, new visitors or new employees – who are either unaware of the house's horrible history or, as in the case of the Lutzes, initially not that bothered by it. There may also be key secondary characters who serve as 'helpers' and either possess knowledge of the house's history or essential insight into the spiritual world more generally.

The plot itself is usually simple, varying only slightly in accordance with the circumstances of the characters in the story, but inevitably involving a slowly escalating series of events, culminating in a dramatic climax which, more often than not, leaves little doubt as to whether or not the house is actually haunted.

For the Lutzes, it began with an infestation of flies in one room in the middle of winter; regularly waking at exactly 3.15 a.m. (supposedly the time of the DeFeo murders); and being unable to keep the house warm, despite George's vigilant stoking of a round-the-clock fire. All of this might have been chalked up to natural phenomena – until the paranormal activity really started ramping up.

By the end of their twenty-eight days in residence, the Lutzes were dealing with full-bodied apparitions (a terrified little boy begging for help in the spare bedroom), serious bodily harm (a window slamming down on the fingers of their eldest son), and potentially demonic entities (the glowing eyes of Jody the pig, seen through their daughter's bedroom window).

At 112 Ocean Avenue, the problems seemed to be endless. Obviously, there was the mass slaughter of the DeFeo family, which the Lutzes knew about and which probably should have been more than enough to trigger a good old-fashioned haunting. But apparently, this was only the tip of the iceberg. Doing a little paranormal detective work, George discovered through chats with the local historical society that a devil-worshipping early settler called John Ketcham was allegedly buried on their land.

Eclipsing Ketcham entirely, however, was a more dubious history: this was supposedly where the Native American Shinnecock tribe traditionally banished their mad and dying. Not quite an Indian burial ground, exactly, but something similar. Except for the facts: the Shinnecock didn't consider Amityville to be their traditional land; there's little evidence that they ever practised this form of tribal expulsion; and there was never an Indian burial (or banishment) ground located there.

The resolution of the haunted house story is usually two-fold. The protagonists must get to grips with the root of the problem in their home. Then they must find a way of exorcising that problem and/or they must get away from it. And so, there are only a handful of options for the finale of the haunted house story. The occupants can banish the bad vibes by means of religious ritual or righting past wrongs, and go on to live happily ever after. Or they can escape the house, more or less unscathed, with or without the house remaining intact. If the house remains, it will more than likely go on to torment others. If it is destroyed – well, we can only hope that that's the end of it. In rarer cases, the house not only survives, but also takes the lives of the occupants. Obviously, this was not the fate of the Lutzes; if it had been, they would not have been around to tell (and sell) their story.

This exact framework has been used to construct nearly every haunted house story of the past 200 years, in everything from Horace Walpole's trailblazing tale *The Castle of Otranto* to Henry James's Victorian Gothic novella *The Turn of the Screw*; from Shirley Jackson's modern mid-century classic *The Haunting of Hill House* to Stephen King's late 1970s supernatural bestseller *The Shining* (though admittedly this last example involves a haunted hotel, not a house).

None of this is to say that *The Amityville Horror* was, beyond a shadow of a doubt, 100 per cent made-up; after all, there are plenty of other examples of alleged real-life hauntings that conform to the same basic formula – the haunting of Borley Rectory, for instance. Rather, the point is that the Lutzes' purported experiences at 112 Ocean Avenue lent themselves so well to the exigencies of Gothic fiction that it seemed to be a foregone conclusion that their story should make its way to print – and eventually, the big screen.

The haunted house goes Hollywood

When producer Samuel Z. Arkoff acquired the film rights to *The Amityville Horror* in spring 1978, he may not have realised he was sitting on a gold mine. Sure, he knew he had a built-in captive audience, which had already helped push Jay Anson's book to the top of the bestseller list, but there was nothing to indicate to him that the film adaptation would go on to spawn four decades of sequels and spin-offs. Rather than a runaway hit, Arkoff probably saw the project as a low-risk investment – a safe bet.

Not only was the production in the capable hands of a veteran director, Oscar-nominated Stuart Rosenberg, but Arkoff had also managed to assemble a roster of fresh, yet familiar, faces in the leading roles. The part of George was given to rugged, moustachioed hunk James Brolin, while the part of Kathy went to the beautiful brunette ingenue Margot Kidder (Lois Lane to Christopher Reeve's Superman). The real (and relatively ordinary-looking) George and Kathy Lutz must have been deeply flattered.

Meanwhile, the role of supporting character Father Francis Delaney was played by character actor Rod Steiger, best known for his role as Al Capone in the eponymous 1959 biopic and his Academy Award-winning turn in the neo-noir crime film *In the Heat of the Night* (1967). Though his bombastic performance as the priest would be slated by critics, Steiger's presence nevertheless added a bit of Old Hollywood panache to the production.

The marketing department would be having an easy time of it too. They had a stellar cast and a sensational story to work with, not to mention a pair of unofficial promotors in the form of the Lutzes, who were continuing to blitz the media circuit in the lead-up to the film's release. At one point, the studio had also planned on further capitalising on the 'true story' angle by attempting to circulate rumours that unexplained events were occurring on the *Amityville* set, hoping that a horror movie 'curse' in the manner of *The Exorcist* (and later the *Poltergeist* trilogy) might drum up still more interest. In the end, the gambit didn't pay off, but it was ultimately unnecessary. The movie poster – featuring the crimson-tinged silhouette of the now-iconic horror house, emblazoned with the tagline 'FOR GOD'S SAKE, GET OUT' in giant white text – proved far simpler and more effective in terms of promotion.

For all intents and purposes, *The Amityville Horror* was, at its core, a tried-and-tested formula for cinematic success. After all, haunted house films had been around for almost as long as film itself.

Widely regarded as history's first horror movie, Georges Méliès's *Le Manoir du Diable* ('The Devil's Manor') was first screened in Paris on Christmas Eve, 1896. The film depicts a pair of wayfaring cavaliers who come upon a castle, where they encounter the devil and a host of ghostly courtiers. Employing a number of pioneering special effects, including the 'substitution splice' – an editing technique used to create the illusion of disappearances and transformations – *Le*

Manoir du Diable was conceived of as a visual magic trick, designed to astonish and amuse early audiences, not actually frighten them.

At just three minutes long, the silent short bears very little resemblance to the modern feature-length haunted house film, though it does hold the distinction of being the first film to incorporate such familiar imagery as a bat transforming into a human being, perhaps making it more accurately the first vampire movie.

There would be several other early entries into the canon of haunted house cinema: George Albert Smith's *The Haunted Castle* (1897), Segundo de Chomón's *La Maison Ensorcelée* ('The House of Ghosts') (1907) and Buster Keaton's *The Haunted House* (1921), among others. But much like their forerunner *Le Manoir du Diable*, these stunt-driven silent shorts seem to have been mostly played for laughs rather than screams.

The haunted house film wouldn't properly hit its stride until the mid-twentieth century, at the height of Hollywood's golden age of psychological thrillers. This was the era of Alfred Hitchcock, the much-lauded 'master of suspense', responsible for such famously spooky fare as *Rear Window* (1954), *The Birds* (1963) and of course, *Psycho* (1960). Although Hitchcock himself didn't contribute to the canon of haunted house films in a straightforward way – the nearest he got was *Rebecca* (1940), based on Daphne du Maurier's classic novel which features a 'haunted' house that lacks a literal ghost – he certainly made a mark on the genre.

The simple plot lines, enriched by gradually escalating psychological tension; the use of plunging darkness and long shadows to imply impending doom; the bleak settings and minimal dialogue – these Hitchcockian trademarks were all usefully employed by makers of haunted house films for decades to come. On top of that, the infamous *Psycho* house – the 'California Gothic' residence of the murderous Norman Bates – has long served as a visual template for cinematic haunted houses, despite the fact that the Bateses' home was not actually supposed to be haunted.

At around the same time, Hitchcock's contemporaries were producing some of the most influential haunted house horror movies of all time. And while, at first glance, the late 1970s 'B-movie schlock' that is *The Amityville Horror* would seem to have very little in common with these more artful earlier films, there are certain shared traits that can be identified in nearly every successful example of the subgenre.

What filmmakers of horror and suspense realised pretty early on was the strength and ease of using a familiar, pre-existing narrative as the basis for their scary movies. In doing so, they could ensure a basic level of interest, approval and awareness on the part of their audience, while remaining free to experiment with techniques in filming, lighting and art direction. One need only look at the early cinematic history of *Dracula* for evidence of this trend (more than two dozen films loosely based on Bram Stoker's novel were released between 1920 and 1960).

Even the most inventive directors understood this simple equation. Hitchcock famously harnessed the power of popular literary works by Daphne du Maurier, Patricia Highsmith and Ethel Lina White, as well as 'true' stories ripped right out of the headlines (*Psycho* was based on both a bestselling novel by Robert Bloch and the notorious real-life murders committed by serial killer Ed Gein).

The makers of haunted house movies would follow suit, with many of the earliest and most lauded films of the subgenre being adaptations of Gothic novels. There was Roger Corman's *The House of Usher* (1960), which was based on Edgar Allan Poe's short story 'The Fall of the House of Usher' (1839); Jack Clayton's *The Innocents* (1961), one of the strongest of a whopping eighteen adaptations of Henry James's celebrated novella *The Turn of the Screw*; and Robert Wise's *The Haunting* (1963), based on Shirley Jackson's *The Haunting of Hill House* (1959), another literary classic that spawned over a dozen cinematic remakes.

In addition to familiar source material, these mid-century haunted house films all possess an eerily effective slow-burning pace; that Hitchcockian build-up of tension before the big reveal – if there even is one. Sometimes we are left to wonder if there are any ghosts at all, or whether the spooky events have been caused by the protagonist's deteriorating mental state, such as in *The Innocents* and *The Haunting*. These films succeed because they leave us guessing.

The most skilled and savvy directors of haunted house films have recognised that they must fight the urge to fall back on gimmicky gore, jump scares and special effects, lest their audience lose the ability to mine the most powerful source of fear of all – the imagination. And though this might have been less of a struggle for filmmakers in the early 1960s, who had less sophisticated movie-making technology at their disposal, for modern ones the temptation is often hard to resist. If you don't believe me, check out Jan de Bont's 1999 CGI car wreck of a remake of *The Haunting*.

According to *Rolling Stone* movie critic Peter Travers, these earlier films are prime examples of the 'less is more' approach to scary movie-making. In his review of the 2005 remake of *The Amityville Horror*, Travers identifies a rarefied category of horror films to which he advises audiences turn their attention rather than wasting their time on the *Amityville* update. He writes:

> *For the real thing, watch* Psycho ... *or* The Shining ... *or* The Haunting ... *or* The Innocents ... *What all those films have in common is precisely what the new* The Amityville Horror *lacks: they know it's what you* don't *see in a haunted house that fries your nerves to a frazzle.*

The *Amityville* reboot clearly failed to live up to these standards; however, it's not impossible for a modern haunted house film to tick all the boxes. In fact, the recipe is pretty simple. Take some compelling source material, hire some skilled actors and set designers, throw in a moody soundtrack, and you're pretty much guaranteed a halfway decent haunted house flick. So long as you don't stray too far from the standard formula, deviate too wildly from your source material, or waste too much time and money on big-budget special effects, you will, at the very least, wind up with something watchable.

Something like *The Amityville Horror*.

Does *The Amityville Horror* deserve its status as one of the most famous haunted house films of all time? For that matter, does the house itself (the *real* one) deserve its enduring reputation as one of the most notoriously haunted homes in America? These are tricky questions. And it's almost impossible to answer the latter without first tackling the former, since the house's reputation is so indelibly tied up with the legacy of the movie. So, for the moment, let's stick with the film.

With its predictable plot, pedestrian performances and threadbare character development, it would be easy to write off *Amityville* entirely, as most movie reviewers did on its original release. But to dismiss it wholesale would be to belie its extraordinary commercial success and enduring impact on the cultural landscape. Clearly, *Amityville* did something right, otherwise we wouldn't still be talking about it today.

Yes, it is formulaic. And as we've established, its familiarity is a big part of its appeal. However, on closer inspection, *Amityville* is not quite the tired old 'paint-by-numbers' haunted house film that critics initially made it out to be. There is some ingenuity and innovation here – just not enough to distract from the time-tested formula.

Obviously, in terms of its set-up and story arc, there is nothing revolutionary about *Amityville*. From the moment Brolin and Kidder appear on screen as the Lutzes on their first viewing of the horror house, we know exactly what's in store for them. Their wide-eyed optimism and carefree canoodling doesn't fool anyone. This couple are about to get seriously haunted. But there's something satisfying about watching it all unfold.

Like all decent haunted house stories, the tension builds slowly. Sure, there are a few frightening flashbacks of the DeFeo murders spliced into the Lutzes' initial tour of the house, but the couple themselves remain blissfully unaware. For the first fifteen minutes or so, not much happens. There are a number of lengthy establishing shots of the house in different lighting. Some scenes with husband and wife exchanging banal banter as they unpack their belongings. Some of the children and family dog playing in the garden. All the familiar, mundane aspects of suburban life that are about to be spectacularly subverted.

The first supernatural scare is set up in direct juxtaposition with this domestic normality. Steiger, as the priest hired to bless the house, arrives at the Lutz residence and discovers they are all outdoors, enjoying their new waterfront home. The clergyman lets himself in and quietly gets to work, setting up shop in a small room on the first floor. He gazes out of the window and observes the Lutz family, frolicking without a care in the world. A faint smile crosses his lips, only to fade quickly, to be replaced by a concerned frown. A swarm of flies has mysteriously amassed on the window pane and the door behind him has slammed shut. Though he senses danger, the priest attempts to perform his duties as the plague of insects descends upon him. Flies crawling up his nose, sweat pouring down his face, holding his hands to his clearly throbbing head, he can barely utter a single prayer. Then that demonic demand: 'GET OUT'.

As an agnostic who grew up in a staunchly secular household, this scene doesn't quite work for me. But for audiences in 1970s America, it was seriously scary stuff. After the success of satanic-themed films such as *Rosemary's Baby* (1968) and *The Exorcist* (1973), the horror movie market was in the grip of devil mania, just as American society at large was on the precipice of the 'satanic panic' – a short-lived but widespread hysteria during which thousands of reported cases of abuse were attributed to satanic cults. At this moment the devil loomed large, so why shouldn't he be invited into the haunted house? And while it's interesting to note that in the 2005 remake of *Amityville*, the priest is reduced to a bit part and the religious references are slim, the demonically possessed house remains a staple of the Hollywood horror movie genre – thanks to *Amityville*.

In spite of its strong religious overtones, the majority of *The Amityville Horror* is centred around the more universally relatable premise of a family in crisis. Throughout the film, the Lutzes attempt to carry out everyday domestic activities. Mum cooks dinner, Dad fiddles with a malfunctioning furnace, they put the kids to bed and try to make love, but are interrupted by a child suffering from nightmares. All of it is perfectly prosaic, but each time they try to carry out an ordinary activity, they are thwarted. We, the audience, know that the source of their problems is paranormal – a problem that most of us are unlikely to have experienced personally – but nevertheless we relate to their frustrations.

In one scene, George complains that the house is constantly cold. He checks the thermostat and finds that it is programmed at a temperate 72°F (22°C). Kathy suggests that there might be a draught coming up from the basement.

'This house is supposed to be well insulated,' George mutters. 'They'll nickel and dime you to death.' Homeowners the world over shudder with a shared sense of financial dread.

In another scene, George, Kathy and their two sons return home from an evening spent at a family wedding. Their daughter, called Amy in the film, has been left in the care of a teenage babysitter, and when they get home they discover that the babysitter has been trapped in a closet for some time. Suspecting that Amy might have been responsible, her parents demand to know why she didn't help the frightened babysitter.

'Jody wouldn't let me,' the child responds. 'Jody is my friend who comes to play with me.'

George snaps. He's heard more than enough about his stepdaughter's meddlesome imaginary friend. 'Jesus, what are we standing here listening to?' he bellows. As the film progresses, we watch George retreat inwards, slowly but surely pulling away from his wife and stepchildren. His fixation on the house's frosty temperature becomes all-consuming, even though nobody else is particularly bothered by the cold. With gritted teeth and an icy glower, George obsessively chops the firewood he needs to heat the house. That his family members seem wholly unappreciative of the pressure he's under as the household's primary protector and provider causes him to withdraw still further. Any attempt to draw him out again is met with sharp rejoinders and menacing glares. He gets colder and meaner as the plot progresses.

Finally, at the film's climax, the now fully possessed George takes up his trusty axe and goes on a rampage, hacking through a locked bedroom door to get at his stepchildren, who are cowering inside. If this sounds familiar, it's because it's strikingly similar to Jack Nicholson's famous axe-wielding scene in Stanley Kubrick's horror classic *The Shining* (1980). Notably, however, Brolin's 'Here's Johnny!' moment predated Nicholson's by a year.

When I first watched it over two decades ago, I failed to recognise all the subtle little ways in which *The Amityville Horror* has informed the modern American haunted house movie. Because I wasn't watching these films in chronological order, I didn't know that George Lutz preceded *The Shining*'s Jack Torrance, or that the Indian burial ground trope wasn't merely recycled in *Amityville*; it originated in that film. And I'm clearly not alone; with the latter, there seems to be some form of collective amnesia that has caused many of us to erroneously attribute the motif to the Steven Spielberg-produced paranormal blockbuster *Poltergeist* (1982) – which doesn't even feature an Indian burial ground, just a run-of-the-mill desecrated cemetery.

So perhaps *Amityville* deserves more credit, after all. Not just because it can claim to have kickstarted a few horror movie clichés, but because it managed to maintain the status quo while offering something ever-so-slightly new. It's well paced, relatable and reassuringly familiar in all the right ways, with just a soupçon of novelty, making it, by horror movie standards (which are admittedly pretty low), a relative success.

Is *The Amityville Horror* the greatest haunted house film of all time? No. But it's quite clearly not the worst.

Shattered dreams and stigmatised homes

The enduring success of *The Amityville Horror* has made it difficult to distinguish fact from fiction. Over forty years since the film's release, it is now almost impossible to separate the cinematic version of events from the real thing. Even the house itself is often confused for its filmic counterpart, with legions of horror movie buffs making the pilgrimage to the Toms River home rather than the Amityville original.

Over time, the 'true story' and the movie have merged into a monolithic myth, leaving us with only one indisputable fact. Half a century ago, a terrible crime took place in an ostensibly ordinary home in the suburbs of Long Island, New York. On 13 November 1974, an assailant – almost certainly Ronald Defeo Jr – took a high-calibre shotgun and executed six members of the same family.

This is the verifiable extent of the so-called 'Amityville Horror'. Everything that happened afterwards is a matter of conjecture. Were subsequent owners besieged by paranormal forces? Did an investigative author dutifully record their testimony and write an authentic account of the haunting, on which the subsequent film would be based? And perhaps most pertinently, would anyone outside Long Island ever have heard of Amityville – town, house or haunting – if the story had not been made into a Hollywood horror movie?

It's doubtful. Yet, behind the iconic façade of the Amityville Horror House, there remains one truth: what happened there to the DeFeo family really *did* happen. A family of six were slaughtered in their own home. And for most of us, that constitutes our worst nightmare. Familicide – the murder of close family members – is an unthinkable crime, particularly when it involves the death of children. It rattles the most seasoned members of law enforcement, shatters communities, and grabs headlines.

When you think about it, it's actually pretty distasteful that the makers of *Amityville* capitalised on a such a horrific crime; a crime that had occurred less than five years before the release of the film. But these types of tragic narrative are so powerful and deeply ingrained in our psyches that we sometimes find it difficult to remember that they are real events, not movies. It's also hard to fight the instinct to transform the sites of these tragedies into phantasmal Gothic settings.

We all tend to assume that such properties are tainted, if not literally haunted. When the crime is recent, fresh in our minds, and of an especially heinous nature, we instinctively feel that the environment has somehow soaked up the dark energy of the event. The more brutal the crime, the more likely it is that the property will be deemed undesirable, perhaps even uninhabitable. And this isn't just a social preoccupation. In some jurisdictions it's a legal issue. In the states of California, Alaska and South Dakota, house sellers are legally required to disclose whether a violent crime has taken place on their property within recent history. In most other states – as well as in the UK – there's no legal requirement to share this information, but it's generally considered good practice to reveal whether a home may be stigmatised.

In estate agent jargon, a 'stigmatised property' is any property that could be devalued on the basis of a non-material factor. This might include a house that was used to conduct criminal activity, such as a drug ring or a brothel; a house where a sudden death occurred, such as murder or suicide; or even a house that is said to be haunted.

Today, prospective American home buyers are bolstered by a legal precedent that was not available to the Lutz family in the mid-1970s. The 1991 landmark case of *Stambovsky* v. *Ackley* – the so-called 'ghostbuster ruling' – saw a buyer in the state of New York successfully petition the court for permission to back out of a sale on the basis that the house he had bought was reputedly haunted.

In an infamous ruling that has since become something of a punchline, Judge Israel Rubin declared: 'As a matter of law, the house is haunted.' Of course, he wasn't actually suggesting that it could be legally proven that the offending house was full of ghosts. Rather, Rubin was supporting the plaintiff's claim that he had not been warned about its reputation, and because it was not something that could be discovered on a routine house inspection, it did not fall under the clause of *caveat emptor* (buyer beware). Whether or not the house was truly haunted was immaterial. The previous owner and new buyer believed it to be so, and the buyer did not want to live in a haunted house. For him, it was tainted. A stigmatised property.

If ever there was a stigmatised property, it was 112 Ocean Avenue, Amityville, New York.

'High Hopes' would, at one time, have hosted pool parties and cocktail receptions; wedding anniversaries and Christmas dinners; modest weeknight meals and quiet nights in. And then, one terrible night in the winter of 1974, it played host to a multiple murder, forever altering its fate as a once ordinary family home. It was thus hardly surprising that, when the Lutzes moved in a year later, they felt more than a little unsettled. It was only natural that they should wonder whether there might be something wrong with their new home. It was no less surprising that the tight-knit community of Amityville – a sleepy borough with a population of just 10,000, with little experience of violent crime or the glare of the media spotlight – would view the Ocean Avenue home with suspicion.

Immediately after the DeFeo murders, it was perhaps inevitable that the house would gain a reputation locally for being haunted. But could anyone have predicted that it would go on to become one of the most notorious haunted houses in the country? The most instantly recognisable stigmatised property of all time? Probably not.

And for this we have producer Samuel Z. Arkoff and director Stuart Rosenberg to thank: filmmakers who were deft enough to recognise a chillingly relatable story when they heard one, but who were not so foolish as to attempt to dismantle some 200 years of Gothic tradition.

The Amityville house of their cinematic creation was at once timeless and timely – the definitive modern American haunted house.

THE WINCHESTER MYSTERY HOUSE

THE ARCHITECTURE OF A HAUNTING

8

> She herself is a haunted house. She does not possess herself; her ancestors sometimes come and peer out of the windows of her eyes, and that is very frightening.
>
> *Angela Carter (1940–1992)*

Lady of mystery

Just before dawn on 18 April 1906, Sarah Lockwood Winchester, the sixty-seven-year-old heiress to the Winchester Repeating Arms Company fortune, was roused from a fitful slumber. Though this was not uncommon for the wealthy widow, whose chronic arthritis made it nearly impossible for her to enjoy a full night's rest, there was something unusual about this nocturnal intrusion.

A deep, ominous rumble reverberated throughout the 500-room San Jose, California mansion, making Sarah's massive mahogany bed frame tremble and groan, as if possessed by some unhappy spirit. The bedroom window panes – elegant pink and red Belgian art-glass panels, ornamented with the flower that was the namesake of Sarah's favourite niece, Daisy – shuddered angrily, threatening to shatter at any moment.

Chunks of plasterwork and timber raining down on her, Sarah scrambled out of bed to the relative safety of the bedroom doorframe. In this moment, the words spoken to her by a Boston-based psychic medium some two decades earlier surely would have returned to her:

> *There is a curse on your life. It is the same curse that took your child and husband, that has resulted from the terrible weapon that the Winchester family created… Build a house not just for yourself but also for the spirits of those who have fallen before that terrible weapon. As long as you build, you will live. Stop and you will die.*

After leaving New England in 1884 and moving some 3,000 miles across country to the last American frontier of California, Sarah *had* built. She built tirelessly and obsessively, creating the architectural magnum opus that was Llanada Villa, a house so monstrously large and strange that it had not only attracted the attention of her bemused neighbours, but also the attraction of local and regional press.

A *Los Angeles Herald* article of April 1895 reported that the widow Winchester's house was constantly under construction because of her fatalistic belief. 'This superstition has resulted in the construction of a mass of domes, turrets, cupolas and towers, covering territory enough for a castle,' the article maintained. But maybe this hadn't been enough. Perhaps she hadn't succeeded in appeasing the spirits, after all.

The Winchester Mystery House seemed to be destined to be haunted. A mad mosaic of turrets and towers, brackets and bargeboards, and spindly white finials that pierce the cobalt northern California sky like dozens of tiny Gothic church spires, the San Jose mansion is all odd angles and asymmetry taken to the wildest extremes. Characteristically high Victorian in its convoluted excess, the Mystery House appears every bit the textbook example of a haunted house – so much so that, even if it lacked a ghostly backstory, it would likely still serve as inspiration for Gothic novelists and Hollywood horror filmmakers. But of course it *does* have a ghostly backstory – and a rather famous one at that.

Today, the legend of the Winchester Mystery House is not just a legend; the story is practically chiselled in stone. It is regularly recounted to the thousands of tourists who traipse through the labyrinthine house each year, mentioned in dozens of ghost story anthologies, history textbooks, documentaries and films, and even described in the property's 1974 application for National Historic Landmark (NHL) status.

The standard narrative, as it appears in the successful NHL application, is as follows:

> *Mrs. Winchester was deeply upset by the deaths of her husband and daughter and seems to have consulted a spiritualistic medium. Reportedly, the medium explained that the spirits of all those who had been killed by the rifles her family had manufactured had sought their revenge by taking the lives of their loved ones. Further, these spirits had placed a curse on her and would haunt her forever. But the medium also stated that she could escape the curse by moving west, buying a house, and continuously building on it as the spirits directed. In this way, she could escape them and perhaps find the key to eternal life.*

For more than a century, these plot points have been presented to the public not as historical possibilities but as immutable facts about the life and legacy of Sarah Lockwood Winchester – the wealthy widow driven mad by grief and guilt.

Now, when I investigate a 'true' haunted house story, I almost always start out by dipping a toe in slowly. Armed with a healthy dose of scepticism, I go in assuming that whatever kernel of truth there may be, the most enduring ghost stories will inevitably have been embellished over time. This has proved true of every single haunted house discussed in this book. Yet, when it came to the Winchester Mystery House, I dived in headfirst. It's not that I genuinely believed that Sarah Winchester was cursed by ghostly gunshot victims, but I did believe that *she* believed it, and for this reason she spent millions of dollars and thirty-eight years of her life on the construction of the 24,000 ft^2 Queen Anne-style mansion which, by the time of her death in 1922, boasted 160 rooms (down from a reported 500, thanks to the 1906 earthquake), 2,000 doors, 10,000 windows, 47 staircases and 13 bathrooms.

Thus, at first glance, I assumed the Winchester Mystery House to be the world's first – and possibly *only* – house purpose-built to be haunted. How wrong I was. The Mystery House – or Llanada Villa, as Sarah called it – wasn't designed to be haunted at all. Rather, it was determined to be haunted (and thought to be the product of a haunted mind) by those who completely misjudged the motivations of its designer.

All the available evidence suggests that Sarah Winchester wasn't mad with grief or guilt. She was simply grieving and in need of an all-consuming diversion. Sarah was a lifelong architecture enthusiast and the daughter of a skilled craftsman. When she suddenly found herself with more money than she knew what to do with, it was only natural that Sarah should find solace in the hobby of house-building. Her San Jose home – actually one of several properties she owned – was not the reflection of a disordered brain. It was an outlet for her creative expression, and a tincture for emotional pain.

There is no concrete evidence that Sarah was interested or involved in spiritualism at all. Seemingly, her enduring reputation as a superstitious hysteric has little to do with the actual person, and everything to do with how she was (and continues to be) perceived by society. Even today, it is apparently impossible to accept the sanity of an independent, single woman.

Because relatively little survives in terms of personal archives, Winchester has been left perilously vulnerable to storytellers and imaginative rewriters of history. What little we know of her has been brought to light thanks to the valiant efforts of historian Mary Jo Ignoffo, whose biography *Captive of the Labyrinth: Sarah L. Winchester, Heiress to the Rifle Fortune* (2010) contains a rare factual account of the construction of Sarah's house, effectively debunking most of the mythology surrounding it.

The historian has been labelled a 'killjoy' by some for attempting to destroy the time-honoured tradition of the Winchester Mystery House. But I don't think that's fair or even accurate because, as it turns out, the real story of Sarah Winchester's uncanny home and how it came to be known as 'the most haunted house in America' is just as fascinating as the fake one.

It is the story of an eccentric, yet highly intelligent woman who unwittingly became the scapegoat for the staggering death toll of the Winchester Repeating Rifle – the world's first firearm capable of firing 15 shots in just over 10 seconds. Partly because she was the primary beneficiary of the money made from selling the deadly weapon, but mostly because she was an unconventional woman who refused to explain herself or justify the size and layout of her home, she was viewed with suspicion by her contemporaries. A reclusive introvert, with little interest in socialising with her high-flying 'Gilded Age' peers, and no apparent plans to remarry after the death of her millionaire husband William Wirt Winchester, Winchester was almost as inscrutable as the blueprints to her mansion.

The lore that surrounds the enigmatic widow does contain some trace elements of truth. Winchester did endure a considerable amount of heartache, losing half a dozen loved ones over fifteen years, including her daughter, her parents and her husband. Her house was the result of these losses, which gave her both the means and motive to build it. But beyond feeling grief for her family members, there is no evidence that Winchester experienced any form of emotional turmoil or existential dread over how her family had made its fortune.

If there is an element of guilt here, it's not personal, but societal. Much like the legends surrounding the Myrtles Plantation, the myth of the Mystery House is, at least in part, a tacit acknowledgement of past atrocities – in this case, as we will learn, the subjugation and mass slaughter of indigenous Americans that occurred during Westward expansion. Somewhere along the line, Sarah Lockwood Winchester became the 'fall guy' for genocide, and the house a simulacrum for its controversial owner.

In all likelihood, the Winchester Mystery House was not purpose-built to be haunted, but it *was* almost fated to become so. In many ways, it is the ultimate haunted house, with all the most familiar ingredients: an eclectic neo-Gothic aesthetic, a good measure of domestic deviation, and of course, a history of death and trauma. What's more, its legend incorporates virtually all the themes and topics we've touched on in previous chapters. There's spiritualism and seances; destruction and desolation; a female central protagonist; and a connection to a problematic past.

Suffice to say, there's a lot to unpack here, and to do so, we're going to have to cover such disparate subjects as Victorian gender ideals, Freudian psychology and genocide to get to grips with one of the most complex, yet archetypal, haunted houses tackled in this book.

Do the ghosts of gunshot victims roam the many rooms of the Winchester Mystery House? Probably not. But it might still be haunted. Perhaps by Sarah Winchester herself. Or maybe by some roving spectres who took one look at it and determined the Mystery House to be the ideal environment for a classic haunting.

Sarah Lockwood Winchester (née Pardee) was an undeniably odd woman, especially by the narrow standards of her day. For starters, Sarah (or Sallie, as she was known to her family) had an unusually sharp intellect and an interest in things that were at the time seen as masculine, including mechanical inventions, woodworking and architecture. She was also somewhat strange in appearance – at least, in her later years. On the rare occasions that Sarah deigned to appear in public, she did so shrouded in a long black veil and wearing full-length gloves. This was partly due to the fact that she was in a perpetual state of mourning; however, it was also said that she hid behind this camouflage to disguise her deformities – a nearly toothless mouth and gnarled fingers crippled by rheumatoid arthritis.

But even though she cut an odd figure in old age, attracting attention for her unusual looks, interests and social habits – not to mention her hefty fortune – Sarah started out life under relatively ordinary circumstances. Born in the summer of 1839 in New Haven, Connecticut, Sarah was the fifth child and fourth daughter of Leonard and Sarah Pardee, a respectable, middle-class couple who were the descendants of some of the town's earliest settlers, able to trace their regional roots back to the late seventeenth century. Though they were never extravagantly wealthy like Sarah's future in-laws, the Pardees were hard-working, prosperous and well connected.

In the late 1840s, when Sarah was a young child, the Pardees became acquainted with their neighbours, the Winchesters. Not yet the powerful firearms tycoon he would go on to be, father Oliver Fisher Winchester had recently co-founded the Winchester and Davies Shirt Manufactory, a clothing company that quickly grew to be one of the most profitable in New England, thanks to its early adoption of the electric sewing machine. Contrary to popular belief, it was shirts, not guns, that made the Winchester fortune, with the textile factory providing the capital to later invest in the arms business.

While the Winchesters' wealth would eventually far eclipse that of the Pardees, in the early days of their acquaintance the two families were of roughly the same social status and income bracket, with children of similar ages, making them natural friends.

It's not clear when Sarah's relationship with the Winchester's eldest son, William, developed from childhood friendship to romance, but whenever it occurred, both families likely approved of the match.

William, of course, was poised to take over the family's lucrative business, and though he lacked his father's drive and ambition, he was nevertheless worldly and intelligent. Sarah was also something of a catch. Not only was she the well-educated daughter of an upstanding old New Haven family, accomplished in language, music and the arts, but she was also, in her youth, an attractive young woman with fashionably porcelain skin and a halo of curly chestnut hair. Petite in stature, keen in intelligence and demure by nature, Sarah was, in short, the ideal Victorian wife.

On 30 September 1862, in the midst of the Civil War, Sarah Lockwood Pardee and William Wirt Winchester were married. And for the first few years of their union, at least, the couple lived a seemingly contented existence in the Winchester family's Court Street home – a temporary living situation while they waited for their marital home to be built in the upscale Prospect Hill area of north New Haven.

As the war raged, Sarah and William were left relatively unscathed by the chaos that swirled around them, even though New Haven was a hotbed of Union support and abolitionist activism. Sarah's own parents were vocal advocates of the cause, and members of both the Pardee and Winchester families served in active combat. However, thanks to William's perennially poor health and important business interests in town, he was spared conscription. The newlyweds were thus able to wait out the war together.

Four years into their marriage, on 15 June 1866, Sarah and William welcomed their first and only child – a daughter called Annie Pardee Winchester, named in honour of William's recently deceased sister. But this joyous occasion for the Winchesters quickly turned to heartbreak. While both mother and daughter fared well during labour, baby Annie struggled to put on weight, even with the aid of an experienced wet nurse. The family physician diagnosed the child with marasmus, a severe form of malnutrition, and within less than a month she was dead.

This marked a turning point in the previously peaceful life of Sarah Winchester.

Much has been made of the death of Winchester's daughter. Together with the death of her husband, it has been suggested as the catalyst for Sarah's subsequent construction of the so-called Mystery House. And while there's no tangible link between the deaths (her daughter died in 1866 and her husband in 1881, but their deaths are often erroneously cited as having happened within a year of each other) and the building project that commenced some twenty-five years later, it certainly seems that Sarah was deeply and irrevocably affected by these losses – especially by the loss of her only child.

That her dearly departed daughter was never far from her mind is demonstrated in the first line of her Last Will and Testament of 1920, which stipulated that $3,000 (about $41,000 today) was to be allocated to the care and maintenance of the family plot in New Haven's Evergreen Cemetery, where Annie was interred. When Sarah herself finally died in 1922, a safe in her San Jose home was opened, to reveal her most cherished possessions: a lock of silken baby hair, along with the obituaries of her husband and child.

In mid-nineteenth-century America, infant mortality was sadly an all too common occurrence, making Sarah Winchester's experience far from extraordinary. Of course, all mothers in this situation would have been heartbroken and would have needed time to grieve, but almost inevitably, they would recover, compelled by a mixture of societal expectation and family obligation to resume their wifely duties. Most women would not have had the luxury to wallow in their grief for long.

Winchester was likely no exception. After all, her husband was set to inherit a fortune and a successful company and, in time, he would be expected to have heirs of his own. But it was not to be. The couple was either unable or unwilling to conceive, and they spent the remainder of their nineteen-year marriage childless. It was probably for this reason that Sarah remained so fixated on her late daughter.

The death of her child was the first in a series of tragedies to befall Winchester. Though there would be a brief respite following Annie's passing, during which Winchester was able to absorb herself in the renovations of her new Prospect Hill home, an expansive Second Empire-style mansion which she and her husband shared with several other adult members of the Winchester family, the Grim Reaper would soon return to claim four more loved ones.

The first of these was the man who had instilled in Sarah a lifelong love for design. Her father, Leonard Pardee, died in June 1869 from a spinal defect likely caused by rheumatoid arthritis, which unfortunately, his daughter would inherit. A little over a decade later, Sarah's mother died of unspecified causes. Six months after that, her father-in-law, Oliver Winchester, by now the president of the highly profitable Winchester Repeating Arms Company, succumbed to complications from a stroke. And finally, in March 1881, Sarah's beloved husband, William, died from the chronic tubercular condition that had plagued him for much of his adult life.

In just ten months, Sarah lost three of the four most important and influential figures in her life, and at the same time, gained more money than most people could spend in a lifetime. As a beneficiary of her husband's and parents' estates, Winchester was suddenly in the possession of a fortune worth an estimated \$20 million (or about \$600 million today). But what was the point of all that money without her loved ones? What would she do with it?

Why, she would build, of course…

Home, strange home: the 'uncanny' Winchester Mystery House

On 11 June 1898, just over a decade into her new life in California, Sarah Winchester wrote to her sister-in-law, updating her on all the developments at Llanada Villa, the 45-acre estate nestled in the verdant Santa Clara Valley that Winchester had named in honour of its resemblance to the Basque region of Llanada Alavesa in northern Spain.

Sarah wrote:

> *I am constantly having to make upheaval for some reason. For instance, my upper hall which leads to the sleeping apartment was rendered so unexpectedly dark by a little addition that after a number of people had missed their footing on the stairs I decided that safety demanded something to be done, so… I took out a wall and put in a skylight. Then I had to have plastering done and as that could not well be done in the heat which succeeded, I had to wait for cooler weather… [But then] I became rather worn and tired out and dismissed all the work-men to take such rest as I might through the winter.*

In this rare historical record, one of only a handful of extant documents to capture the true voice of Sarah Winchester, we see a woman who is dramatically different from her popular image. Neither hysterical nor obsessive, the author of this letter appears to have been methodical, pragmatic and, above all, lucid in her approach to building. Ghosts didn't dictate the plan and schedule of her house construction; practical concerns such as safety and weather conditions did. What's more, contrary to claims that she employed an army of builders to work on the property for thirty-eight years straight, Sarah evidently allowed them to have much-needed breaks.

And yet, however sensible she may have been, the fruits of Winchester's architectural labours were decidedly unconventional. What started out as a modest eight-room farmhouse mushroomed into a twenty-six-room mansion within just six months of Winchester's purchase of the property in 1886, sparking speculation about the owner's motivation and intentions. For what possible reason could a widowed, childless woman require a house that would eventually grow large enough to accommodate a family of forty? And why would she choose to construct it on a relatively remote tract of land on America's last frontier, rather than in the more developed, dignified environs of her native New England? It is a fixation that persists to this very day.

But it isn't simply the sheer scale of the house or its position that invites curiosity. It is its ostensibly illogical layout and preponderance of peculiar fittings and features that have earned the property its popular moniker the 'Winchester Mystery House' – a name that has been associated with it since at least the 1930s, when it was owned and operated by fairground impresarios John and Mayme Brown. The Browns had originally intended to construct one of the nation's first rollercoasters on the site, but when they discovered that the home itself was effectively a carnival funhouse, they abandoned plans for the fairground ride.

Modern visitors to the Mystery House are invited to ponder the dead-end doorways, switchback staircases and stained-glass windows that are designed to enlarge and distort everything beyond them. These disorienting features, it is commonly suggested, were implemented by the widow Winchester to foil the angry spirits that stalked her throughout the sprawling estate. Of course, Sarah never actually said that this was the impetus for her unorthodox architectural plans, but then, she didn't say much about anything, leaving the door wide open to conjecture.

According to Carl Ferrigno, a San Jose native who worked as a tour guide at the Mystery House as a teenager in the early 1970s, at the time the staff were not provided with an official script but were definitely encouraged to put forward a certain narrative.

'All the guides told similar, but not precisely the same, stories,' he recalls. 'We all privately believed what we wanted to, and espoused what was expected. Some cared about the truth, and others not so much.'

For his part, Ferrigno did not buy into the legends: 'I have no belief in hauntings by victims of the Winchester rifle. Poppycock, as they would say. But is it haunted? Maybe…' More from Carl later.

In reality, there are plenty of plausible explanations for the Winchester Mystery House, and as many of them stem from asking 'why not?' as from asking 'why?'

Why not build in northern California, where land was relatively cheap compared to the more densely populated East Coast? The pleasant climate would be good for a sufferer of chronic arthritis. Besides, Sarah had once holidayed in the Bay area with her husband; the location likely held happy memories.

Why wouldn't someone with time, money, and interest in ambitious architectural projects build such a large structure? After all, though her home stood largely empty, with only one other occupant living with Winchester for any length of time – her adult niece, Daisy Merriman – Sarah had originally conceived of it as a family home. Not for a nuclear family, mind you, but for several of the extended family members who had followed her to the West Coast in the late 1880s: her sisters, Belle, Estelle and Nettie, together with their husbands and children.

As for those peculiar fittings and features, most of these have logical explanations. A zig-zagging staircase that uses 44 tiny steps to rise just 9 feet was constructed to accommodate Winchester's arthritic knees. The mysterious 'doors leading nowhere' would have, at one point, led somewhere. Many of them were sealed off following the 1906 earthquake as a safety precaution. Still other peculiarities were simply experiments in design. Because Sarah was untrained in architecture and refused to hire a professional to oversee her project, the implementation of her plans often had mixed results. If she was unhappy with an outcome, she would simply cease construction and move on somewhere else.

While it's admittedly eccentric, there is nothing about the Mystery House that is intrinsically inexplicable. It's only because its owner neglected to offer any kind of explanation for it that rumours were able to germinate, then flourish. This began within Winchester's lifetime, with a series of articles that appeared in the California press in the 1890s. The stories started out curious and speculative, but eventually turned derogatory, painting Winchester as a delusional neurotic, forever in fear of the wrath of spirits that perpetually followed her.

Perhaps, if she had been more approachable and made a greater effort to ingratiate herself within her new community in California, Sarah might have been spared. If she had been willing to perform the role of society hostess; if she had publicly backed a political candidate, or opened her doors to either of the two American presidents who visited the area (William McKinley and Theodore Roosevelt); if she had used her supposedly ill-gotten gains to support a worthy cause, or at the very least, to bail out her bankrupt brother-in-law when creditors were after him, Winchester might have been viewed differently.

Incidentally, Sarah did make major charitable contributions later in life, most of which were anonymous, but included the very public foundation of the William Wirt Winchester Tubercular Hospital in New Haven in 1918. By this point, however, her fate was all but sealed.

One has to wonder, though: if Winchester had been a man and had behaved in precisely the same manner, would all the sensational stories about her still have been written and circulated? Western society has long struggled to know what to do with a single woman, and never was this more true than in the Victorian era at the height of 'the cult of domesticity' or 'the cult of true womanhood': a belief system that promoted the home as the woman's rightful sphere of influence. Here, a woman would oversee the general management of the household: supervising servants, food preparation, cleaning and child-rearing all came under her purview. A woman's remit was home-making, not house-building; the latter was a distinctly masculine undertaking.

Based on these criteria, Sarah Winchester was clearly lacking in key areas. She was childless, but also seemingly uninterested in assuming any of the other suitably 'feminine' roles that were available to her: socialite, philanthropist or wallflower.

According to historian Barbara Welter, one of the first scholars to advance the study of the 'cult of domesticity', the ideal 'true' woman was thought to be frail, physically and intellectually incapable of any pursuit outside the home, and dependent on a husband or father to protect her within that home. And while Winchester did stay mostly confined to her house, she had no such male figure in her later years. She was strong-minded, independent and personally responsible for the construction of the shelter that provided her protection. In essence, she was an aberration in the eyes of most of her contemporaries.

It is surely no coincidence that haunted house narratives, particularly those of nineteenth-century American Gothic fiction, are largely populated by single women. If the haunted house represents the inverse of the ideal family home – or what French modernist philosopher Gaston Bachelard terms the 'oneiric house' (the house of dreams or fantasies), then it makes sense that the canonical central character of the haunted house story should be the opposite of the ideal woman. Childless and unmarried governesses, boarding-house matrons, adult daughters and widows feature heavily in works by Henry James, Nathaniel Hawthorne, Edith Wharton and Mary E. Wilkins Freeman, among others.

To be sure, there is no direct link between these authors' ghost stories and the Winchester Mystery House. However, there is some suggestion that Sarah's home served as the inspiration for a much later haunted house narrative: Shirley Jackson's *The Haunting of Hill House*.

Set against the backdrop of post-Second World War America – an era that witnessed women's return from the factory to the homestead, and consequently the resurgence of 'the cult of domesticity' – the novel focuses on the interior world of its central protagonist, Eleanore Vance, a thirty-two-year-old single woman. Having spent her entire adult life caring for her invalid mother, Eleanore views her trip to Hill House as an opportunity to explore her new-found freedom. She yearns for independence and belonging. She fantasises about having a home of her own: a dream house notable for its conspicuous absence of family ('I could live there all alone, she thought. No one would ever find me there, either, behind all those roses'). Though initially frightened by the labyrinthine, Winchester-like Hill House, Eleanore soon comes to view it as her ultimate destiny. Her true home.

In this modern American Gothic classic, the main character is cast as both victim of and rebel against the patriarchal system that allowed the 'cult of domesticity' to flourish – an iconoclastic figure not wildly dissimilar to the real-life Sarah Winchester.

In so many ways, Winchester's home is abnormal. Aesthetically, it is a mishmash of styles, incorporating the Romanesque and Gothic, the Italianate and Spanish, and even East Asian influences. Practically speaking, it is unusual too, lacking a logical layout or clear-cut plan for construction. And ideologically, it obviously lacked a crucial component: a family. Altogether, it is a strange bit of work. One might say it's an *uncanny* piece of architecture.

'Uncanny' is a term frequently employed to describe the haunted house. On the face of it, this is fairly self-explanatory, considering the most commonly understood meanings of the word are as follows: 1) something 'strange or mysterious, often in a way that is slightly frightening'; 2) something or someone possessing qualities that are 'beyond what is normal or expected'; or 3) something that is 'difficult or impossible to explain'. In short, the perfect descriptor of the haunted house.

However, there is an alternative understanding of the word – a slightly more esoteric one that, while less well known, is perhaps still more applicable to the haunted house and to the Winchester Mystery House in particular.

In German, the word for 'uncanny' is *unheimlich*, which translates as 'unhomely' or something that is 'not of the home or familiar'. It is this definition of the word that has formed the basis for the psychoanalytical theory of 'the uncanny'– the experience of an event, environment or object that feels at once oddly familiar yet discomfortingly foreign (think, for instance, of the sensation of déjà vu).

Most famously espoused by Sigmund Freud in his 1918 essay *'Das Unheimliche'*, which uses the example of humanoid objects such as dolls, waxwork figures and automatons to illustrate the anxiety that can be caused by something simultaneously ordinary and extraordinary, the theory of 'the uncanny' has since been used by scholars working in a range of disciplines, and applied in a multitude of different contexts – including in reference to haunted houses.

Given the etymology of the German word, along with its popular associations, it seems strange that Freud didn't focus his own study of 'the uncanny' on the haunted house. After all, what's more familiar than the home? And what could be more unsettling than a haunted one? The analyst freely acknowledges this omission about halfway through his essay, writing:

> *We might indeed have begun our investigation with this example, perhaps the most striking of all, of something uncanny, but we refrained from doing so because the uncanny in it is too much mingled with and in part covered by what is purely gruesome.*

Not wishing to confuse the experience of 'the uncanny' with that of full-blown horror, Freud quickly drops the subject of haunted houses, leaving it for other academics to pick up decades later.

For the purposes of our discussion, there are two modern variants of 'the uncanny' theory that are particularly relevant: domestic uncanny and architectural uncanny.

The former denotes the experience of a dwelling that either lacks the requisite components of the ideal family home or that is somehow discordant with the feeling of 'being at home', while the latter describes an architectural space that is constructed in a manner that seems to be at odds with the ways in which its occupants would ordinarily use or enjoy the space. Both are characterised by sensations of surprise, tension, disorientation and defamiliarity. Both seem to perfectly encapsulate the unique environment of the famously haunted Winchester Mystery House.

From the moment visitors cross the threshold of the Mystery House, whether they are aware of the uncanny theory or not, they become immersed in the house's theoretical framework. Visitors on guided tours are ushered through an oddly circuitous route of the house, which seems to have been deliberately designed to disorient, traversing what feels like miles up and down staircases and corridors, only to end up back where they started. At every turn, their attention is drawn to numerous oddities, all of which work to defy their expectations of the conventional house: a tiny cabinet door that opens up to a maze of thirty rooms beyond; a cache of priceless Tiffany glass windows stored in a space where no light can pass through them; a hatch that leads to a 15-foot drop into the garden; and of course, all those 'dead-end' doorways and staircases. All the while, the tour guide tells them about the childless widow Winchester and her unorthodox approach to home-making.

In 'Designs for the Haunted House', a tongue-in-cheek essay that appeared in *Uncommon Structures, Unconventional Builders* (1971), an architectural guide aimed at a popular audience, author-illustrator Alan Van Dine inventively reimagines the design and construction of the Mystery House in terms that are likewise markedly uncanny:

> *Design conferences took place in the Seance Room, where Mrs. Winchester sat each evening, apparently alone. Her ghostly consultants were numerous but untrained, capricious, often vague, and utterly insatiable – demanding room after room, balcony after balcony, chimney after chimney... The place was being designed by ghosts and for ghosts. At first these makeshift blueprints were nearly indecipherable and often unbuildable. As time went on, however, the drawings improved – even if their logic did not.*

Of course, as we now know, this is not at all how the construction of the Winchester Mystery House took place. There were no spirit architects, no nightly seances, or even a seance room (it was, as it turns out, the gardener's attic bedroom). And yet, even if we strip away all this supernatural set-dressing, we are still left with something strange and surprising. A house that is undeniably uncanny.

The gun that won the West

When Sarah Winchester arrived in California in 1886, it had been 350 years since European explorers first set foot in the region, a century since it had been colonised by the Spanish, and 40 years since it had seceded from Mexico during the Mexican-American War (1846–8). The discovery of gold in Coloma, California in 1848, at the start of American occupation, brought a tidal wave of immigrants into what was then still a largely 'unsettled' region – and I use quotations, as it is highly debatable whether these new arrivals actually brought anything like peaceful settlement to what would soon become the nation's thirty-first state. During the gold rush of the late 1840s the territory was virtually lawless, characterised by rampant theft, property damage, prostitution, violence and murder; it earned its popular moniker the 'Wild West'.

By the time Sarah set down roots here, however, much had changed. In a relatively short time the 'Wild West' had been effectively tamed and the state had made major inroads in revamping its once unsavoury image. Middle- and upper-class Easterners like Winchester were enticed to travel west by the promise of cheap land, mild weather and the opportunity to invest in the resource-rich state.

At the time, there were a number of major marketing campaigns spearheaded by Californian chambers of commerce and business interests to promote the state and reassure new settlers of its now stable status. In promotional materials such as Charles Nordhoff's *California for Health, Pleasure and Residence: A Book for Travelers and Settlers* (1872), terms such as 'settled', 'safe', 'peaceful', 'orderly' and 'lawful' are strategically peppered throughout the text.

As a worldly, well-read woman, Winchester would have been acutely aware of the sustained period of violence that had preceded her move to California. She would've known that many men, women and even children had died by gunshot in the highly chaotic process of Westward expansion, a process idealistically branded by contemporary politicians as 'manifest destiny' – the belief that American settlers were divinely preordained to expand west across the entire North American continent.

But what almost certainly wouldn't have been on Sarah's radar was her own loved ones' potential culpability in the whole bloody ordeal. And to be fair to her, this wasn't necessarily a case of wilful ignorance. The Winchester Repeating Rifle – previously known as the Henry rifle in honour of its designer, Benjamin Tyler Henry – which Sarah's father-in-law invested in and ultimately brought to market in 1860, wasn't widely available or used until the 1870s. By this point, much of the dirty work in terms of 'winning' the West was already done.

As well as treacherous terrains, renegade outlaws and rampant disease, the main obstacle that American settlers in the mid-1800s faced in California was the large population of indigenous people, estimated to number in the tens of thousands, if not more. Though their colonial predecessors, the Spanish, had subdued much of the native population through forced religious conversion and indentured servitude, there remained a sizeable number of free indigenous Americans, many of whom actively resisted the invasion of their land and the depletion of its natural resources. Considered an inherent threat to 'manifest destiny', the Californian Indian came to be viewed as the American colonist's number-one enemy.

On 6 January 1851, in a speech to the California Senate, First Governor Peter Burnett put popular sentiment and government policy on indigenous Californians into words:

> *That a war of extermination will continue to be waged between the races until the Indian race becomes extinct must be expected. While we cannot anticipate this result but with painful regret, the inevitable destiny of the race is beyond the power or wisdom of man to avert.*

Here, Governor Burnett plainly articulates the genocidal intentions of the American government. Californian Indians would have to be eradicated – and they very nearly were between the years of 1846 and 1873, during what historians now refer to as the California genocide, a period which saw the government-sanctioned systematic murder of an estimated 16,000 indigenous people (though some scholars put the figure as high as 100,000). They were killed in all manner of gruesome ways – hanging, stabbing, beating, bludgeoning and burning – but the most common method by far was by firearm. Quite simply, it was the fastest and most efficient way to get the job done – especially after the advent of the repeating rifle.

However, the Winchester Repeating Rifle wasn't sold until 1860. The model marketed as 'The gun that won the West' in a 1919 advertising campaign and later made famous by actor Jimmy Stewart in the Western film noir *Winchester '73* (1950) wasn't available until

1873 – what historians generally consider to be the last year of the genocide. To be sure, the Model '73 was responsible for more than its fair share of bloodshed, including the murder of many indigenous Americans. But it was not the key instrument of destruction in the California genocide.

Suffice to say, Sarah Winchester was not responsible for the California genocide. In fact, despite serving as a board member and major stakeholder of the Winchester Repeating Arms Company, she had very little to do with her late husband's business. Her personal feelings about gun ownership are unknown, but it's unlikely that she would have felt anything other than complete neutrality.

When America was in its infancy, and still primarily a rural country, very few people would have questioned the ownership or use of guns. Firearms were considered essential to survival and safety – a necessary tool to fend off wild animals and indigenous enemies. It was only after the growth of cities in the 1880s and 1890s that guns would have been looked upon by some as dangerous and unnecessary.

Crucially, it was also around this time that the American press began to articulate some form of collective guilt about the brutal treatment of indigenous people in the mid-nineteenth century. And it was also around this time that stories began to circulate about Sarah's unusual home. The widow Winchester had somehow come to personify the controversial issue. But why?

It partly comes down to being in the wrong place at the wrong time. For all it had going for it, California was perhaps not the best place for the heiress of a firearms company to live. As the dust settled in the aftermath of Westward expansion, many ordinary Californians, now enjoying peaceful lives in modern enclaves in the former untamed wilderness, were finally able to reflect on the period of anarchy that had led to their current circumstances. All that chaos and carnage seemed a world away, but they knew it had all taken place within living memory. Sarah's neighbours needed to assuage their guilt; they needed someone to point the finger at – and who better than an obscenely wealthy gun baroness who was splashing out millions on a bizarrely constructed mega-mansion?

It was also about name recognition. For although the Winchester Repeating Rifle was not the sole – or even primary – weapon used to annihilate indigenous people, it was certainly the best known at the time. As a pricey status symbol costing about $100 (around $2,500 today), wielded by celebrated gunslingers such as Buffalo Bill and Annie Oakley, the weapon had considerable cachet.

In sharing the same name with the (in)famous firearm, Sarah Winchester was virtually powerless to prevent the connection between herself and the death toll of the 'gun that won the West'.

There are no ghost stories involving indigenous Californians associated with the Winchester Mystery House, at least not explicitly. If, according to the standard mythology, Sarah Winchester really was haunted by the victims of the Winchester Rifle, then this would naturally include a fair few Native Americans. But it has always been suggested that this particular haunting is somewhat abstract. There are no full-bodied apparitions of Apache warriors, only the residual energy of their unhappy souls.

Intriguingly, however, there *is* a resident American Indian at the Mystery House: a garden sculpture known as *Chief Little Fawn*, which Winchester is said to have erected as a form of atonement for her family's role in the California genocide (though it should be noted that the 'noble savage' was a common motif for cast-iron statues at the time, and Sarah also displayed statuary of classical gods and goddesses, cherubs, birds and beasts, suggesting that the presence of the statue was purely decorative). But while tour guides sometimes suggest that the sculpture depicts a real-life victim of a Winchester firearm, the only record of a historical person named Little Fawn that I could find was a Native American woman who died in Massachusetts some 200 years before the invention of the repeating rifle.

Whoever he is, Chief Little Fawn does not appear to be haunting the Winchester Mystery House. Not literally, anyway.

Generally speaking, indigenous people do not figure prominently in traditional Anglo-American ghost stories prior to the second half of the twentieth century.

Of course, Native Americans have their own centuries-long tradition of supernatural folklore. Each of the 574 federally recognised indigenous tribes in America has a subtly different system of spiritual belief, all of which are underpinned by supernatural legends that have been passed down orally over the generations. The majority of these bear very little resemblance to the standard Anglo-American ghost story and are virtually unknown outside tribal communities, with perhaps the sole exception being the Algonquin legend of the wendigo – a malevolent spirit of the wilderness, known for stalking and possessing its human victims – which was borrowed (or appropriated) by British ghost story author Algernon Blackwood in 1910. But this is a rare example of a Native American-themed supernatural tale that managed to permeate popular Western culture before the late twentieth century – and perhaps the only example to draw any inspiration from actual indigenous belief.

As with the legacy of slavery in the American South, the collective guilt over the events of Westward expansion would eventually go on to inspire ghostly legends, but it would take some time for Native Americans to break free of negative stereotypes to become the more sympathetic – and tragic – figures we know today. Even now, though, Americans' guilt seems to be fixated on the seizure of indigenous land rather than their barbaric treatment of the actual people. This, we will learn, has had a unique effect on the modern Native American-themed ghost story.

Public expressions of remorse over the treatment of Native Americans were already being voiced before Sarah Winchester set foot in California. One such voice was bestselling author Helen Hunt Jackson. Like Winchester, Jackson was a well-to-do New England widow who, following the untimely deaths of her husband and infant child, travelled west in search of a new life, as well as relief from a consumptive condition, first settling in Colorado before relocating to southern California in the late 1870s. It was here that she developed a keen awareness of the plight of the Californian Indian.

In addition to writing fictional and non-fictional accounts of the maltreatment of indigenous people, Jackson served as an official government agent tasked with investigating the living conditions of the local indigenous population. Her exhaustive research resulted in a 35-page report on the 'Conditions and Needs of Mission Indians of California', as well as a full-length book entitled *A Century of Dishonour* (1881), a searing indictment of the administration that allowed the torture and murder of thousands of natives in the name of 'manifest destiny'.

Finding that cold hard facts did relatively little to alter public opinion or effect real change, Jackson turned her attention to fiction. Inspired by her friend Harriet Beecher Stowe's *Uncle Tom's Cabin* (1852), a sentimental novel that had a profound impact on popular attitudes towards slavery, Jackson set to work on a historical romance that grappled with the issues that were dear to her.

'If I could write a story that would do for the Indian one-hundredth part what *Uncle Tom's Cabin* did for the Negro, I would be thankful the rest of my life,' Jackson declared.

The result was her best-known work, *Ramona* (1884). Set in southern California following the Mexican-American War, the novel follows the trials and tribulations of the titular character, Ramona, a mixed-race Scottish-Native American orphan struggling to survive during the period of American annexation.

Though somewhat maudlin (or 'sugar-coated', as the author herself worded it), the book proved to be a huge hit, with more than 150,000 copies sold within the first ten months of its publication. But as successful as it was, Jackson's novel ultimately failed in its true aim. It did next to nothing to raise awareness for the plight of indigenous people, with readers focusing on the book's romanticised historical setting, location and love story, rather than its racial message.

The real barrier that Jackson and other activists of the period kept coming up against was a deep-rooted and long-lasting prejudice. That much of the general public continued to view indigenous people with contempt is made clear in a contemporary critique of Jackson's novel in which the journalist remarks that she finds it hard to believe that such 'lazy, cruel, cowardly, and covetous' people as the Mission Indians could produce 'specimens of physical beauty and mental sublimity' like Ramona and her paramour, Alessandro.

In spite of the efforts of figures such as Jackson, it would take decades for indigenous Americans to gain widespread public sympathy, or anything close to respect. At best, they were afforded benign, yet simplistic, roles in popular culture, roles like Tonto (a Spanish word which translates as 'fool' or 'silly'), the faithful sidekick in the TV series *The Lone Ranger* (1933–56). At worst, they were relegated to the role of the savage foe to the all-American hero, as seen in John Wayne films such as *Stagecoach* (1939) and *The Searchers* (1956).

It wouldn't be until the late 1960s, at the height of the Civil Rights movement, that the tide began to change. In 1968 the 'Indian Civil Rights Act' was passed into law and the first Native American studies programme was established at the University of Minnesota. In 1970, historian Dee Brown published his groundbreaking history of Californian Indians, *Bury My Heart at Wounded Knee*. And in 1973, actor Marlon Brando famously protested against the portrayal of Native Americans in film by sending actress Sacheen Littlefeather, dressed in full Apache attire, to the Academy Awards in his stead.

All of this not only set the stage for more respectful representation of indigenous peoples in popular culture, but also prepared them for their entrée into the realm of ghostly folklore. Unsurprisingly, when indigenous people first started to appear in Anglo-American ghost stories in the 1970s and 1980s, they assumed virtually the same role as the African American slave: the ghost as embodiment of past atrocities.

In Dolores Riccio and Joan Bingham's 'true' ghost story anthology, *Haunted Houses USA* (1989), such figures feature in three narratives, including one that takes place at La Purisima Mission in southern California, in which the ghosts of Chumash Indians are described as being seen 'dressed in rags with long dirty matted hair'. Sightings of these spectral Chumash parishioners in such 'wretched' conditions were said to be in jarring contrast to how the Mission museum officially presented them to the public, suggesting that their manifestation was some sort of posthumous act of protest. A solemn reminder of their true experience under the brutal Spanish regime in the late eighteenth century.

If you're unfamiliar with this ghost story – or indeed, with anything remotely like it – that's not so surprising; although there are plenty of similar stories out there, they aren't the most widely circulated examples of the Native American-themed supernatural legend. But chances are you will have come across a tale involving a cursed Indian burial ground, a trope inaugured and made famous by *The Amityville Horror*.

Sometimes it's suggested that the curse – and subsequent supernatural activity – is the consequence of building a home on sacred (stolen) land, sometimes it's suggested that it is caused by the desecration of the graves beneath, but more often than not, it's not fully explained at all. And rarely, if ever, do we actually encounter an apparition of an indigenous person.

Now, no one has ever explicitly suggested that the Winchester Mystery House was built on an Indian burial ground, but there are some subtle commonalities between the Mystery House mythology and the Indian burial ground trope, as well as a shared timeline in terms of their development as a kind of *mea culpa* for past injustices perpetrated against indigenous peoples. In both, the Native American is simultaneously ever-present, yet conspicuously absent. A long, dark shadow cast by a faceless, nameless form. And perhaps this is to be expected, since the history of relations between Native Americans and white settlers is a history of erasure. That the Native American ghost seldom appears in the haunted house is probably a reflection of the fact that, unlike African American slaves, indigenous people rarely set foot inside white men's homes. What's more, they were banished from the very land on which such houses stood, relegated to life on isolated reservations – that is, if they were allowed to live at all.

In the 2018 supernatural thriller *Winchester*, a film loosely based on the Mystery House mythology and starring Helen Mirren as Sarah Winchester, the American Indian is finally invited indoors. About halfway through the film, in a sequence depicting a parade of ghostly gunshot victims, we glimpse the figure of a bare-chested Indian, lurching out of a closet with a tomahawk raised above his feather-crested head. Afforded no dialogue and only a split-second of screen time, there is little to indicate that this vengeful spirit is meant to represent a particular individual. However, if we look carefully, buried deep in the final credits, we find that Cherokee actor Red Horse Rivera is listed in the role of a character with a name. A character called Chief Little Fawn.

So, just who is Chief Little Fawn? He is no one and everyone. He's the silent, ephemeral embodiment of all the thousands of American Indians who perished at the hands of white settlers, some of whom were wielding the notorious Winchester Repeating Rifle.

The most haunted house in America?

If you google 'most haunted house in America', the search engine will compile a handy little list of top candidates for you. There's the

Myrtles Plantation ranked at number four; the LaLaurie Mansion (former home of the sadistic Madame Delphine LaLaurie) at number six; the Amityville house at number seven; and several other worthy contenders. But most significantly, at the top, holding the coveted number-one position, is the Winchester Mystery House.

It is a strange set of circumstances that has led to this property being declared the 'most haunted house in America': an unlikely intersection of gun violence, misogyny, racism and experimental architecture. And yet, all these disparate parts seem to come together to build a pretty convincing haunted house.

But is the Winchester Mystery House actually haunted? As I do with all the houses discussed in this book, I leave that up to the reader to decide. However, I find it interesting that even the historian widely credited for debunking the Mystery House myth is reluctant to completely dismiss the notion.

'The people who have told me about their supernatural experiences at the house believe them to be true,' says Mary Jo Ignoffo. 'Who am I to say they aren't? I am a person of faith, and I believe humans sometimes have mystical experiences. I just don't think they are as likely to happen at a place that charges a hefty fee and tells you when to look for the spirits.'

Clearly, Ignoffo has never experienced anything other-worldly at the Mystery House, but plenty of others have, including those who similarly disbelieve the canonical narrative, and who did not come to the property in search of the supernatural.

When former tour guide Carl Ferrigno started working at the Mystery House in the summer of 1970, he came without any preconceived notions about Winchester and little to no interest in the subject of ghosts. He says:

> *To be blatantly honest, I just wanted a part-time job to make some pocket money while going to school. But of course, it sounded much more interesting than a job at McDonald's. Over time, I grew to have great respect for Sarah Winchester and a disdain for the carnival-type atmosphere of the tourist operation.*

During his four years there, Ferrigno never bought into the silly superstitious stories about the home's former owner. And yet he managed to rack up three separate supernatural experiences. One involved the sound of heavy breathing, heard while on a surreptitious sleepover with a friend in the notorious Seance Room. Another involved hearing footsteps crossing the roof of a porch. The third involved an inexplicably terrified guard dog cowering in a corner of the empty basement.

Ferrigno's best anecdote by far, however, comes to him second-hand from his wife of thirty years, Jenna, who visited the Winchester Mystery House in 1990, many years after Carl's time there. At this point, the couple had not yet started dating and were simply colleagues in the Purchasing Department at Philips Electronics. Jenna was aware that Carl had once worked at the Mystery House, but knew little else about him, apart from the fact that he was 'well-dressed, handsome and quite prolific with his negotiating skills'.

While touring the house with her sister and family, Jenna was suddenly overcome with an uncanny feeling.

> *As we were guided through the many rooms, I became acutely aware that I was being overwhelmed with intense feelings of attraction, as if I was suddenly in love and the person I was visualising was Carl. It was as if a spell was being cast and Sarah was laying my future right out in front of me. From that moment on, I was in love with Carl. That's how our history together began... And I owe it all to Sarah Winchester.*

I would very much like this story to be true. I'd like to believe that, rather than gunshot victims and casualties of racial genocide, the Winchester Mystery House is instead haunted by the home's former owner, the indomitable Sarah Winchester. And she's not overcome by grief or guilt, forever trapped in a maze-like prison of her own making; she's simply sticking around to keep an eye on her architectural labour of love, helping others find love in the process.

GLOBAL GHOSTS

THE HAUNTED HOUSE AT HOME AND ABROAD

9

The world is full of ghosts, and some of them are still people…

Peter Straub (1943–2022)

The others: alternatives, anomalies and also-rans

This book has focused on a particular cultural construction: the modern haunted house. This is the iconic structure that emerged from British and American Gothic fiction of the eighteenth and nineteenth centuries. Inspired by Anglo-American Protestant beliefs, underpinned by middle-class mores, and coloured by local and regional history and folklore, these are the haunted houses of our collective imagination.

The ghostly legends attached to these houses were shaped by the themes and narratives of Gothic literature, as well as by period- and location-specific social preoccupations: the myth of the Myrtles Plantation feeds off the anxieties surrounding the antebellum past and the racial tensions that continue; the ghosts haunting Raynham Hall represent the decline of the English aristocracy and their golden age of social dominance and grand architectural construction; and the apparitions in Amityville embody the fragility of the so-called 'American dream' and our deep-rooted fear of familial destruction.

Architecturally speaking, all of these houses are relatively distinct. Granted, the Gothic Revival movement has played an important role in the development of the iconography, owing to the fact that the style is so strongly linked to the concurrent rise of Gothic literature. But a haunted house need not be a Victorian neo-Gothic mansion. It might be a medieval castle, a Palladian manor, an antebellum plantation house, or even a comparatively modern American suburban home. While typically old, dark and dreary, often rural and remote, and very rarely urban and new, these characteristics are not compulsory requirements. Rather, what these haunted houses have in common is their function as a domestic residence, past or present.

They are *all* homes with a history – usually a dark one.

Based on this admittedly loose criterion, it obviously leaves the door open for thousands – if not millions – of homes in Britain, America and indeed around the world to fall into the potential category of haunted house. And there are scores of other houses that might have been included in our survey. Unfortunately, there are simply too many haunted houses and too little time.

In the course of writing this book, I was frequently asked if I planned on including such-and-such a haunted house. Colleagues and acquaintances in Sussex in the south-east of England, where I currently live, often ask me if I will be writing about Preston Manor, a Brighton-area medieval manse locally renowned for its ghostly inhabitants, including an excommunicated nun and a Grey Lady. Friends and family back home in Canada wonder if I will be including Casa Loma, a neo-Gothic mansion in Toronto purported to be haunted by its former owner. Even my own father, an avowed sceptic with little interest in the subject of haunted houses, asked if I would be covering Newstead Abbey in Nottinghamshire, the ancestral seat of famed Romantic poet Lord Byron, who is said to still roam its halls.

Ultimately, however, I chose to focus on cases that can best and most expediently be used to illustrate the fundamental tenets of our current understanding of the haunted house. But there are, of course, many, many more examples: some that conform with all the typical traits we've discussed thus far, and others that deviate in certain ways.

This final chapter is dedicated to the outliers.

One of the more potentially glaring omissions in a study largely focused on British haunted houses is the absence of properties in Wales, Scotland and Northern Ireland. Or for that matter, the Republic of Ireland. As any resident of these nations will tell you, they are chock-a-block with haunted houses, some of which are very famous indeed.

The only excuse I can offer for not paying them greater attention is that, as we now know, the origins of the modern haunted house lie squarely in England, with the birth of 'gloomth' at Horace Walpole's twee Twickenham castle, Strawberry Hill House. Its further development and maturation took place across the pond in America, where the Gothic Revival movement in literature and domestic architecture reached its zenith and where, later, the Hollywood film industry took the haunted house to a mainstream audience of millions.

But the other countries within the United Kingdom have made notable contributions to the canon. With their own distinctive folkloric heritage, tempered – though never entirely quashed nor subsumed – by the arguably more dominant Anglo culture, the haunted houses of the Celtic nations deserve due acknowledgement.

'Scotland has a notoriously rich and diverse cultural tradition when it comes to the supernatural,' writes Rosemary Gray, an anthologist of Scottish ghost stories. 'From the Highlands to the Lowlands, from blasted heath or remote glen to wretched hovel or austere castle, the very topography lends itself somehow to the strange and unexplainable.'

She's certainly not wrong. Like Northumberland, its English neighbour to the south-east and home to Chillingham Castle, the Scottish landscape is littered with ancient edifices, many of which are popularly assumed to be haunted. Perhaps none is so infamous as Glamis Castle – a fifteenth-century citadel in the county of Angus, said to have been Shakespeare's inspiration for Macbeth's castle (although in the time of the real historical figure it had not yet been built).

Nestled in the lush lowland valley of Strathmore, Glamis Castle has been the home of the Bowes-Lyon family, earls of Strathmore and Kinghorne, for the past six centuries. Built in 1400 on the site of a much earlier hunting lodge – where, in 1034, King Malcolm II died from injuries sustained during a fight with a gang of bandits – the current building retains much of its late medieval appearance, despite extensive renovations in later centuries. Its quintessentially Gothic look – thick, time-weathered sandstone walls, crenelated battlements, towers and turrets – combined with its colourful history make Glamis the perfect setting for a classic ghost story.

Reflecting on an overnight stay there as a young man, novelist Sir Walter Scott evocatively captured the castle's haunting atmosphere, writing: 'As I heard door after door shut [that night]… I began to consider myself as too far from the living and somewhat too near to the dead.'

Except Glamis's most famous occupant is not actually a ghost. As well as being known for being the childhood home of the Queen Mother, the castle is most commonly associated with its resident monster – the 'Monster of Glamis'.

The story goes that within the bowels of this ancient fortress lies a secret chamber, and within that chamber is (or, at one point, *was*) a grotesque creature. A hideous blight to the honour of the castle's owners, the beast is alleged to have been kept imprisoned there by the Bowes-Lyon family in the nineteenth century.

'If you could even guess the nature of this castle's secret, you would get down on your knees and thank God it was not yours,' the 13th Earl of Strathmore (and grandfather of the Queen Mother) is reported to have said.

According to the Victorian rumour mill, this was no ordinary monster. It was one with noble blood. Well beyond Scotland, even as far afield as America, gossip columnists flooded the popular press with reports of an aristocratic scandal, with the *New York Sun* reporting in 1883 that the 'monster' was, in fact, 'an elder son of the House of Lyon, who was born of a monstrous shape and grew to a monstrous size'. This secret son was apparently 'the rightful heir to the Strathmore estates, and if he got loose or his existence had been verified, the control of the property would have been taken away from those that enjoyed it'.

So, it would seem that the 'Monster of Glamis' wasn't really a monster at all; it wasn't a fearsome supernatural being but rather a flesh-and-blood human child – albeit a disfigured and horrifically mistreated one.

Or was it?

What the American columnist writing for the *New York Sun* was probably unaware of was the strong folkloric tradition in Scotland – as well as in Ireland, Wales and parts of northern Europe – of the changeling: a strange human-like being that is left behind in place of an ordinary child who has been kidnapped by a supernatural entity, such as a fairy or demon.

Prior to modern advances in medical science, this myth functioned as an ameliorating explanation for birth defects, degenerative diseases and other abnormalities that might befall a much-prayed-for child. But what is particularly fascinating here is that these beliefs persisted, to some extent, well after the Age of Enlightenment. In Scotland – a world leader in medical science in the nineteenth century – the superstition apparently clung on even among the aristocratic elite.

What the legend of Glamis Castle demonstrates is that, even in an era of scientific advancement and age of cultural supremacy for the English, the traditional Gaelic myths lived on. At once, a regionally specific folk tale and a story of aristocratic disfunction that could have been ripped from the pages of a Gothic novel, the 'Monster of Glamis' was effectively a hybrid: ancient and modern in equal measure.

This is a common trait among the haunted houses of Celtic countries, where Gothic ghosts and folkloric entities such as changelings, faefolk and banshees often cohabit. What's more, within these nations where the Protestant Reformation took longer to take effect (or had minimal to no effect at all), it is also not uncommon for supernatural legends to incorporate traditional religion.

Consider, for example, the legend of Loftus Hall, a neoclassical manor house in County Wexford, Ireland, built atop the site of a medieval castle. Once the ancestral seat of the Loftus family, the marquesses of Ely, the historic home's best-known supernatural tale takes place in the eighteenth century. As it is traditionally told, on a dark and stormy night in the winter of 1775, a ship unexpectedly docked at the Hook Peninsula, not far from the hall. A lone man disembarked the vessel and sought refuge from the storm in the Loftus home. Anne, the eldest daughter of the then-Viscount Loftus, became infatuated with the handsome stranger and soon grew close to him.

One evening, not long after the mysterious man's arrival, Anne and her family were playing cards with their guest when something unexpected occurred. When she dropped one of her cards, Anne bent down to retrieve it from the floor. When she glanced under the card table, she saw that the stranger had a cloven foot. She screamed out in terror, alerting the rest of the family to her ghastly discovery. With that, the man shot up through the hall's ceiling in a ball of flames, leaving behind a gaping, smoke-scorched hole.

Traumatised by her encounter with the presumed devil, Anne is said to have become catatonic. Embarrassed by her delirious state, the family locked her away in a chamber, where she eventually died of starvation. It is Anne's ghost who is believed to haunt Loftus Hall today.

If this story sounds familiar, it is because it's actually a fairly well-travelled one within the Celtic nations. Similar versions are said to have occurred at the Hell-Fire Club in Dublin, in the village of Rhuddlan in Wales, and most notably at Glamis Castle in Scotland. Whereas in the more secular nation of England, Gothic ghosts are rarely joined by demonic entities, they are a frequent fixture elsewhere in the British isles, much like they are in the United States.

All of this isn't to say that in England, traditional mythology and religious superstition are all but dead. It's just that the form of haunted house dreamed up by Horace Walpole and carried forward by his predominantly Protestant, Enlightenment-era followers tended to eschew such subjects in favour of the 'pure ghost' – the soul of a once living person. In Scotland, Ireland and Wales, however, they preferred to mix and match their supernatural legends to create haunted house hybrids, such as we've seen with Glamis Castle and Loftus Hall.

Far from being impervious to the influence of Gothic literature, the Celtic nations simply added its ingredients to their own arsenals of spooky stories.

An uncanny empire: the spread of the Anglo-American haunted house

Beyond the borders of Great Britain, across the turbulent waters of the English Channel and North Sea, we find in Europe many more haunted houses that broadly conform with our standard model. And this isn't surprising when we consider the strong and enduring cultural ties between the UK and its closest continental neighbours.

Over the course of several millennia, invasions, immigration, ethnic mixing and cross-cultural exchanges have resulted in a rich melting pot of pan-European folklore. Yet the migration of the modern haunted house from its native England to the European mainland may have had just as much to do with a more recent and direct cultural transference.

Within a few short years of its publication in 1763, *The Castle of Otranto* – history's first Gothic novel – began to pop up elsewhere in Europe. Before the century was up, it had been translated into at least four other languages (French, German, Dutch and Spanish). Today, it has been printed in sixteen languages, including almost every major European language.

Somewhat ironically, however, one of the first foreign editions to hit international bookshelves in 1767 was the French translation, which appeared not long after the Seven Years' War, at the height of diplomatic tensions between the conflict's leading combatants (and traditional adversaries), England and France. Political differences aside, the two nations continued to have a strong cultural dialogue, and the translation of Walpole's novel would lay the foundations for France's own Gothic movement: a movement that would thrive during the French Revolution of the 1790s – particularly during the tumultuous early phase known as 'the reign of terror', during which an estimated 17,000 'enemies of the Revolution' (predominantly members of the nobility, aristocracy and clergy) were beheaded by the infamous 'Madame Guillotine'.

On both sides of the Channel, it was widely recognised that many of the themes of the Gothic novel (or *roman noir*, as it was called in France) were frighteningly relevant in relation to the events unfolding in the French capital. Violence, chaos, social upheaval and aristocratic decay were no longer simply the stuff of fiction.

As the controversial author, the Marquis de Sade, opined during this period, 'The novel was as difficult to write as it was monotonous to read. In order to confer some interest on their productions' it was necessary for novelists 'to appeal to hell for aid and to find chimeras in the landscape'. In other words, the everyday reality of the French Revolution was so shocking that it forced writers to invoke the demonic or supernatural just to get a reaction from their readers.

French Gothic novels of the late eighteenth and nineteenth centuries are, in some ways, subtly distinct from their English counterparts, reflecting the tastes and sensibilities of the French. They are often more explicitly violent and sexual in nature, and tend to focus on grotesque figures (such as the titular figure of Victor Hugo's *The Hunchback of Notre Dame*) or supernatural beings (such as the first female vampire, Clarimonde, written by Théophile Gautier) rather than ghosts. However, what they most assuredly do have in common is setting: old, often crumbling buildings, such as castles, monasteries and mansions. And again, this is not at all surprising given that France, like the UK – and much of the rest of Europe – is awash with evocative ancient edifices. After all, the eponymous setting of the first Gothic novel, *Otranto*, was a continental castle, not an English one.

Outside of fiction, the most famous haunted house in France is probably the Château de Brissac, a seventeenth-century baroque palace in the Loire Valley, which boasts seven storeys and a soaring north tower, making it one of the tallest castles in the country. Built on the site of an eleventh-century fortress, the property has changed ownership several times over the centuries, but since the early 1600s it has remained in the hands of the Cossé-Brissac family, continuing to serve as the seat of the Duke of Brissac to this day.

While the chateau has played host to many dramatic events – including a ferocious ransacking during the French Revolution – the most notorious episode of violence to take place there occurred in the fifteenth century. No mere myth, the murder of Charlotte de Brézé, the illegitimate daughter of King Charles II, on the night of 1 June 1477 is a historically documented fact. Believing that she had been engaged in an adulterous affair with one of his huntsmen, Charlotte's husband Jacques de Brézé, Comte de Maulévrier, strangled her to death before throwing her out of an upper-storey window.

The subsequent legend, on the other hand, is more dubious. It is also suspiciously familiar. Following her murder, it is said that Charlotte underwent a terrifying transformation from living mistress of Château de Brissac into '*la dame verte*' or the 'Green Lady', the castle's resident spectre, known for the shade of her dress and the hollow holes in place of her eyes.

Remarkably, this legend is virtually identical to that of the Brown Lady of Raynham Hall in Norfolk, England. Two houses separated by some 500 miles; two women living in different countries, during different centuries, and yet they are near-mirror images. Contrasting methods of murder and colour of attire aside, their legends are clearly cut from the same supernatural cloth.

And there are countless others like these across Europe: the legends of Germany's Wolfsegg Castle ('White Lady'), Norway's Akershus Castle ('woman in black'), Malta's Verdala Palace ('Blue Lady'), Estonia's Haapsalu Castle (another White Lady), and so forth. So ubiquitous is this type of castle-based haunting that we might question whether the origins of the modern haunted house really do lie in the UK after all. Rather than being invented by the English, perhaps it was simply first recorded in popular fiction by an English author.

Whatever the case, the cultural boundaries of the European nations were – and are – extremely porous, allowing myths, legends, and the haunted house as we understand it to migrate at will.

At its height in the early twentieth century, the British Empire ruled roughly a quarter of the Earth's land surface and governed approximately 450 million people, making it the largest empire in human history, beating the Romans (at their peak) by about 10 million square miles and 360 million subjects. Once optimistically referred to as the 'empire upon which the sun never sets', Britain eventually lost its hold over its global dominions in the aftermath of the two world wars, but not before it made an irreversible impact on the countries over which it had presided.

Traditional history textbooks generally devote the most attention to the social, political, religious and infrastructural changes introduced by the British Empire (good and bad); however, no one could deny its cultural impact. Not even America, the wayward (and long-lost) child of Great Britain, with an empire of its own, would be able to argue against the powerful influence of its Founding Fathers.

The shared literary and architectural heritage of England and America has, as we now know, led to the growth of the Gothic movement in both architecture and literature, and the development of the modern haunted house. But what many of us are unaware of is the immense global reach of the Western-style haunted house, thanks to the sprawl of the British Empire.

As mentioned in the introduction, there are relatively few territories outside Britain and North America that have long-standing native traditions of the haunted house. While some global cultures have a strong sense of hauntedness being rooted to place, few have so many ghost stories that are tethered to domestic dwellings. It was for this reason that, during the course of my research, I was surprised to discover a good handful of characteristically Anglo-American examples located in some far-flung and unlikely locales.

Almost without exception, these houses are to be found in Commonwealth nations – former territories of the British Empire. Most of them were built during the late colonial period and thus possess that quintessential haunted look (Victorian neo-Gothic). And while some of them incorporate the architectural aesthetic and local traditions of their host countries, they remain, for the most part, heavily anglicised.

Some examples include Charleville Mansion, a Tudor Revival home in Simla, India, said to be haunted by its former owner, Charles Pratt Kennedy, a British-born officer in the Bengal Artillery, who died there under mysterious circumstances; Kellie's Folly, an unfinished castle ruin in the Kinta district of Malaysia, once belonging to Scottish planter, William Kellie-Smith, and now believed to be haunted by a host of spectral inhabitants, including Kellie-Smith himself, who perished before his castle was completed; and Rose Hall, an eighteenth-century plantation house in Montego Bay, Jamaica, which is thought to be cursed by the so-called 'White Witch' of Rose Hall, the voodoo-practising wife of the plantation's original owner.

Markedly, all of these houses once belonged to white people with British ancestry and are believed to be haunted by white ghosts (with the exception of Rose Hall, which is said to be haunted by the plantation's white mistress and the black slaves she is said to have mistreated). The legends attached to these properties circulated – at least, initially – among the Anglo expat communities in their respective host countries. It is, however, unclear what the native population made of the nascent myths at the time: did they believe the stories to be true or dismiss them as a product of their foreign invaders' belief system? Certainly, in all these nations, there would be a common understanding of the concept of ghosts, but not necessarily a strongly held belief that they stuck around in their old homes.

At any rate, over time, the legends have been absorbed into local folklore, and today the properties are widely considered to be 'haunted houses' by both foreigners and natives alike.

Of all the properties I stumbled across in my global hunt for haunted houses, I found Erasmus Castle perhaps the most intriguing. It is an imposing three-storey mansion built on the summit of a hill in Pretoria, South Africa, between 1892 and 1903, for the family of a wealthy farmer, Jochemus Johannes Petrus Erasmus. He was not a British colonial, but an Afrikaner – that is, an African of Dutch extraction.

Erasmus Castle is often described as being in the 'art nouveau' style – an art and architectural movement characterised by rich ornamentation and sinuous organic motifs, most commonly associated with artisans working in the urban centres of Western Europe at the close of the nineteenth century. But this is something of a misnomer. Erasmus is a prime (if somewhat out-of-place) example of Eastlake architecture, an offshoot of the neo-Gothic movement and subset of the Queen Anne style, named after English designer Charles Locke Eastlake. It is an almost exclusively domestic form of architecture, typically found in the Victorian suburbs of North America.

If you search the internet for an image of Erasmus Castle, you will be confronted with one of the most haunted-looking houses you've ever seen. A steeply gabled, high Victorian mansion which you would be forgiven for confusing with the likes of Carson Mansion in Eureka, California – that iconic, over-the-top, Queen Anne manor house discussed in the introduction. As far as I'm aware, Erasmus is the only surviving building of its type in Pretoria, if not in all of South Africa, making it a real fish out of water.

The early history of the mansion is fairly unremarkable. Jochemus Erasmus, an affluent landowner, required a big house for his growing brood, and so he enlisted a team of professionals to get the job done. Frans van der Ben, a Dutch architect, together with an English draughtsman and an Italian builder, were hired at a contract price of £7,500 (or about £615,000 in today's currency).

Nothing especially dramatic is known to have occurred in the house, apart from the premature death of a young daughter, Enslin, who is lovingly memorialised on a tombstone in the family cemetery with the phrase *'Onze Zonnestraaltje'* ('our ray of sunlight'). Otherwise, the Erasmuses seem to have lived peaceably in their home until Jochemus's death in 1940. Then, the tide began to turn.

In the decades following the patriarch's passing, the Erasmus family fell on hard times. Financial struggle and familial dispersal caused the house to fall into disrepair, and eventually it was abandoned. Already possessing the trademark 'gloomth' of a Gothic structure, the house, now empty and derelict, began to take on the unmistakable aura of hauntedness.

In 1960, Jochemus's descendants sold the Erasmus estate to the local authority, which planned to demolish the mansion to make way for a new motorway. These plans ultimately fell through, and Erasmus Castle sat empty for a further fifteen years. By the time Armscor (the arms procurement agency of the South African Department of Defence) purchased the house in 1975 to turn it into offices, it had reached such an advanced state of decay that it had attracted the attention of locals. Fittingly, they dubbed it *'Die Spookhuis'* or 'the haunted house'.

Today, Erasmus Castle remains the headquarters of Armscor, and though it is not officially open to the public, the agency occasionally indulges in requests for private tours. The fortunate few to gain access claim to have experienced a range of paranormal events, including mysterious smells, sounds, and even the sighting of a little girl in Edwardian clothing (perhaps the ill-fated Enslin).

In many ways, I struggle to wrap my head around Pretoria's *Spookhuis*. How does it fit in with the other houses we've discussed in this book? Unlike most of the others, Erasmus Castle does not have a clearly defined legend attached to it – although there was once a rumour that two of the Erasmus children, who suffered from leprosy, had been kept locked in the attic. This has since been disproven. In truth, Erasmus was never the site of a shocking or scandalous event. According to the living descendants of the family, 'the house had always been one of love and laughter amidst a busy farmyard'.

What's more, despite its oddly Anglo-American Gothic appearance – which made it look as though it had been lifted out of the San Francisco suburbs and plunked down halfway across the world in Pretoria – the mansion has no direct link to the cultural origins of the haunted house. For although a unified South Africa would eventually become part of the British Empire, Pretoria itself was founded by Afrikaners as the capital of an independent Boer Republic. As such, even after British conquest in 1909, the dominant influence in the region remained Netherlandish. Like most of their neighbours, the Erasmuses were the descendants of Dutch farmers who emigrated to South Africa more than a century before the Gothic movement swept Europe.

One wonders what might have been running through Jochemus Erasmus's mind when he settled on the design for his family home. Perhaps on the advice of his English draughtsman, J. W. Leslie Simmons, he picked a style that was popular at the time in England and America, lending his mansion an air of exotic urbanity. Or the style choice may have been made at the insistence of his wife, Johanna, by all accounts a cultured and creative woman, who had seen and admired the grand Gothic mansions in the upscale (and predominantly British) Parktown neighbourhood of Johannesburg. It's possible that, as a well-educated man, Jochemus would have been aware of the origins and associations of the style he selected. But then again, maybe he wasn't.

One thing is for certain, though. By the time Erasmus Castle had been abandoned in the mid-twentieth century, the people of Pretoria were very much familiar with what they were looking at – a *Spookhuis*. For one thing, it was desolate and decaying – the universal indicator of a haunting – and, for another, it looked exactly like every other haunted house they'd seen in the movies. And not just in Hollywood movies, which had been screened in South Africa since the first decades of the twentieth century, but in films of their own. In September 1950, South African Pictures released *Hier's Ons Weer*, a slapstick comedy about a bank robber on the run who is forced to take refuge in an abandoned haunted house.

The house that appears in that film is Erasmus Castle.

So, while Pretoria may seem a strange place for the quintessential haunted house, and the original owners may never have expected it to become one, thanks to the power of both literal and cultural imperialism, we find that the tenets of the Anglo-American haunted house are just as deeply entrenched in places like Sub-Saharan Africa as they are here at home.

East creeps west: the Japanese haunted house

The last stop on our ghostly global tour is Japan, a nation that holds the unique distinction of being perhaps the only other country on the planet that possesses its own strong native tradition of the haunted house.

As we've established, scores of other countries have their own famously haunted homes – some of which are distinct from the Western model – but I can think of no other nation that has had such an enduring fascination with the concept as Japan. A concept termed *obake yashiki* (literally, 'monster' or 'spook house') can refer either to an actual haunted house or to a kind of amusement park-style 'house of horrors', a hugely popular cultural pastime in Japan for the past several decades.

The phrase itself can be traced back over many centuries. However, it wasn't until the Edo period (1603–1868) that the *obake yashiki* came to the forefront of cultural consciousness. In popular plays, literature and artwork of the late eighteenth and nineteenth centuries, the *obake yashiki* established itself as a standard setting for scary stories, making the Japanese haunted house an exact contemporary of the Anglo-American Gothic one. This is an especially intriguing case of cultural synchronicity, given that Japan, an isolationist state for over 200 years, was essentially closed off from the rest of the world for almost the entirety of the Edo period.

In this section, in an admittedly cursory survey of a rich and complex subject, we will explore how the Japanese haunted house both conforms to and deviates from the Western model. We will see how the Japanese version fits into a far more intricate tapestry of traditional supernatural beliefs, which differs greatly from our own, and yet sometimes lines up with them in strange and surprising ways. As we will learn, not all Japanese ghosts are tied to their former places of residence – or even to one place in particular – but some of them are homebodies, and these are the ghosts that have the most in common with their Gothic brethren.

To be sure, the Japanese haunted house *is* foreign, but it is also oddly familiar…

Ghosts (or *yurei*) are ubiquitous in Japanese folklore. They come in myriad forms, some roughly analogous to their Western counterparts, some completely unrecognisable. *Zashiki-warashi*, for example, are ghost children. Like their Anglo-American cousins, they tend to be mischievous and playful rather than dangerous – though they're still pretty scary.

But then there's the less familiar *ubume*, who are the ghosts of dead mothers, who have returned to the earthly realm to care for their abandoned offspring, often bringing them sweets and toys.

There are *funayūrei*, the spirits of sailors who died at sea, sometimes taking the form of mermaid-like creatures. *Goryō*, who are angry aristocratic ghosts with chips on their uppity shoulders. And *ikiryō*, who aren't really ghosts at all, but supernatural energies released from living creatures, humans and animals alike.

The list goes on.

There's a whole *yurei* taxonomical system. Countless books, plays, pictures, films and video games are devoted to their stories. And even though they are a vestige of a centuries-old folkloric belief system, they continue to play a powerful role in Japanese culture today.

Yurei have their own annual holiday – the festival of Oban, or the Feast of the Dead, in which families prepare parties for their dearly departed, who return home once a year in August, when the divide between the land of the living and the land of the dead is porous enough to let the dead back in.

This is along the same lines as All Souls Day in medieval Europe or Días del Muerte in modern Mexico, or indeed, any of the other global traditions that pay homage to dead ancestors. But in Japan, perhaps, there's just a bit more emphasis on the guests of honour, the *yurei*, who are guided home by the light of small bonfires or lanterns.

So revered are the *yurei*, they even have their own shrines and public monuments. The biggest and best-known is the Yasukuni Shrine, a 200-year-old temple in Tokyo devoted to the worship of over 2 million spirits who died while serving the Japanese nation (conspicuously including several war criminals). These military spectres are a ghostly genus of their own, known as *kami* or *eirei*, meaning 'heroic spirits'.

So, ghosts run rampant in Japan. But where are all these *yurei*? As it turns out, their natural habitat is a little harder to pin down. And that's mainly because not all Japanese ghosts have a designated place of residence. While the haunted house – or *obake yashiki* – is widely recognised in Japan to be a natural environment for ghosts, only certain types of ghost are believed to reside there.

There are two main categories of Japanese ghost: the *jibakurei*, the kind of ghost that is linked to their place of death; and the *fuyurei*, or free-travelling spirit, which are more common.

A classic example of the *fuyurei* appears in *Yotsuya Kaidan*, a kabuki play first staged in 1825, which has gone on to become one of the most famous Japanese ghost stories of all time. The title roughly translates as 'The Bewitching Apparition of Yotsuya', named for its setting, a historic neighbourhood in Tokyo. In the grisly tale of a poisoned and hideously disfigured wife who rises from the grave to hunt the husband who killed her, the 'haunted' husband is never free from his tormentor. Even when he flees Yotsuya to a remote mountain retreat, the angry ghost follows.

This Edo-era play has been adapted for the screen no less than twenty times and is said to have been the inspiration for countless modern cinematic ghosts, including Kayoko, the antagonist in the popular horror movie *The Grudge* (more on this influential film later). The embittered wife in *Yotsuya Kaidan*, and Kayoko in the modern movie, represent the archetypal *onryō* or vengeful spirit. They even possess the archetypal *onryō* look: a white dress representing a burial kimono, long, black matted hair and a chalky white face that traditionally signals a *yurei* in kabuki plays.

While less common than the free-wheeling *fuyurei*, the location-rooted *jibakurei* also abound. And they can theoretically be found just about anywhere an untimely death has occurred – hospitals, roads, bridges, skyscrapers, middle-class homes. But what about in spooky old mansions?

Dr Michael Crandol, a lecturer in Japanese studies at the University of Leiden in the Netherlands, explains:

> *In Europe and America we have a strong sense that a building that is hundreds of years old would naturally have a ghost attached to it, but in Japan, there are very few buildings that are more than 100 years old, since brick and stone were not common building materials in such an earthquake-prone country. [Instead] old schoolhouses and hospitals are more often thought to be haunted, as they tend to be concrete, cavernous and rather uninviting-looking buildings.*

Anyone who has ever watched a YouTube video on the practice of urban exploring (or 'urbexing' for short) will recognise such a structure. In both East and West, we associate abandoned institutional buildings such as prisons, sanatoriums and schools with ghostly goings-on; however, in the West, we wouldn't properly consider them examples of 'haunted houses' – because they're not. By contrast, in Japan, they might fall into the broader category of *obake yashiki* simply because the nation doesn't have many old homes to work with.

But there is a notable exception. A well-known example that much more comfortably fits with our Western conception. A place that seems almost purpose-built to house a few *jibakurei*. That place is Himeji Castle.

Perched on a hilltop high above the city of Himeji in the Kansai region of south-central Japan, the glimmering white edifice of Himeji Castle has loomed over the landscape for aeons. Defying all odds, including its precarious placement and flimsy timber foundations, the castle has remained in place for nearly 700 years. Neither the firebombing of the Second World War nor the Great Hanshin earthquake of January 1995 could make it tumble.

Many believe that the castle is guarded by a supernatural force; a power emanating from its distinctive ceramic tiled roof. These special tiles, lovingly restored by local master craftspeople in 2009, take the form of *onigawaras* or ogres (basically Japanese gargoyles), the mythical protectors of the castle. Of course, it doesn't hurt that these *onigawaras* act to prevent leaks by covering key joins in the ordinary tiles underneath.

Built in 1333 for the powerful samurai Akamatsu Norimura, the massive castle complex, currently consisting of eighty-three structures, has been renovated and expanded at least five times in its seven-century history. Its present-day appearance is most reflective of its early-seventeenth-century remodelling under Ikeda Terumasa, a *daimyō* or feudal lord, who had been gifted the palace as reward for his success in battle. Ikeda demolished the original three-storey keep and completely rebuilt and extended the castle between 1601 and 1609.

Mirroring the owner's military prowess, the castle became a

sophisticated defensive structure, boasting three moats, eighty-four gates, numerous ramparts and turrets, and a maze-like path leading to the main six-storey tower. Today, visitors are guided to the entrance via extensive signposting, but in Ikeda's day they'd have been left to their own devices.

Potential marauders would naturally have been wary of the *ish-iotoshi* (small holes in the walls of the main complex that allowed soldiers to throw stones or pour scalding water onto uninvited guests). There were also *sama*, slits from which arrows and rifles were shot, much like the arrow slits found in Himeji's European counterparts.

And if that wasn't scary enough, like any castle worth its salt, Himeji had ghosts. The oldest of the ghostly legends attached to Himeji is associated with the medieval castle keep razed by Ikeda in 1608. But destroying the building where a *jibakurei* resides doesn't always solve the problem. Shortly after erecting a new tower to replace the earlier structure, Ikeda fell seriously ill. It was believed that he was cursed; someone (or something), it seems, wasn't happy about the modern renovations – a typical grievance of ghosts inhabiting old buildings.

The ghost in the tower at Himeji is known as Osakabehime. Though her identity and origin are unknown, her name – which loosely translates as 'Princess Punishment' – suggests she was a high-born woman associated with the castle. In most versions of her legend, she's described as a sort of princess oracle – a hermit spirit who remains hidden away in her tower, apart from once a year, when she descends the stairs to inform the lord of the castle's fate. She's sometimes described as a beautiful young woman, sometimes an old crone. She's either a wraithlike Rapunzel or a spectral sorceress, depending on your source.

In the eighteenth-century miscellany *Rōō Chabanashi* ('Tea-time Gossip of Old Ladies') (1742), for example, she is envisioned as the former. She cuts a romantic figure in a tale about a young page who went on a dare to see if the *yokai* of Himeji Castle really existed. He is said to have come upon an ethereal noblewoman in a sumptuous twelve-layered ceremonial kimono. When asked why he had come to her tower, he explained to Osakabehime it was a test of his bravery. Impressed with his courage and candour, the ghostly princess gifted him a *shikorobuki*, the neck guard of a helmet, as a reward.

Conversely, in *Konjaku Gazu Zoku Hyakki* ('Illustrated One Hundred Demons from Past and Present') (*c.* 1779), the roughly contemporary work of author-illustrator Toriyama Sekien, the *yokai* is referred to as simply Osakabe and is depicted as an old witch-like figure with pet bats. She is a misanthrope who hates society, and thus remains cloistered in her tower with only her familiars for company.

Some 300 years later, the creators of the popular video game *Fate/ Grand Order*, combined elements of both variants of the legend to form their own Osakabehime. A standard *Sailor Moon*-type manga character, this princess looks like a cross between a Catholic schoolgirl and a high-class prostitute. She's childlike, yet hypersexualised, donning a micro-mini skirt, knee-high socks, and what appears to be a witch's cloak. Naturally, her sidekick is a small purple bat.

In spite of Osakabehime's incredible longevity and continued influence on contemporary popular culture, she is not even the best-known ghost at Himeji Castle. That honour goes to Okiku – the infamous ghost in the well.

Another female *jibakurei*, only of a much lower order, Okiku is said to have been a beautiful servant girl who met an untimely end at the bottom of a well. Again, her origin and identity are unknown, and there are several versions of her legend. In fact, there are several Okikus – other similarly named well-ghosts found all over Japan – making her a bit like the Eastern equivalent of the 'White Lady' of European folklore. Apparently, just like in the West, the Japanese haunted castle is dominated by female phantoms.

Himeji Castle is a fascinating case study. Its history, architecture and supernatural myths are simultaneously specific to Japan and fairly general in the context of the global haunted house. However, as stated, Himeji is the exception to the rule, rather than the norm.

If you were to ask the average Japanese person to describe the classic haunted house, they likely wouldn't cite the castle as an example (though they would definitely know of it). They might, as Dr Crandol suggests, describe a modern urban structure like an abandoned schoolhouse. Or they might have a more historicised version in mind.

According to Dr Koichi Kato, a Professor of Architecture at the University of Tokyo, 'Traditional Japanese *obake yashiki* are small, shabby, old wooden houses.' Think of an American 'cabin in the woods' or a British hikers' bothy. But because such flimsy structures rarely survive, modern audiences would only recognise them from antique watercolours and woodblock prints, or contemporary artists' renderings in manga and movies.

Or they might picture something different altogether.

'In Japan, two main types of haunted houses exist,' contends Dr Kato. 'The traditional Japanese one and the Western-style one.'

Thanks to the Treaty of Kanagawa, signed by the United States and Japan on 31 March 1854, the floodgates opened to both foreign trade and cultural influence. Though Japan's own folkloric heritage remained intact, the country then opened to other traditions and, in turn, the world was introduced to Japan's traditions. A two-way cultural dialogue between East and West was struck up not long after, with the first anthology of Japanese ghost stories appearing in English in 1904 and the first Gothic novels cropping up in Japan by 1906.

The rise of international film only amplified this dialogue, so that today the Japanese fully recognise our haunted house, just as we too know a little about theirs. Once again, through the magic of cinema, the globe gets a little smaller, and the haunted houses of the world move ever closer together.

On 22 October 2004, the supernatural thriller *The Grudge* hit cinemas in America, just in time for Halloween. A fortnight later, on Guy Fawkes Night, it opened in the UK.

Based on director Takashi Shimizu's original cult hit *Ju-On*, the film was one of the first in a series of successful adaptations of Japanese horror movies. Though not a shot-for-shot remake, the Western reimagining was fairly faithful to its source material, retaining the same basic plot, the same setting and even the same haunted house. The only notable difference was that the core cast was now populated by white Americans.

Sarah Michelle Gellar – of *Buffy the Vampire Slayer* fame – might seem an odd choice for the part of a domestic carer working in suburban Tokyo, but perhaps the director felt that Western audiences needed a relatable touchpoint: a familiar face in a foreign land.

The plot is fairly straightforward. A deranged husband kills his wife, son and pet cat in a jealous rage. Their former family home is thus cursed, and anyone who enters it is doomed to be frightened to death by a woman with inordinately long black hair and a chalk-white face (the classic *onryō*). Occasionally, her creepy kid (a *zashiki-warashi*) does some of the work, and even the howling demon cat pulls her weight.

The bulk of the story follows the expat American nurse Karen, who comes in to care for the house's elderly new occupant, Emma. Karen has to solve the mystery of the curse, all the while dodging the lead ghost, Kayoko, who seems hell-bent on strangling everyone with her long, knotted locks. Sophisticated it is not, but it's definitely good for a few scares.

Perhaps unsurprisingly, *The Grudge* had mixed reviews. One critic summed it up as 'a watchable yet erratic Hollywood remake'. In spite of its weak critical reception, however, *The Grudge* was a major box office success, banking £151 million in global ticket sales and spawning three sequels. What's more, it launched a cultural phenomenon. Kayoko's ghastly white face and stringy black hair became instantly iconic, a popular Halloween costume in the West for years to come. And suddenly Japanese horror films (or J-Horror) were all the rage, with many more Hollywood remakes scheduled for release in quick succession.

For all its flaws, *The Grudge* succeeded in introducing Western viewers to something somewhat new – much like *The Amityville Horror* had some twenty years earlier. By and large, English-speaking audiences found the Japanese-inspired film strange and scary: foreign, yet familiar. And perhaps it was this tension between foreignness and familiarity that was one of the keys to its success.

In an early scene in the film, we watch our American protagonist, Karen, nervously navigating her way through the heaving streets of central Tokyo. Her flaxen hair and casual clothing stand out in a sea of raven-haired businessmen. When she stops in a fruit market to ask for directions in stilted Japanese, a young child peers uneasily at her from behind his mother's legs. It's not clear whether he finds her foreign appearance alarming, or whether he senses that she is in danger.

Karen soon turns down a side street, away from the hum of the commercial district. She's on a quiet suburban cul-de-sac. The street is deserted. Out of the glare of the electric neon lights, the atmosphere becomes darker; the sky seems greyer than it did before.

As she slowly approaches her final destination, the wind picks up, swirling dead leaves around her ankles. The ominous orchestral soundtrack fades to a barely audible drone. She's arrived.

The camera zooms in on her face so that we can't see what she sees, but we know that she has seen something that clearly troubles her. Then the angle changes to her point of view, and at last we see it: the haunted house. Only it's unlike any haunted house we've seen before.

Now, obviously, viewers should not expect to find a medieval castle or a neo-Gothic manor house in suburban Tokyo. But the house isn't even a mansion; it's not especially old. Instead, it is a relatively modest two-storey home with dingy white stucco walls, a cantilevered roof and a small Juliet balcony above the front entrance. It isn't exotic, exactly. In fact, we might stumble upon a similar sort of house in a mid-twentieth-century suburb in America. It's just not what we have come to expect of a home harbouring wrathful spirits. Sure, it has some of the familiar trappings – namely its dark and vaguely decrepit appearance – but it's a far cry from Castle Dracula, or even Himeji Castle.

The *Grudge* house, or Saeki House as it is popularly known (Saeki being the surname of its ghostly inhabitants) is, in fact, a real house. Though the American version was filmed on a soundstage, it was closely modelled on the real location used in the Japanese original: a detached two-storey home in the Suginami ward of western Tokyo.

According to Dr Kato, Saeki House is a fairly typical example of domestic housing in an affluent suburban area in Japan. 'It seems to be enclosed by a fence and has a small wooded yard,' he notes. 'So it could be considered more of an upper-middle-class house.'

Other than that, it's fairly ordinary. Perhaps its relative normality is what makes it so scary. The house looks to be an ordinary family home – again, not unlike 112 Ocean Avenue in *Amityville*.

Of course, Karen immediately senses there's something amiss, but she's working on instinct. The house doesn't come with all the obvious warning signs of a conventional – or conventionally Western – haunted house. No bats or cobwebs or broken windows. While it's run down, it's superficially habitable.

'The film seems to be based on the idea of stigmatised property,' suggests Dr Kato. Here, he refers to the term estate agents use to describe a house deemed undesirable based on reasons other than physical conditions or features.

In a flashback scene in *The Grudge*, we watch as the Williams family, the incumbent owners of Saeki House, are shown around the property by a cheerfully nervous estate agent. Though there's a language barrier between the American buyers and their Japanese guide, it's clear that the agent is aware he's poised to make a sale. But he also knows there's something he's not telling them.

While the family excitedly explore the house, the agent ducks into a bathroom, where he finds the bath full of water. Not wanting anything to spoil his impending commission, he tentatively reaches into the tub to release the plug. His hand comes up holding some dark, tangled hair and he's soon face to face with a half-submerged ghost child. He recoils in fear. Moments later the buyers come in to announce they're making an offer. The agent smiles and says nothing.

As we know, the concept of the stigmatised property is hardly unique to Japan. It's a controversial subject that has been plaguing estate agents, home sellers and buyers the world over for quite some time. And so, for this reason, the dilemma faced by the characters in *The Grudge* is a relatable one. In Japan, the matter of 'stigma' is governed by fairly strict laws. Any property that is 'stigmatised' must be legally disclosed to the buyer. And while there is quite a wide range of potential 'stigmas', the term typically applies to places where people have died suddenly or violently. These are known as *jiko bukken*, or 'black properties'. An estate agent must tell you if a house is a *jiko bukken*, though they sometimes get round it by using a legal loophole: they are only obligated to disclose this information to potential buyers for the first two years after the incident. So, it would appear that the agent in *The Grudge* might have been bending the rules.

Above all, it seems, Japanese home buyers are paranoid about winding up with a property infested with *jibakurei* – those pesky earthbound spirits who have suffered a terrible death and are peeved about being stuck in their place of demise. And prospective buyers are right to be wary of each property they tour because a *jibakurei* could be hiding anywhere. Unlike their Gothic counterparts, they don't necessarily end up trapped in a spacious manor house.

'For places haunted by *jibakurei*, there is no particular building type,' reiterates Japanese folklore expert Zack Davisson. 'It can be modern apartments in towering skyscrapers – the Sunshine 60 building in Tokyo is famously haunted; or it can be an ancient castle like Himeji. There is a lot of variety.'

So, in the end, the Japanese haunted house seems to be almost any house (or building) where something bad has happened. It might be a medieval castle, a Western-style neo-Gothic mansion, a modern high-rise, a decrepit timber cabin or a contemporary family home, like the one in *The Grudge*. So long as something sinister has taken place there, it could be haunted. And in this respect, it is not so vastly dissimilar to the Anglo-American haunted house.

On 15 April 1983, the Haunted Mansion at Tokyo Disneyland opened its doors to the public for the first time. Initially planned for inclusion in Westernland – an area of the park modelled after the early-American pioneer-themed section in the California original – the Japanese horror house attraction was ultimately erected in Fantasyland, a fairy-tale-based zone. This change in location largely came down to space, but it also seems to indicate that the Japanese planners deemed it unnecessary for the mansion to be located in the explicitly American-themed area of the park, as visitors would recognise it for what it was, with or without context.

It was obviously a haunted house. Not a traditional *obake yashiki*, of course, but an easily identifiable archetype that the Japanese public would have known well.

Architectural professor Koichi Kato, who was a primary school lad when the attraction opened, tells me that most of his contemporaries would have quickly associated the mansion with the structures they'd seen in American TV imports such as *The Addams Family*.

Tokyo's Haunted Mansion is pretty much a carbon copy of the version in Walt Disney World's Magic Kingdom in Orlando, Florida: a labyrinthine red-brick neo-Gothic manor based on domestic architecture popular in upstate New York in the late nineteenth century. Curiously, the few changes made in the Japanese attraction have absolutely nothing to do with their own folkloric traditions. Instead, they only serve to reinforce the connections with its Anglo-American inspiration. For example, the mansion's main gates are adorned with griffins, a traditional motif in English heraldic imagery. The names of fictional phantom characters emblazoned on portrait labels and gravestone epitaphs have been changed, but they remain English in origin. And most notably, the queue area, which is designed to look like an unfinished wing of the house, is said to have been inspired by the perpetually unfinished Winchester Mystery House in San Jose, California.

As acknowledged in the introduction, Disneyland might seem a strange place to source evidence for the impact of the haunted house, but the fact is, it is a powerful barometer of global culture. A wildly popular entertainment attraction, now found in locations across the world, Disneyland is designed to attract children and adults of all ages, and of all ethnic, cultural and socioeconomic backgrounds, who will instinctively understand the imagery they see there.

If this is the case, then the Anglo-American haunted house has, most assuredly, conquered the world.

Postscript

In the preface to this book, I wrote that I have never seen or experienced a ghost. I must admit, I wrote this section fairly early on in the research process, before I had the chance to visit many of the haunted houses I cover in this book. And while the statement remains fundamentally true, I must now add a caveat. I've still never seen a ghost, but I can say that on a research trip to the American South – what was meant to be a simple reconnaissance mission to gather historical information and environmental detail pertaining to purportedly haunted plantation houses – I came close to experiencing what some might consider to be a supernatural event. I'm still not really sure what happened, but I do know that it was extremely unnerving.

Let's return to the notoriously haunted Myrtles Plantation in St Francisville, Louisiana.

It's a sultry summer's night, around 10 p.m., and my husband and I are getting ready for bed in our twee, antique-filled guest suite on the upper floor of the 200-year-old plantation house. Although I initially planned on staying up late to conduct some amateur ghost-hunting experiments for a bit of fun, we're both incredibly tired after a long car journey and a recent bout of gastroenteritis (let me tell you, that was not particularly fun on a road trip).

When my husband leaves the room to brush his teeth, I decide to make one last half-hearted attempt to contact the spirits before retiring to bed. I pick up my phone and record a video of the room, panning from side to side, getting good shots of the mantlepiece upon which is displayed a group of Victorian porcelain dolls (rumoured to move of their own accord) and a mirrored armoire across from it. I intend to review the footage the next day to see if the dolls decide to reorganise themselves or if Chloe, the Myrtles' resident slave spirit, makes a surprise appearance in the mirror's reflection.

'Well, we're going to bed now, ghosts,' I say to the empty room. 'If you're going to make yourself known, you better do it now, because we'd like to have a good night's sleep.'

Silence.

Moments later, my husband returns, and we turn in for the night. It's reasonably quiet (apart from a humming air conditioner and the distant chatter of other house guests) and the dolls seem to be behaving themselves, remaining stationary and in their original positions. As such, I'm not feeling remotely frightened. I fall asleep quickly and easily.

But a couple of hours later, I suddenly awake with the distinct feeling that someone or something is standing directly above me. Though the room is not completely dark, I can't actually see anything. And yet I sense it strongly. Within seconds, I become overwhelmed with a feeling of dread like nothing I've ever experienced before. I *know* that something bad is about to happen. Then, there it is: the unmistakable sound of someone crying – either a child or a young woman. Not even the sound of my own son sobbing has ever moved me this much; I feel an unbearable mixture of terror, sorrow and helplessness. All I can do is shrink away from the weeping presence and scream at the top of my lungs: 'Help me!'

Next thing I know, my husband is cradling me in his arms. 'It was just a nightmare,' he reassures me.

Was it? Was what I experienced at the Myrtles Plantation just a run-of-the-mill nightmare? Or the somewhat less common but no less natural experience of sleep paralysis? Granted, I was able to move, so perhaps it was a related parasomnia, such as a night terror. Or is it possible that I had my first – and hitherto only – supernatural encounter?

When we return to the UK after our visit to the Myrtles, I decide to reach out to Frances Kermeen, the plantation's former owner and author of a 'true ghost story' book devoted to her experiences there, to see what she makes of this episode. Does it line up with hers or others' experiences in the house?

'Yes, that is very typical for the nursery wing,' she says, referring to the part of the house we were staying in. 'I was in the adjoining room when I woke up, and actually saw a black woman leaning above me.' Apparently, many other overnight guests have had similar experiences there – several of whom reported hearing the same spectral sobbing that I did.

Sometimes, opines Kermeen, 'it's easier for ghosts to "manifest" in that twilight dream state'. She may be right. According to Dr Simon Sherwood, a lecturer in psychology at Derby University who specialises in hypnagogic/hypnopompic states (those between waking and sleep and sleep and waking, respectively), there is a school of thought that supports Frances's theory. 'There have been claims that such states are conducive to paranormal processes,' he says. 'A variety of different paranormal experiences have been reported during them.'

But what does Dr Sherwood make of my encounter? 'My initial inclination, based on what you've told me, would be that it is a normal hypnopompic experience,' he states. He goes on to explain that these episodes are relatively common, and while they differ from the ordinary dream in the sense that the person is conscious and fully aware of their surroundings, they are simultaneously experiencing dream-like hallucinations: 'vivid imagery in a number of sensory modalities', such as visual and auditory, or possibly feeling a presence.

'These kinds of imagery can be shaped by our knowledge and expectations,' Sherwood further explains. 'Given your interest in haunted houses and knowledge of the alleged haunting at the Myrtles, this might have influenced your hypnopompic imagery.'

Although I was not previously aware of the accounts of a crying phantom in the area of the house where I was staying, I suppose I was, as Dr Sherwood contends, primed for such an experience. I may not have gone to bed frightened, but my psyche certainly wasn't settled.

As I slipped from the waking world into the realm of slumber, my subconscious mind was surely cogitating on the fact that I was now occupying a space where countless people had once suffered. Black men and women forced into bondage; white men and women who lived in constant fear of violent retribution; and mothers and fathers, husbands and wives, who mourned the premature loss of their loved ones due to disease, war and random acts of violence.

I should probably also mention that, on the night in question, I had consumed a fair amount of alcohol, was potentially suffering from jet lag, and was not exactly sleeping in the most ideal environment. But regardless of its cause, this nocturnal episode felt incredibly real at the time. I still frequently think about it, trying to remind myself of the peculiarly alarming sensation I felt, the likes of which I have never experienced before or since. I ask myself, again and again: '*Was* it just a dream?'

I know the answer is probably yes. I know it because I have spent years studying supposedly haunted houses, and I recognise all the social, cultural, psychological and environmental factors that can lead to a property developing this kind of reputation.

Yet, my experience at the Myrtles still managed to throw me for a loop, demonstrating the power of the haunted house. For in the end, it seems, even a sceptic armed with an arsenal of facts and logic can still fall under its spell.

Bibliography

Introduction

Blunt, A., and Dowling, R., *Home*, Routledge, London, 2022.
Lang, A., *The Book of Dreams and Ghosts,* Longmans and Green, London, 1897.
Owens, S., *The Ghost: A Cultural History,* Tate Publishing, 2017.
Taylor, D., 'Spaces of transition: New light on the haunted house', *At the Edge,* vol. 10, 1998.

Chapter 1: Strawberry Hill House

Bacon, S. (ed), *The Gothic: A Reader,* Peter Lang Group, Lausanne, 2018.
Chambers, P., *The Cock Lane Ghost: Murder, Sex & Haunting in Dr Johnson's London,* Sutton Publishing, Stroud, 2006.
Davoli, S., *Lost Treasures of Strawberry Hill,* Scala Arts and Heritage Publishers, London, 2018.
Radcliffe, A., *The Mysteries of Udolpho: A Romance*, G. G. and J. Robinson, London, 1794.
Reeder, C., 'The Phantastical Gothic Ghost of Horace Walpole', via https://academia.edu.
Reeve, M. M., 'Gothic architecture, sexuality, and license at Horace Walpole's Strawberry Hill', *The Art Bulletin,* vol. 95, no. 3, 2013, pp. 411–39.
Walpole, H., *Aedes Walpolinae or a Description of the Collection of Pictures at Houghton-Hall in Norfolk,* London, 1758.

Walpole, H., *The Castle of Otranto, A Gothic Story,* John Murray, London (third edition), 1769.
Walpole, H., The Yale Edition of Horace Walpole Correspondence, electronic version, https://libsvcs-1.its.yale.edu/hwcorrespondence.

Chapter 2: Chillingham Castle

Barham, R. H., *The Ingoldsby Legends, or Mirth and Marvels,* Richard Bentley, London, 1840.
Crow, C., *The Night Side of Nature: or Ghosts and Ghost-Seers,* G. Routledge & Co. London, 1848.
Ingram, J. H., *Haunted Homes and Family Traditions of Great Britain,* Gibbings and Co. Ltd., London, 1886.
Lipman, C., *Co-habiting with Ghosts: Knowledge, Experience, Belief and the Domestic Uncanny,* Routledge, Abingdon-on-Thames, 2016.
Melchi, A., *Servants of the Supernatural,* Arrow Books, London, 2008.
Tankerville, L., *The Ghosts of Chillingham Castle,* Wooler, J. W. Brand, 1925.

Chapter 3: Borley Rectory

Adams, P., Underwood, P., and Brazil, E., *The Borley Rectory Companion: The Complete Guide to 'The Most Haunted House in England',* The History Press, Cheltenham, 2016.
Blum, D., *Ghost Hunters: William James and the Search for Scientific Proof of Life After Death,* Penguin Group (USA), New York, 2006.
Clarke, A., *The Bones of Borley,* https://www.foxearth.org.uk/BorleyRectory.
Clarke, R., *A Natural History of Ghosts: 500 Years of Hunting for Proof,* Penguin, London, 2012.
O'Connor, S., *The Haunting of Borley Rectory: The Story of a Ghost Story,* Simon and Schuster, London, 2022.
Price, H., *Fifty Years of Psychical Research, a Critical Survey,* Longmans, Green and Co., London, 1939.

Price, H., *The Most Haunted House in England: Ten Years' Investigation of Borley Rectory,* Longmans, Green and Co., London, 1941.
Price, H., *Search for Truth: My Life for Psychical Research*, Collins, London, 1942.
Price, H., *The End of Borley Rectory,* G. G. Harrap & Company, London, 1946.
Wallace, A. R., *On Miracles and Modern Spiritualism,* J. Burns, London, 1875.

Chapter 4: Hampton Court

Ainsworth, W. H., *The Tower of London,* George Routledge & Sons, 1840.
Bordo, S., *The Creation of Anne Boleyn: A New Look at England's Most Notorious Queen*, Houghton Mifflin Harcourt, Boston, 2013.
Edwards, A., *"There are things going bump in the night all over this town": Gothic Tourism, Haunted London, and the Geographies of Haunted Space*, PhD thesis, Manchester Metropolitan University, Manchester, 2022.
Harper, C. G., *Haunted Houses,* Senate Publishing, Rickmansworth, 1994.
Law, E., *The History of Hampton Court in Tudor Times,* George Bell and Sons, London, 1885.
Law, E., *The Haunted Gallery at Hampton Court and its Associations with Shakespeare,* Hugh Rees, London, 1918.
McEvoy, E., *Gothic Tourism,* Springer, New York, 2016.
Parker, J., *Reinvention and Continuity in the Making of an Historic Visitor Attraction: Control, Access and Display at Hampton Court Palace, 1838-1938*, PhD thesis, Kingston University, Kingston-upon-Thames, 2009.
Russell, G., *Young and Damned and Fair: The Life and Tragedy of Catherine Howard at the Court of Henry VIII*, HarperCollins UK, London, 2017.
Russell, G., *The Palace: From the Tudors to the Windsors, 500 Years of British History at Hampton Court*, Simon and Schuster, New York, 2023.

Chapter 5: The Myrtles Plantation

Gordon, A., *Ghostly Matters: Haunting and the Sociological Imagination,* University of Minnesota Press, Minneapolis, 2008.
Gorn, E. J., 'Black Spirits: The Ghostlore of Afro-American Slaves', *American Quarterly,* vol. 36, no. 4, autumn 1984, pp. 545–65.
Harper, C. W., 'Black Aristocrats: Domestic Servants on the Antebellum Plantation', *Phylon,* vol. 46, no. 2, 1985, pp.123–35.
Jacobs, H., *Incidents in the Life of a Slave Girl,* Thayler & Eldridge, Boston, 1861.
Kermeen, F., *The Myrtles Plantation: The True Story of America's Most Haunted House,* Warner Books, New York, 2005.
Miles, T., *Tales from the Haunted South: Dark Tourism and Memories of Slavery from the Civil War Era,* University of North Carolina Press, Chapel Hill, 2015.
Pirok, A., 'Specters of the Mythic South: How Plantation Fiction Fixed Ghost Stories to Black Americans', *Southern Cultures*, vol. 29, no. 4, 2003, pp.16–31.
Pirok, A., *The Common Uncanny: Ghostlore and the Creation of Virginia History*, PhD thesis, University of South Florida, Tampa, 2017.
Pittman, R. F., *The History and Haunting of the Myrtles Plantation,* Wonderland Publications, 2016.
Riccio, D., *Haunted Houses, USA,* Simon and Schuster, New York, 1989.
Robb Larkins, E., 'Violence and Recreation: Vacationing in the Realm of Dark Tourism', *Anthropology and Humanism,* vol. 34, 2009, pp. 51–60.

Chapter 6: Raynham Hall

Boyington, A. and Draper, K., 'A Concise Architectural History of Raynham Hall, Norfolk', *Art and the Country House*, https://doi.org/10.17658/ACH/RNE568.
Postle, M., 'The Curious Case of the Townshend Heirlooms Sale', *Art and the Country House*, https://doi.org/10.17658/ACH/RNE571
Tinniswood, A., *The Long Weekend: Life in the English Country House, 1918–1939*, Random House, London, 2016.

Tinniswood, A., *The Power and the Glory: Life in the English Country House Before the Great War*, Basic Books, New York, 2024.
Townshend, G., and Ffoulkes, M., *True Ghost Stories,* Senate, Rickmansworth, 1994.
Yarker, J., ' "The noblest pyle among us": Raynham in its Local Context', *Art and the Country House*, https://doi.org/10.17658/ACH/RNE573.

Chapter 7: *The Amityville Horror*

Anson, J., *The Amityville Horror,* Prentice Hall, Hoboken, 1977.
Bailey, D., *American Nightmares: The Haunted House Formula in American Popular Fiction*, University of Wisconsin Press, Madison, 2011.
King, S., *Danse Macabre*, Simon and Schuster, New York, 2010.
Meehan, P., *The Haunted House on Film: An Historical Analysis*, McFarland, Jefferson, 2019.

Chapter 8: The Winchester Mystery House

Gutierrez-Perez, R., 'Sarah Winchester & the Winchester Mystery House, or Confronting the Ghosts of Genocide & White Guilt', *Cheers from the Wasteland,* 2017.
Harter, W. L.,*The Phantom Hand, and Other American Hauntings*, Prentice Hall, Hoboken, 1976.
Ignoffo, M., *Captive of the Labyrinth: Sarah L. Winchester, Heiress to the Rifle Fortune,* University of Missouri, Columbia, 2010.
Jackson, H. H., *A Century of Dishonour,* Roberts Brothers, Boston, 1895.
Jenkins, J., *Failed Mothers and Fallen Houses: Gothic Domesticity in Nineteenth-century American Fiction*, The University of Arizona, Tucson, 1993.
Junker, C., 'The Domestic Tyranny of Haunted Houses in Mary Wilkins Freeman and Shirley Jackson', *Humanities,* vol. 8, no. 2, 2019, pp.107–20.

Van Dine, A., *Unconventional Builders,* J. G. Ferguson Pub. Co., Chicago, 1977.

Chapter 9: Global Ghosts

Davisson, Z., *Yurei: The Japanese Ghost,* Chin Music Press, Seattle, 2015.
Gray, R., *Scottish Ghosts,* Lomond Books, Broxburn, 2009.
Paulson, R., 'Gothic Fiction and the French Revolution', *Elh,* vol. 48, no. 3, 1981, pp. 532–54.

Acknowledgements

When I first sat down to write this book at the height of the global pandemic, I saw it as little more than an amusing diversion in a trying time. But it quickly became a kind of obsession (or *possession*?), spurred on by the support of friends and family, and eventually a wider network of professional backers.

The first of these backers was Eli Keren of Curious Minds Agency, one of only a few literary agents I nervously reached out to with an admittedly *very* rough book proposal. To my astonishment, he responded within hours of receiving my email and has worked tirelessly ever since to get this book on the shelves. I'm eternally grateful to Eli for never giving up, even when it all felt a bit slow to start, and some publishers seemed to struggle to understand our vision.

Additionally, the research and writing of this book required the assistance of many others who had little to no investment in the project, but who were nevertheless kind enough to offer their time, advice and knowledge.

I would like to thank the following: Carole Tucker, Librarian at Strawberry Hill House; Sir Humphry Wakefield, present owner of Chillingham Castle; Mark Trotter, retired tour guide at Chillingham; Tracy Barlow and James Tate, visitors to Chillingham, who shared their experiences with me; Andrew Clarke, historian with the Foxearth & District Local History Society; Ian Franklin, retired State Apartment Warder at Hampton Court; Karey Draper, Curator of Historic Buildings at Hampton Court; Frances Kermeen, author and former owner of the Myrtles Plantation; Mary Jo Ignoffo, historian and biographer of Sarah Winchester; Carl Ferrigno, former guide at the Winchester Mystery House; Zack Davisson, author and Japanese folklore expert; Dr Koichi Kato, Professor of Architecture at the

University of Tokyo; Dr Michael Crandol, Assistant Professor in Japanese Studies at the University of Leiden; and Dr Simon Sherwood, Senior Lecturer in Psychology at Derby University.

Finally, I must thank my husband, Bobby, and parents, Karen and Gerry, who have patiently listened to me rattle on about haunted houses for what must feel to them like an eternity.